Wheat-Free, Gluten-Free, Reduced-Calorie Cookbook

Connie Sarros

Mc Graw Hill

New York Chicago San Francisco Lisbon London Madrid Mexico City
Milan New Delhi San Juan Seoul Singapore Sydney Toronto

Library of Congress Cataloging-in-Publication Data

Sarros, Connie.
    Wheat-free, gluten-free, reduced-calorie cookbook / Connie Sarros.—1st ed.
        p.   cm.
    Includes index.
    ISBN 0-07-142375-3
        1. Wheat-free diet—Recipes.   2. Gluten-free diet—Recipes.   3. Low-calorie diet—
    Recipes.   I. Title.

    RM237.87S273   2003
    641.5'63—dc21
                                                                        2003012698

8 9 10 11 12 13 14 15 16 17 18 19 20 21 22 23 24 25 WFR/WFR   0

ISBN   978-0-07-183669-2
MHID   0-07-183669-1

Interior design by Sue Hartman
Interior illustrations by Jacqueline Dubé and Dean Stanton, copyright © 2000, 2001 by
Birch Design Studios

McGraw-Hill books are available at special quantity discounts to use as premiums and sales
promotions, or for use in corporate training programs. For more information, please write to the
Director of Special Sales, Professional Publishing, McGraw-Hill, Two Penn Plaza, New York, NY
10121-2298. Or contact your local bookstore.

Contents

Preface

S ince you are looking at this cookbook, it is likely that you or someone you know is gluten intolerant or has celiac disease (CD). To explain the condition in simplified terms, if you have CD and eat gluten, your body can't absorb the nutrition from the foods you eat. This may cause lower-tract distress and may lead to further serious health problems. The only means of controlling CD is a gluten-free diet. The destructive gluten is protein found in wheat, barley, malt, and rye. Oats are gluten-free but are not recommended because of the high risk of cross-contamination. There are glutens in rice and other grains (for example, millet and teff), but these glutens are not harmful. Even if you have celiac disease or are gluten intolerant, you don't have to give up your favorite foods; you just have to make some adjustments in how they are prepared.

Many people on gluten-free diets complain that the "safe" foods are often high in calories. Today we are far more educated about the importance of proper nutrition than at any other time in our history. We are constantly being told to watch our intake of sodium, fat, cholesterol, and carbohydrates. The good news is that this does not necessitate giving up good taste.

This is not a weight-loss diet cookbook; it is a life maintenance book. Your body converts the food you eat into usable materials needed by the cells that make up your body. Many weight-loss diets deprive your body of some nutrients or food groups; this deprivation may impair your health over a prolonged period of time. Your body's chemistry cannot make the right materials for your cells unless it gets the right foods to work with. Keep the following points in mind when planning your own meals:

- Eating foods rich in protein, vitamins, and minerals is better than consuming mostly high-starch foods.
- Cut down on the *amount* of food you eat. The majority of people consume far more than their bodies need to stay healthy.
- Never skip breakfast.
- Drink eight glasses of water a day.

"Low-calorie" cooking is designed for people on a strict diet to trim calories and lose weight. The aim of this cookbook is to provide *lower*-calorie or *reduced*-calorie recipes, designed to provide a new lifestyle of eating that is lower in fat, carbohydrates, cholesterol, and sugar. Many recipes in this cookbook are low-calorie; others are reduced-calorie, which means the caloric content has been significantly reduced from traditional versions of those recipes. Sugar and fats are often eliminated or significantly reduced; extra spices are frequently added to maintain taste integrity.

Become an avid, educated label reader. This point cannot be emphasized enough. When in doubt about ingredients, contact the manufacturer. The ingredients listed in this book are, at the time of printing, all gluten-free. The recipes in this cookbook offer you the means to eat "safe" foods while maintaining a healthful, reduced-calorie diet without sacrificing any of the taste.

Cookbooks are organized by groupings, usually by type of food (meat, vegetable, salad, etc.). However, that is not how we eat. We eat a meal consisting of a variety of foods with an entree (such as meat, fish, or poultry), a salad, a vegetable, and perhaps a starch. So this book organizes the recipes by types of meals. It is important to consume a variety of foods at each meal to maintain a balanced and nutritious diet. The foods selected for each meal take into consideration preparation time for each dish, inclusion of the various food groups, and plate presentation (a variety of colors, textures, and tastes for appeal).

How I Started Writing Wheat-Free, Gluten-Free Cookbooks

Becoming the author of gluten-free cookbooks is nothing I planned; it just happened! In 1993 my father, at the age of seventy, became very ill. In a period of two months, he went from 165 pounds down to 127 pounds, and the doctors could not find the cause. Even though my father was eating, his body was not absorbing any of the nutrients of the foods; he was literally starving to death. After seeing thirteen doctors, he was finally diagnosed with celiac disease. We had never heard the term before and had no idea what it entailed.

Having a computer in my home, I immediately went to the Web for some help and information. Anyone can post anything to the Web, so I had to be very careful when considering the validity of the source of any information. But I did find a wealth of reliable sources, including the St. John's listservice. As a member of the listserv, I could post any questions I had, and doctors or people who had lived with celiac disease for years would answer them.

I became involved with the CD support groups. Eventually, I was asked to be the Northeast Ohio representative for the St. John's listservice, which entailed helping "newbies" (those newly diagnosed with CD)—clarifying the diet restrictions and passing along gluten-free lists by brand names, gluten-free prescription lists, names of gluten-free mail-order companies, and so on.

In the meantime, my mother was busy at home trying to adjust to Dad's new diet. She was concentrating on preparing "safe" meals and had not yet tackled desserts. Mother's Day was approaching, and I thought it would be novel to present Mom with a gluten-free dessert cookbook of the family's favorite dessert recipes. So I began experimenting. Like most novices, I thought that all I needed to do was substitute rice flour for the wheat flour called for in a recipe. The results of the first two desserts I tried were a total disaster—very heavy, grainy, and gritty. Obviously, just substituting rice flour wasn't going to be enough. I began to add a variety of gluten-free flours; then I added the mysterious ingredient "xanthan gum" to help hold the pastries together. I still wasn't pleased with the results, so I began adding additional flavorings and additional leavening. Slowly, through trial and error, the desserts began tasting more like their wheat counterparts. Finally, when both my husband and I were pleased with the results, I began to type up recipes. Eventually, I had 25 converted recipes, which I printed off my computer. I punched two holes on the left side of the pages, made a cover, then tied it together with a ribbon, and presented it to my mom for Mother's Day.

People talk. When my parents would go out to dinner, their friends would ask Dad about his restricted diet. When some of them heard him mention celiac disease, they would reply that they had a niece or child or neighbor or friend with CD. Mom would tell them about the dessert cookbook I had made her for Mother's Day, and they would ask for a copy to send to whomever they

To my husband, Ted, who has been so patient with me.
Coming up with new recipes involves a lot of experimentation.
Once something looks good on paper,
the concoction must be prepared and taste-tested.
If the taste, consistency, or presentation is not perfect,
then the recipe must be adjusted and remade.
This process is often repeated four or five times
until the ultimate result is achieved.
Ted would come home from work,
night after night, week after week,
never quite sure what I would present for dinner.
But he was always such a good sport
and kept encouraging me to continue with this book.

knew with CD. I would run off the copies. Then those friends would tell others . . . who told others . . . who all requested a copy. Meanwhile, I was still experimenting in my kitchen, and the 25-recipe book had grown to 50 recipes, then to 150 recipes, until finally it reached 400 dessert recipes. Printing the copies at home, getting them spiral bound, then giving or shipping them to the appropriate people became not only very time consuming, but expensive. It reached the point where I had to decide whether to stop taking requests or begin taking the book seriously and make it into a commercial enterprise. In September 2000, I left my job to publish and promote the *Wheat-Free, Gluten-Free Dessert Cookbook* full-time. I have never regretted that decision.

Unfortunately, man does not live by cake alone. I have done a lot of cooking for my father and realized that many gluten-free recipes are high in calories, sugar, fat, cholesterol, and sodium. My father has had two open-heart surgeries and has to watch his fat, cholesterol, and sodium intake closely. Once again, I began experimenting, trying to substitute ingredients and come up with new ideas for breakfasts, lunches, and dinners that are gluten-free and heart-healthy. I began writing down these new recipes, and the *Wheat-Free, Gluten-Free, Reduced-Calorie Cookbook* was born.

I enjoy giving speeches to support groups throughout the country. The talks center around cooking and baking in a gluten-free kitchen and the special dietary needs of celiacs, with a portion of my discussion devoted to the benefits of increasing media exposure. Writing, editing, publishing, and promoting my own cookbooks and speaking to support groups has been an incredible journey, and it has enabled me to meet so many wonderful people around the country. A special thanks to all who have supported me in this venture.

Hints for Successful Gluten-Free Cooking

Most traditional recipes containing gluten may be converted to gluten-free with excellent results. Cooking gluten-free is not difficult, but it does require some adapting and adjusting.

The Myth of the Mystery Flour Mixture

Baking without wheat flour is no mystery; many alternative flours may be used. The problem is that many alternative flours are often more gritty or heavier than wheat flour and not as tasty. To combat this, combine a variety of different gluten-free flours. Each alternative flour has its own unique properties: some are lighter, some are tastier, some help hold the product together better. By combining flours, you can achieve an end product that is very close to the properties of wheat flour. Readily available at health food stores and even some traditional grocery stores are rice flour, potato flour, potato starch flour, tapioca flour, and a variety of bean flours. Cornmeal, corn flour, and cornstarch are also used frequently in combination with the other flours. The secret (if there is one) is to find a combination of flours that will result in a lighter, less grainy texture.

In this cookbook, many desserts are made with Gluten-Free Flour Mixture. Gluten-free baking will be easier and more convenient if you make up a large batch of the flour mixture, then freeze it in a plastic bag. The mixture will be loose enough to measure straight from the freezer each time you need it. Let the measured amount come to room temperature, then sift again before mixing it with other ingredients.

Gluten-Free Flour Mixture

2½ cups rice flour
1 cup potato starch flour
1 cup tapioca flour
¼ cup cornstarch
¼ cup bean flour
2 tablespoons xanthan gum

Sift together the rice flour, potato starch flour, tapioca flour, cornstarch, bean flour, and xanthan gum into a large bowl. Sift the ingredients until completely mixed. Transfer the mixture to reclosable plastic freezer bags, and store in the freezer. *Makes 5 cups.*

Experiment with the bean flours. Mung bean flour is available at Asian grocery stores and is a wonderful addition to the light-textured dessert recipes. Chick-pea, or garbanzo bean, flour also is light. Fava bean flour, found at health food stores, is a nice addition for denser desserts, like pound cakes, fruitcakes, and sweetbreads. Additional flours that are gluten-free are sweet potato flour, sweet rice flour, sorghum flour, buckwheat flour, and pea flour. Xanthan gum, despite its intimidating name, is a white powder sold in pouches or small jars at health food stores. It helps to bind the pastry and keep it from crumbling. If you are allergic to corn, omit the cornstarch from the flour mixture.

Baking Hints for Converting Recipes

Gluten-free flours do not have as much taste as wheat flour. If you are converting a wheat recipe to a gluten-free one, it helps to add flavorful ingredients to the batter or dough. Possibilities include orange juice, cinnamon, raisins, fresh or dried fruits, chocolate chips, a bit more vanilla or almond extract—something to enhance the flavor.

A few brands of packaged cut-up fruits are dusted with flour to keep the pieces from sticking together. If you add dried fruits such as dates, you are always "safe" when you chop your own. The easiest way to chop dried fruit is to use scissors dipped in hot water. Soak raisins, dates, and other dried fruits in warm water 15 minutes before using, then drain well; this will soften and plump them. After draining, dust them with Gluten-Free Flour Mixture so they distribute evenly throughout the dessert instead of sinking to the bottom or floating on top.

Here are some additional ways to adapt the ingredients in conventional recipes:

- If you don't have xanthan gum, you may substitute double the amount of unflavored gluten-free gelatin in the recipe (1 teaspoon xanthan gum = 2 teaspoons unflavored gluten-free gelatin).
- In cake and muffin recipes, add 1 tablespoon of gluten-free mayonnaise for a lighter texture.
- If you are converting a traditional wheat flour recipe to a gluten-free version, replace the wheat flour with Gluten-Free Flour Mixture. Add 1 extra egg and half again as much baking soda or gluten-free baking powder as the recipe calls for.

- For a lighter texture, use applesauce in place of some of the liquid called for in the recipe, or use buttermilk in place of regular milk.
- If baking with rice flour exclusively, combine it with the liquid called for in the recipe, and heat until warm (do not boil), stirring, then cool. This will eliminate most of the grittiness.
- You may want to substitute the liquid called for in a conventional wheat recipe. Adding carbonated drinks tends to make baked products lighter. Fruit juices add flavor.
- If a recipe calls for flour as a thickening agent, such as in creamed mixtures, substitute equal amounts of cornstarch or potato flour.

Gluten-free baking requires some adaptations to procedures:

- Gluten-free flours contain no preservatives. Therefore, refrigerate or freeze any flour mixture you are not using immediately.
- Bake gluten-free products at a slightly lower temperature than baked goods made with conventional recipes.
- Wheat products get a nice golden brown on top when baked; unfortunately, gluten-free baked goods tend not to brown as much. Don't depend on color as a guide to when your cake or cookies are done. Use the toothpick test on cakes. For cookies, touch the tops lightly. When your finger leaves no imprint and when the bottoms of the cookies are beginning to brown, the gluten-free cookies are done.

Cookie Hints

- When rolling dough, if the dough is too soft, refrigerate it 1 hour, then roll again.
- If the dough is too dry, work in a little cream or milk or whatever liquid the recipe calls for.

- Refrigerating cookie dough for 1 hour prevents drop cookies from spreading too much.
- If your cookie dough is sticky, dip your spoon and fingers into warm water frequently while forming cookies.

Piecrust Hints

- Gluten-free crusts are more fragile than their wheat counterparts. It helps if you roll the crust between two pieces of waxed paper.
- For a shiny top crust, brush the top with milk before baking.
- For a sweet top crust, brush the top with water, then sprinkle generously with sugar before baking.
- For a glazed top crust, whip together an egg yolk with a little water, then brush it on the crust before baking.

Hints for Healthy Eating

Weight control is a learned behavior. The recipes in this book and the tips that follow can help you learn to eat healthier and to control your weight.

Hints for Curbing Your Appetite

- Eat what you like—just eat smaller portions and prepare food with fewer calories. You won't stick to your new program if you are forced to eat foods you don't like and give up those you enjoy.
- Sit down. Train yourself to sit and enjoy your meal. Never eat at the counter standing up. Never walk out of the door while holding a sandwich in your hand.
- Don't starve. Crash diets don't work for prolonged periods, and they could affect your health.

- Serve meals attractively; garnish your plates. A pretty plate presentation will make even plain food look appealing.
- Before eating something, ask yourself, "Am I really hungry, or am I just bored?" If you are just bored, chew a piece of sugarless gum, and jog around the block.
- Don't skip meals. Skipped meals often lead to an out-of-control appetite before your next mealtime.
- If you get really hungry between meals, snack on healthful, low-calorie snacks (carrot sticks, plain popcorn, or a few raisins).
- Skip the "extras": Don't put butter on your bread. Butter doesn't fill you—it just adds calories and fat. Don't add sugar to your cereal or coffee or tea. Use skim milk in your coffee instead of cream or cream substitutes. Many cream substitutes contain tropical oils that are very high in fat.
- Incorporate a minimum amount of starch into your diet, but do not eliminate it totally. Your body needs some carbohydrates.
- Incorporate more fiber into your diet. Roughage will keep your system operating efficiently.
- The key to healthful nutrition is to select the least-processed foods possible. For example, eat an apple instead of drinking apple juice or eating applesauce; eat a baked potato instead of potato pancakes or whipped potatoes. Get your carbohydrates by eating fruits and vegetables instead of eating pasta and breads.

Hints for General Good Health

To stay healthy, exercise. Don't use the excuse that you don't exercise because you can't afford a membership at a health club. You can do floor exercises at home or walk up

and down stairs at home or at a public building. The excuse about not having the time to exercise doesn't work either. Do you have an hour for lunch at work? Take half of that time to walk the corridors of your building. You will make time if you want to badly enough.

Begin by walking. While it won't perform overnight magic, walking promotes a lifetime of good health. In the beginning, forget stopwatches, heart rates, and technique. Just go for a walk at a comfortable pace for 30 minutes. When you are at ease with this, increase your pace and/or the length of time for your walks. Finally, refine your method of walking. The correct posture, arm swing, and stride add up to a higher-intensity exercise and a lower risk of injury.

Eat a wide variety of foods. Eating many different foods assures you of getting a full range of nutrients. In particular, eat an abundance of vegetables and fruits. Every day, adults should consume a minimum of three servings of vegetables and two servings of fruit—more is even better.

Five things may affect your buildup of cholesterol: high blood pressure, smoking, family history of heart disease, diabetes, and obesity. You cannot control family history, but you do have some control over the other four factors. Here are some guidelines that most experts agree on:

- Reduce saturated fat in your diet. Eat less red meat. When you do eat red meat, trim any fat before cooking, and limit the amount to 3 to 5 ounces. Read food labels. Avoid foods

that contain large amounts of hydrogenated vegetable oils, such as cocoa butter, coconut and palm oils, and beef fat or lard. Eat low-fat cheese, such as part-skim mozzarella. Cook with egg whites when possible instead of whole eggs. Limit portions of meat, fish, and poultry to no more than 6 ounces a day. Organ meats (liver, brain, kidney) have very high amounts of "bad" cholesterol; they are also sources of concentrated toxins. Eliminate these from your diet.

- Eat unsaturated fats (olive oil, corn oil, sunflower seed oil, safflower oil). Polyunsaturated oil lowers your total blood cholesterol. Monounsaturated oil (olive oil) lowers the bad cholesterol (LDL) but leaves the beneficial cholesterol (HDL) intact.

- Cut down on salt consumption by flavoring foods with herbs and spices.

- Limit your use of butter and gluten-free margarines, which are high in saturated fats. Instead of sautéing vegetables in butter, spray the pan with gluten-free nonstick spray. Another alternative is to precook onions, celery, bell peppers, and other vegetables by simmering them in a little water or broth, then draining.

- Stir-frying allows you to cook small amounts of meat with lots of fresh vegetables and very little (if any) fat.

- Beware of focusing only on "fat-free" foods. Shrimp has almost no fat or calories, but it is higher in bad cholesterol than many other foods. A "fat-free" dinner may have excessive amounts of sugar and salt, which may be just as bad for you as fats.

- Beware of focusing too much on calorie consumption. If you just count calories, you could eat four pieces of candy in one day, avoiding all other foods. Obviously, four pieces of candy will not give your body the nutrition it needs, even though you are within your calorie limitations. While caloric intake is a consideration, so are other factors, such as getting the proper vitamins, minerals, protein, and fiber.

Hints for Eating Out

- Select entrees that are steamed, poached, broiled, grilled, or roasted in their own juices.
- Fish and chicken are far lower in calories, fat, and cholesterol than beef.
- Be wary of "Diet Platters." These often contain tuna salad made with high-calorie mayonnaise, cottage cheese with fruit canned in heavy, sugared syrup, or iceberg lettuce (which has minimal nutrients).
- Instead of asking the server about ingredients and methods of preparation, call ahead and speak directly with the chef.
- Order Asian dishes only if you confirm that cornstarch is used as a thickener instead of wheat flour, no soy is used, and the wok is cleaned after each use.
- Limit portions. Restaurant portions are notoriously large. Eat half of the meal and bring the rest home for tomorrow's dinner.
- Instead of ordering deep-fried, greasy french fries, select a baked potato, baked sweet potato, or steamed vegetables as a side dish.
- If you must eat fast food, instead of ordering french fries and a milkshake (640 calories, 12.6 g saturated fat), opt for a packaged garden salad and a small orange juice (140 calories, 1 g saturated fat).

Cooking Basics

This chapter provides lists of measurement equivalents, substitutions, and terms and guidelines, along with their explanations. These are intended to help you better understand gluten-free cooking and terms used throughout this book.

Measurements

1 tablespoon = 3 teaspoons
1 fluid ounce = 2 tablespoons
1 jigger = 3 tablespoons
¼ cup = 4 tablespoons
⅓ cup = 5⅓ tablespoons
½ cup = 8 tablespoons
1 cup = ½ pint = 16 tablespoons
1 cup = 8 fluid ounces
1 pint = 2 cups
1 quart = 4 cups = 2 pints
½ gallon = 2 quarts
1 gallon = 4 quarts

½ stick butter = 4 tablespoons = ¼ cup
1 stick butter = 8 tablespoons = ½ cup
1 pound butter = 4 sticks = 2 cups
1 pound = 16 ounces
1 pound granulated sugar = 2¼ cups
1 pound brown sugar = 2¼ cups, packed down
1 pound confectioner's sugar = 3½ cups
1 square baking chocolate = 1 ounce

Emergency Substitutions

If you are missing an ingredient, check this list to see if you can substitute something else:

1 square gluten-free unsweetened chocolate = 3 tablespoons cocoa + 1 tablespoon butter or gluten-free margarine

1 square gluten-free semisweet chocolate = ⅓ cup chocolate chips

2 tablespoons Gluten-Free Flour Mixture for thickening = 1½ tablespoons cornstarch

1 teaspoon gluten-free baking powder = ¼ teaspoon baking soda + ½ teaspoon cream of tartar + ¼ teaspoon cornstarch

1 cup corn syrup = 1 cup sugar + ¼ cup liquid (same type as liquid used in the recipe)

1 tablespoon cornstarch (for thickening) = 4 teaspoons quick-cooking tapioca

1 cup sugar = 1 cup honey or 1 cup maple syrup (reduce other liquid in recipe by ⅓ cup)

1 cup half-and-half = 1 cup evaporated milk = ½ cup milk + ½ cup cream

1 cup milk = ½ cup evaporated milk + ½ cup water

1 cup buttermilk = 1 tablespoon apple cider vinegar + enough milk to make 1 cup

1 cup firmly packed brown sugar = 1 cup white sugar + 2 tablespoons molasses

1 cup firmly packed brown sugar = 1 cup brown sugar substitute (sold near granulated sugar in grocery stores)

1 package gluten-free active dry yeast = 1 tablespoon gluten-free active dry yeast

3 tablespoons cream of tartar = 2 tablespoons gluten-free baking powder + 1 tablespoon baking soda

1 cup ketchup = 1 cup tomato sauce + ½ cup sugar + 2 tablespoons cider vinegar

1 cup canned tomatoes = 1⅓ cups cut-up fresh tomatoes simmered 10 minutes

1 tablespoon fresh herbs = 1 teaspoon dried herbs

1 clove garlic = ⅛ teaspoon garlic powder

Terms and Guidelines

Alcoholic Beverages: Some alcoholic beverages contain gluten. Several of the recipes in this book contain white domestic wine. White wine that has not been fortified is "safe." (Fortified means that nongrape ingredients are used in the distillation process. American domestic wine is not fortified; most imported wines are fortified.) Other gluten-free alcoholic beverages that are used in this book are rum, crème de menthe, crème de cacao, coffee-flavored liqueur, and domestic brandies. When in doubt, check with the manufacturer to be certain of the gluten-free status of alcoholic beverages.

Baked Products: Traditional baked goods made from wheat flour tend to stay fresher longer than those baked with substitute flours. Gluten-free products are generally best when eaten the same day they are prepared. Most may be frozen. Freeze them right away to retain freshness.

Canola Oil: Canola oil is technically gluten-free. A few people are concerned about cross-contamination issues, and canola oil may act as a laxative in some individuals. Using canola oil is a personal option. While safflower oil may be used in salad dressings, avoid using it for cooking. Heat breaks down the components of safflower oil and may cause it to become carcinogenic.

Cheese: Some commercial grated cheeses have been found to contain a small amount of flour as part of the spice flavoring or to help prevent the cheese shreds from caking. Read the list of ingredients carefully.

Chicken: Most of the fat on a piece of chicken is right beneath the skin. Cook chicken with the skin on to retain the flavor, but remove the skin before eating to lower fat and cholesterol consumption. When a recipe in this cookbook calls for chicken breast, it means half of a whole double breast. If a whole double breast is used, the recipe will state that specifically.

Cocoa: Whenever cocoa is listed as an ingredient, it refers to unflavored, unsweetened. powdered, natural cocoa. Do not substitute hot chocolate mixes, because they are presweetened, and many of them contain gluten.

Eggs: Pasteurized eggs are available in some areas, but due to the increasing concern of salmonella, all of the recipes in this cookbook call for cooking eggs.

Fat: Many recipes include small amounts of fat, usually in the form of olive or corn oil. These two oils, especially olive oil, help clean out arteries and raise HDL. The saturated fats have been reduced or eliminated from these recipes. Remember that *all* oils and fats, even the "good" ones, should be used sparingly.

Flours: Rice flour is the most common substitute for wheat flour. However, rice flour alone may give the finished product a heavy, grainy taste. It is best to use a combination of flours. Some grocery stores carry tapioca, potato starch, or garbanzo bean flours. Gluten-free flours also may be purchased at health food stores or through mail order. Because these substitute flours are heavier than wheat flour, cooks must sift the flours together before adding them to liquid ingredients. Even if you are using only a small amount of flour, take the time to sift it. For foods and desserts calling for Gluten-Free Flour Mixture, use the flour recipe in the Hints chapter.

Do not confuse sweet rice flour with rice flour. Sweet rice flour is used more as a thickener, like cornstarch, but often cannot be substituted for rice flour in these recipes. Potato flour (a thickener similar to cornstarch) should not be substituted for potato starch flour.

Gluten-Free Bread: Some recipes call for gluten-free bread slices, cubes, or crumbs. The plain rice bread, which may be purchased from health food stores, is too dense for most of these recipes. Bread that is more porous will yield much better results. You may use homemade gluten-free bread, or you may purchase a gluten-free almond or pecan rice bread from health food stores. These latter two are more porous, and moisture will saturate them better. When using gluten-free bread in a recipe, cut off and discard the crusts and end pieces.

Natural Ingredients: While I attempted to use as many "natural" ingredients as possible, I did use substitutes (such as gluten-free margarine) to lower fat and caloric content. Some recipes call for egg substitutes to reduce cholesterol levels. Check with the manufacturer to be certain that the egg substitute you are using does not contain gluten. In an effort to stay away from foods with a lot of added chemicals, I did not use sugar substitutes.

Pork: Whether a recipe calls for chops, roast, or other pork cut, look for pork that is lean. In most meat counters, you will find pork labeled Lean Generation. Its fat content is less than for traditional cuts of pork.

Reduced Calorie: Most recipes in this book are "low calorie." Some, however, are merely lower in calories than their traditional counterparts.

Rice: Brown rice is more healthful than white rice. Some brands of instant rice contain gluten, so read the labels carefully, or check with the manufacturer. There are pros and cons to presoaking rice. When rice is presoaked, most of the starch is washed away, which prevents the kernels from sticking together and clumping; but you also wash away many of the nutrients.

Spices: While most plain spices are gluten-free, a few spices, like chili powder and curry powder, contain small amounts of flour to keep contents from clumping. This is especially true with spice blends. No prepackaged spice blends are used in this cookbook.

Xanthan Gum: The first time you see this name, you may become intimidated. Don't be. When wheat flour is replaced by alternative flours in baked goods, the finished product, whether bread, cookies, or cake, often tends to fall apart. Wheat flour binds ingredients better than the alternative flours. Xanthan gum (produced from the fermentation of corn sugar) is a powder that is added to many gluten-free baked goods to help with this binding. It is a light powder that comes in a pouch or small jar and may be readily purchased at almost all health food stores. Usually, anywhere from ¼ teaspoon (for small batches of cookies) to 2 to 3 tablespoons (for large loaves of bread) is enough to bind the baked product together.

1

Breakfasts and Brunches

E ating a hearty, nutritious breakfast will speed up your metabolism and give you energy throughout the day. This chapter features both simple breakfasts, such as eggs or cereal, and more elaborate brunches.

Pancake Breakfast

Cornmeal Pancakes

You can make the pancakes ahead of time. Then stack them with sheets of waxed paper between the pancakes. Cover and refrigerate. Just before breakfast, set two pancakes side by side on a dish. Cover with a dampened paper towel, then warm in the microwave for about 25 seconds, or cover with foil and reheat in a toaster oven. (Upright toasters are not recommended for reheating these pancakes because they crumble easily.)

¾ cup Gluten-Free Flour Mixture (See the Hints chapter.)

½ cup cornmeal

2½ tablespoons sugar

2 teaspoons gluten-free baking powder

¼ teaspoon salt

½ teaspoon cinnamon

3 egg whites, slightly beaten

¾ cup skim milk

1 teaspoon corn oil

Sift together the flour mixture, cornmeal, sugar, baking powder, salt, and cinnamon. In a small bowl, whisk together the egg whites, milk, and corn oil. Add the liquid ingredients at once to the dry ingredients; stir just till blended. Spray a griddle with gluten-free nonstick spray. Preheat the griddle over medium heat. For each pancake, pour a scant ¼ cup of batter onto the hot griddle. Cook till bubbles appear on the surface of the pancakes and the edges are slightly dry (1 to 2 minutes). Turn the pancakes over; cook another 1 to 2 minutes till golden brown. *Makes 4 2-pancake servings.*

One serving–Calories: 147; Total fat: 1.8 g; Saturated fat: 0.3 g; Cholesterol: 8 mg; Sodium: 26 mg; Carbohydrates: 28.3 g; Fiber: 0.8 g; Sugar: 6.5 g; Protein: 6.7 g

Cinnamon Apple Pancake Syrup

The syrup may be made up to 5 days ahead. After cooking the syrup, let it cool; cover and refrigerate. Reheat before serving.

⅔ cup apple juice

⅓ cup water

¼ cup grated apples

1½ teaspoons cornstarch

¼ teaspoon cinnamon

1½ tablespoons light brown sugar

In a small saucepan, combine the juice, water, apples, and cornstarch. Stir to dissolve the cornstarch. Add the cinnamon and brown sugar. Bring to a boil, stirring constantly, over medium-high heat. Serve warm. *Makes 4 ¼-cup servings.*

One serving—Calories: 26; Total fat: 0.2 g; Saturated fat: 0 g; Cholesterol: 0 mg; Sodium: 2 mg; Carbohydrates: 9.4 g; Fiber: 0.2 g; Sugar: 6 g; Protein: 0.2 g

Maple Sausage

To further reduce calories, broil the sausage on a rack, turning frequently, instead of browning it in a skillet.

> 8 links gluten-free turkey sausage
>
> 1 teaspoon maple syrup

Over medium-low heat, cook the sausage in a skillet, turning frequently, till cooked through and browned. Brush the maple syrup over the sausage, and continue cooking 1 minute till glazed. *Makes 4 2-sausage servings.*

One serving—Calories: 133; Total fat: 10.1 g; Saturated fat: 2.1 g; Cholesterol: 34 mg; Sodium: 328 mg; Carbohydrates: 5.3 g; Fiber: 0 g; Sugar: 0.5 g; Protein: 8.6 g

Greek Scramble Breakfast

Greek Scramble

To further lower the calorie and cholesterol intake, you may use an egg substitute or all egg whites in place of the whole eggs called for in this recipe. If using an egg substitute, read the label to be certain it is gluten-free.

> 3 eggs
>
> 3 egg whites
>
> ¼ teaspoon pepper

¼ teaspoon salt

¼ teaspoon oregano

4 tablespoons 1% milk

½ onion, chopped

3 teaspoons olive oil

1 small zucchini, shredded

1 tomato, chopped

3 tablespoons crumbled gluten-free feta cheese

In a bowl, whisk together the eggs, egg whites, pepper, salt, oregano, and milk; set aside. In a skillet, sauté the onion in the oil 3 minutes or till softened. Add the zucchini; sauté 3 minutes. Add the tomato and the egg mixture. Stir gently until the eggs are almost set. Stir in the feta cheese, and continue stirring until the eggs are cooked. *Makes 6 ⅔-cup servings.*

One serving—Calories: 77; Total fat: 4 g; Saturated fat: 1.4 g; Cholesterol: 108 mg; Sodium: 205 mg; Carbohydrates: 2.4 g; Fiber: 0.2 g; Sugar: 0.5 g; Protein: 5.6 g

Lemon Almond Muffins

For the finishing touch, sprinkle the tops of the muffins with grated lemon zest or sesame seeds just before baking.

1 cup Gluten-Free Flour Mixture (See the Hints chapter.)

2 teaspoons gluten-free baking powder

1 teaspoon baking soda

⅛ teaspoon salt

⅓ cup light brown sugar

2 teaspoons corn oil

½ cup skim milk

3 egg whites, lightly beaten

2 teaspoons grated lemon zest

1 tablespoon gluten-free, low-fat mayonnaise

1½ tablespoons lemon juice

¼ teaspoon vanilla

½ teaspoon almond extract

2 tablespoons coarsely chopped almonds

Preheat oven to 350°F. Sift together the flour mixture, baking powder, baking soda, and salt. In a medium bowl, mash the brown sugar and oil together with a fork until smooth. Stir in the milk, egg whites, lemon zest, mayonnaise, lemon juice, vanilla, and almond extract until well blended. Stir in the dry ingredients and almonds just till mixed. Spray muffin tins with gluten-free nonstick spray. Spoon the batter into the muffin tins. Bake about 18 minutes, until very lightly browned or until a toothpick inserted in the center of a muffin comes out clean. Remove the muffins to a wire rack. *Makes 12 muffins.*

One muffin—Calories: 88; Total fat: 2.6 g; Saturated fat: 0.4 g; Cholesterol: 0.5 mg; Sodium: 94 mg; Carbohydrates: 12.4 g; Fiber: 0.4 g; Sugar: 4.5 g; Protein: 3.6 g

Old-Fashioned Country Breakfast

Country Eggs

In place of the sausage, try adding lean ham or leftover lean corned beef.

3 small links gluten-free turkey sausage

1 tablespoon gluten-free margarine

1 cup diced cooked potatoes

½ onion, diced

½ green bell pepper, diced

3 eggs

3 egg whites

3 tablespoons skim milk

Dash salt

Dash black pepper

Brown the sausages in a nonstick skillet. Remove the sausages from the skillet; cut each into six pieces. Use a paper towel to wipe out the skillet. Melt the margarine in the skillet, and brown the potatoes, onion, and green bell pepper. Add the sausage. In a bowl, whip together the eggs, egg whites, milk, salt, and black pepper; pour into the skillet. Cook, stirring constantly, until the eggs are set. *Makes 4 ¾-cup servings.*

One serving—Calories: 150; Total fat: 8.2 g; Saturated fat: 2.5 g; Cholesterol: 140 mg; Sodium: 254 mg; Carbohydrates: 8.3 g; Fiber: 0.2 g; Sugar: 0.6 g; Protein: 9.9 g

Cranberry Muffins

For a glaze that adds very few calories, stir together ½ cup of sifted confectioner's sugar and 2 teaspoons of orange juice; drizzle the glaze over the tops of the hot muffins.

> ¾ cup dried cranberries
>
> 1 ½ cups Gluten-Free Flour Mixture (See the Hints chapter.)
>
> ⅔ cup plus 1 ½ tablespoons sugar
>
> 3 teaspoons gluten-free baking powder
>
> 1 teaspoon cinnamon
>
> ½ teaspoon salt
>
> 1 teaspoon baking soda
>
> ⅔ cup buttermilk or skim milk
>
> 3 tablespoons gluten-free margarine, melted
>
> 2 egg whites
>
> 1 egg
>
> 4 teaspoons finely grated orange zest
>
> 1 ½ teaspoons vanilla

Preheat oven to 375°F. Put the cranberries in a small bowl, and cover with tepid water to soak. Over a large bowl, sift together the flour mixture, ⅔ cup of the sugar, and the baking powder, cinnamon, salt, and baking soda. In another bowl, whisk together the buttermilk, margarine, egg whites, egg, orange zest, and vanilla until blended. Drain the cranberries; mix them with 1½ tablespoons of the sugar to coat. Stir the cranberries into the flour mixture. Pour the liquid ingredients into the dry ingredients, and stir just until blended. Spray 12 muffin tins with gluten-free nonstick spray. Spoon the batter into the muffin tins. Bake 20 minutes or until a toothpick inserted in the center of a muffin comes out clean. These are best when served warm. *Makes 12 muffins.*

One muffin—Calories: 112; Total fat: 2.6 g; Saturated fat: 0.7 g; Cholesterol: 18 mg; Sodium: 152 mg; Carbohydrates: 19.7 g; Fiber: 0.9 g; Sugar: 7.5 g; Protein: 2.8 g

Rice Cereal Breakfast

Breakfast Rice Cereal

On a cold winter day, there is nothing better than a bowl of hot cereal to keep you warm. Breakfast Rice Cereal will keep in the refrigerator, covered, for 4 days.

1½ cups plus 2 tablespoons water

½ cup apple juice

1 cup quick-cooking brown rice

¼ teaspoon salt

¾ cup skim milk

2 tablespoons chopped walnuts

1 McIntosh apple, peeled, cored, and diced

¼ cup light brown sugar

¼ cup raisins

¾ teaspoon cinnamon

1 egg

Nutmeg

In a saucepan, combine 1½ cups of the water and the juice, rice, and salt. Bring to a boil. Reduce heat to low, cover, and cook 15 minutes or until the rice is tender. Add the milk, walnuts, apple, brown sugar, raisins, and cinnamon. Return to a simmer, and cook uncovered 15 minutes more, stirring occasionally. Beat the egg and remaining 2 tablespoons of water in a small bowl. Stir about 1 cup of the rice mixture into the egg, then stir the egg mixture into the rice in the saucepan and simmer for 2 minutes more, stirring constantly. Serve hot or cold, sprinkled lightly with nutmeg. *Makes 4 ¾-cup servings.*

One serving—Calories: 197; Total fat: 2.9 g; Saturated fat: 0.6 g; Cholesterol: 53 mg; Sodium: 179 mg; Carbohydrates: 37.8 g; Fiber: 2.5 g; Sugar: 17.3 g; Protein: 4.1 g

Broiled Cinnamon Grapefruit

This delicious grapefruit may be eaten warm or cold. Try topping it off with a scoop of gluten-free cottage cheese.

   2 grapefruit

   4 teaspoons gluten-free white wine (optional)

   2 teaspoons light brown sugar

   ¼ teaspoon cinnamon

Cut the grapefruit in half; with a grapefruit knife, cut the sections to separate. Cover a baking sheet with foil. Place the grapefruit halves on the baking sheet. Drizzle the wine over the fruit; sprinkle with brown sugar and cinnamon. Broil 8 minutes or till top is glazed. *Makes 4 ½-grapefruit servings.*

One serving (with wine)—Calories: 60; Total fat: 0 g; Saturated fat: 0 g; Cholesterol: 0 mg; Sodium: 12 mg; Carbohydrates: 14.4 g; Fiber: 0.2 g; Sugar: 12.9 g; Protein: 1 g

Apple Pancake Breakfast

Apple Pancakes

You can make these pancakes ahead of time and freeze them. After the pancakes are cooked, stack them with 2 pieces of waxed paper between each pair, and wrap them in heavy-duty foil. To reheat, slightly overlap the frozen pancakes on a dish, cover them with a damp paper towel, and warm them in the microwave on High for 40 seconds.

½ cup Gluten-Free Flour Mixture (See the Hints chapter.)

¼ teaspoon salt

¾ teaspoon gluten-free baking powder

2 tablespoons sugar

½ teaspoon cinnamon

2 eggs

¼ teaspoon vanilla

⅔ cup skim milk

1 cup peeled, shredded apple

Maple syrup

Sift the flour mixture, salt, baking powder, sugar, and cinnamon into a medium bowl. In a large bowl, whip the eggs with a whisk until light and fluffy. Stir in the vanilla and milk. Gradually whisk in the dry ingredients until well blended. Stir in the apple. Preheat a griddle or large skillet; spray with gluten-free nonstick cooking spray. Pour about ¼ cup of batter per pancake into the skillet. Cook, turning once, until golden on each side. Repeat until all batter is used. To serve, drizzle maple syrup over the pancakes. *Makes 4 2-pancake servings.*

One serving (without syrup)—Calories: 138; Total fat: 2.7 g; Saturated fat: 0.7 g; Cholesterol: 107 mg; Sodium: 200 mg; Carbohydrates: 22.4 g; Fiber: 1.5 g; Sugar: 10 g; Protein: 6.2 g

Baked Bananas

This healthy, sweet treat is also great cooked on the grill.

  2 bananas, peeled

  2 teaspoons honey

  3 teaspoons gluten-free creamy peanut butter

Preheat oven to 350°F. Cut each banana in quarters, then cut each quarter in half lengthwise. Stir together honey and peanut butter; spread on the cut side of eight pieces; top with the remaining eight pieces. Cover a baking sheet with foil. Set the banana pieces on the baking sheet; bring up the sides of the foil, and seal the packet. Bake 10 minutes. Serve warm. *Makes 4 2-piece servings.*

One serving—Calories: 94; Total fat: 2.5 g; Saturated fat: 0.2 g; Cholesterol: 0 mg; Sodium: 15 mg; Carbohydrates: 17.4 g; Fiber: 1.7 g; Sugar: 2.9 g; Protein: 1.6 g

Layered Breakfast

Layered Breakfast Sandwich

This dish is so versatile! Try adding a layer of baked hash brown potatoes, use gluten-free mozzarella slices or shredded cheddar cheese in place of the feta, or sprinkle the tomatoes with crumbled cooked gluten-free sausage or bacon instead of the ham.

  4 slices Irish Potato Bread (See Index.)

  4 slices tomato

  ¼ teaspoon pepper

  4 thin slices low-fat, gluten-free ham

  4 tablespoons crumbled gluten-free feta cheese

  4 eggs

  4 tablespoons skim milk

  ⅛ teaspoon salt

  ½ teaspoon gluten-free margarine

Preheat oven to 350°F. Top each slice of bread with a slice of tomato. Sprinkle the tomatoes with pepper. Lay a slice of ham on top of each tomato; sprinkle the cheese on top of the ham. Cover a baking sheet with foil. Lay the open-face sandwiches on the baking sheet. Warm in the oven for 5 minutes. While the sandwiches are baking, whisk the eggs, milk, and salt in a bowl until frothy. Melt the margarine in a skillet; add the egg mixture. Cook, stirring constantly, until the eggs are set. Spoon the eggs on top of the cheese. *Makes 4 sandwiches.*

One sandwich—Calories: 190; Total fat: 8.9 g; Saturated fat: 3.2 g; Cholesterol: 221 mg; Sodium: 543 mg; Carbohydrates: 15.2 g; Fiber: 1.3 g; Sugar: 2 g; Protein: 12.1 g

Tortilla Flower Brunch

Eggs in Tortilla Flowers

The tortilla shell is an attractive way to present eggs. Don't feel wasteful when you throw out egg yolks. Most of the egg's nutrition, including a high protein content, is the white. The yolk mostly contains fat and cholesterol.

- 4 corn tortillas
- 1½ teaspoons corn oil
- 3 eggs
- 3 egg whites
- 2 tablespoons skim milk
- ¼ teaspoon black pepper
- ½ red bell pepper, finely chopped
- 2 green onions, sliced
- 2 teaspoons gluten-free salsa

Preheat oven to 325°F. Invert four small custard cups on a baking sheet, and coat the bottoms with gluten-free nonstick spray. Brush each tortilla with ⅛ teaspoon of the corn oil, then cut eight evenly spaced 2-inch slits around the edge of each. Center each tortilla, oiled side up, on top of a cup, letting the cut edges drape down the sides. Bake 20 minutes or until crisp. In a bowl, beat together the eggs, egg whites, milk, and black pepper. Spray a large skillet with gluten-free nonstick spray; add 1 teaspoon of corn oil, and heat for 1 minute on low heat. Add the red pepper and green onions; cover and cook over medium heat for 4 minutes or until softened. Add the egg mixture, and cook, stirring, until the eggs are set. Remove the tortillas from the cups, and invert them onto serving dishes. Fill each tortilla with the egg mixture. Top each with ½ teaspoon of the salsa. *Makes 4 tortilla flowers.*

One flower—Calories: 122; Total fat: 6.9 g; Saturated fat: 1.7 g; Cholesterol: 159 mg; Sodium: 131 mg; Carbohydrates: 6.1 g; Fiber: 0.4 g; Sugar: 0.4 g; Protein: 9.8 g

Baked Canadian Bacon

Most Canadian bacon is already fully cooked. If the bacon you buy is not, preheat oven to 325°F, and line an 8-inch square baking pan with foil. Add ½ cup of water and the Canadian bacon; bake 1 hour. Remove the meat from the pan, and continue the recipe as directed.

    ½ pound lean Canadian bacon
    1 8-ounce can gluten-free jellied cranberry sauce

Preheat oven to 350°F. Slice the meat into eight thin slices. Place ¼ cup of water in a baking pan; layer the meat in the pan so the slices barely overlap. Cut the cranberry sauce into 8 slices; tuck each slice of cranberry sauce between slices of bacon. Cover and bake 15 minutes. *Makes 4 2-slice servings.*

One serving—Calories: 173; Total fat: 11 g; Saturated fat: 1 g; Cholesterol: 27 mg; Sodium: 589 mg; Carbohydrates: 28 g; Fiber: 0.7 g; Sugar: 21.8 g; Protein: 9.6 g

Eggs Florentine Brunch

Eggs Florentine

While this dish has some cholesterol and sodium, the counts are far reduced from traditional Florentine recipes.

- 2 cups cooked chopped spinach
- 4 eggs
- ⅛ teaspoon salt
- ⅛ teaspoon pepper
- 3 tablespoons grated gluten-free cheddar cheese
- 1 4-ounce can low-fat evaporated milk
- ¼ cup gluten-free dried Corn Muffin crumbs (See Index.)
- 2 teaspoons gluten-free margarine, melted

Preheat oven to 350°F. Spray four ½-cup custard cups with gluten-free nonstick spray. Drain the spinach well. Spread the spinach in the bottom of the custard cups; cover with foil and bake 5 minutes to warm the spinach. Remove from oven. Make a small well in the center of the spinach; drop an egg into each well, and season lightly with the salt and pepper. Put the cheese and milk in the top of a double boiler; heat over boiling water until the cheese is melted, stirring frequently. Drizzle the hot cheese sauce over the eggs. Stir together the corn bread crumbs and margarine until the crumbs are evenly coated; sprinkle over the cheese and eggs. Bake about 20 minutes until the eggs are firm. *Makes 4 ½-cup servings.*

One serving—Calories: 168; Total fat: 8.6 g; Saturated fat: 2.8 g; Cholesterol: 220 mg; Sodium: 328 mg; Carbohydrates: 10.8 g; Fiber: 2 g; Sugar: 4 g; Protein: 12.8 g

Miniature Blueberry Muffins

This recipe contains no eggs, yet the muffins hold together beautifully. Overstirring the batter makes the muffins tough; stir only until the wet and dry ingredients are evenly moistened.

1 cup Gluten-Free Flour Mixture (See the Hints chapter.)
¼ cup light brown sugar
1 teaspoon gluten-free baking powder
½ teaspoon baking soda
⅛ teaspoon salt
½ cup buttermilk
¼ teaspoon vanilla
¾ cup blueberries

Preheat oven to 375°F. Sift the flour mixture, brown sugar, baking powder, baking soda, and salt into a bowl. Stir in the buttermilk, vanilla, and blueberries just till blended. Spray 40 miniature muffin tins with gluten-free nonstick spray. Spoon the batter into the muffin tins. Bake for 18 minutes or until lightly browned and a toothpick inserted in the center of a muffin comes out clean. *Makes 40 muffins.*

One muffin—Calories: 16; Total fat: 0.1 g; Saturated fat: 0 g; Cholesterol: 0 mg; Sodium: 2 mg; Carbohydrates: 3.5 g; Fiber: 0.2 g; Sugar: 1.1 g; Protein: 0.4 g

Peach Popover Brunch

Tomato Eggs

The tomatoes need to be very ripe for this recipe so they will bake and be soft enough in the time it takes the eggs to bake.

6 ripe tomatoes
1½ teaspoons gluten-free margarine
Dash salt

Dash pepper

6 eggs

6 romaine lettuce leaves

Preheat oven to 350°F. Cut a thin slice off the top of each tomato. From the center of each tomato, cut out a hollow large enough to hold an egg. Spray an 8-inch square baking pan with gluten-free nonstick spray. Set the tomatoes in the baking pan. Add ¼ teaspoon of the margarine and a dash of salt and pepper to each hollow. Break an egg into each tomato. Sprinkle the top of each egg with a dash of salt and pepper. Bake 15 to 20 minutes until the eggs are firm and the tomatoes still hold their shape. When serving, place a leaf of lettuce on each plate; place a tomato on the lettuce. *Makes 6 stuffed tomatoes.*

One stuffed tomato—Calories: 97; Total fat: 6 g; Saturated fat: 1.7 g; Cholesterol: 212 mg; Sodium: 80 mg; Carbohydrates: 3.7 g; Fiber: 1 g; Sugar: 0 g; Protein: 7 g

Honey Ham

If you bake your own ham, remove all visible fat, and slice the pieces very thin.

1 ½ teaspoons gluten-free margarine

6 slices (¾ ounce each) gluten-free lean cooked ham

2 teaspoons honey

Spray a large skillet with gluten-free nonstick spray. Melt the margarine in the skillet. Brush both sides of each ham slice with the honey. Place the ham in the skillet, and brown quickly on both sides. *Makes 6 ¾-ounce servings.*

One serving—Calories: 46; Total fat: 1.7 g; Saturated fat: 0.5 g; Cholesterol: 6 mg; Sodium: 253 mg; Carbohydrates: 1.3 g; Fiber: 0 g; Sugar: 1.3 g; Protein: 4.5 g

Peach Popover

For a change, substitute a fresh pear, banana, or apple for the peach. One 4-ounce can of peaches may be used instead of the fresh peach; drain canned peaches well.

    1 tablespoon light brown sugar

    ¼ teaspoon cinnamon

    2 eggs

    ½ cup skim milk

    ¼ teaspoon vanilla

    ½ cup Gluten-Free Flour Mixture, sifted (See the Hints chapter.)

    ⅛ teaspoon salt

    1 tablespoon gluten-free margarine, melted

    1 fresh peach, peeled and sliced very thin

    1 tablespoon finely chopped pecans

Preheat oven to 400°F. In a small bowl, combine the brown sugar and cinnamon; set aside. Place a 9-inch pie plate in the preheated oven to warm. In a bowl, beat the eggs till fluffy and light. Add the milk and vanilla. Gradually beat in the flour mixture and salt. Remove the pie plate from the oven; spread the bottom and sides with margarine. Pour in the batter. Arrange the peach slices over the batter. Sprinkle the peaches with the cinnamon-sugar mixture. Sprinkle with the pecans. Bake about 25 minutes till puffy and golden brown. Cut into 6 wedges. *Makes 6 servings (wedges).*

One serving—Calories: 98; Total fat: 4 g; Saturated fat: 0.9 g; Cholesterol: 71 mg; Sodium: 105 mg; Carbohydrates: 11 g; Fiber: 0.6 g; Sugar: 2.5 g; Protein: 4 g

Baked French Toast Brunch

Baked French Toast

Use the most porous gluten-free bread available. Prepare the bread, then cover and refrigerate it for 6 hours, or overnight. This will allow the egg mixture to be absorbed better.

2 eggs

3 egg whites

⅛ teaspoon salt

1 cup skim milk

1½ tablespoons granulated sugar

1 teaspoon vanilla

8 slices gluten-free bread

½ teaspoon confectioner's sugar

½ teaspoon cinnamon

Blueberry Syrup (Recipe follows.)

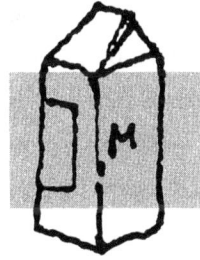

Preheat oven to 400°F. In a bowl, whisk together the eggs, egg whites, salt, milk, granulated sugar, and vanilla; pour into an 8″ × 12″ baking dish. Lay the bread in the mixture, and let stand for 15 minutes. Turn the bread over, and let stand 10 minutes or until moisture has been absorbed. Place a baking sheet in the preheated oven for 5 minutes. Remove the heated baking sheet from the oven, and spray lightly with gluten-free nonstick spray. Lay the bread on the baking sheet, and bake for 7 minutes. Turn the bread over, and bake 6 minutes more or until golden. In a small bowl, mix together the confectioner's sugar and cinnamon; sift lightly over an entire serving dish. Lay the French toast on the dish, then drizzle each slice with 1 tablespoon of Blueberry Syrup. *Makes 4 2-slice servings.*

One serving—Calories: 173; Total fat: 4 g; Saturated fat: 1.2 g; Cholesterol: 107 mg; Sodium: 366 mg; Carbohydrates: 22.4 g; Fiber: 1.5 g; Sugar: 7.3 g; Protein: 11.2 g

Blueberry Syrup

If you have any leftover syrup, drizzle it over gluten-free frozen yogurt for a quick dessert after dinner.

    ¾ cup apple juice

    4 teaspoons honey

    ½ teaspoon sugar

    1 tablespoon cornstarch

    ⅛ teaspoon powdered ginger

    ⅛ teaspoon cinnamon

    2 cups blueberries

    1 teaspoon lemon juice

    ¼ teaspoon gluten-free almond extract

In a saucepan, stir together the juice, honey, sugar, cornstarch, ginger, and cinnamon until the cornstarch dissolves. Add the blueberries, and simmer, stirring, for 2 minutes. Remove from heat and stir in the lemon juice and almond extract. Serve warm. *Makes 4 3-tablespoon servings.*

One serving—Calories: 74; Total fat: 0.5 g; Saturated fat: 0 g; Cholesterol: 0 mg; Sodium: 8 mg; Carbohydrates: 18.5 g; Fiber: 1.7 g; Sugar: 15.3 g; Protein: 0.7 g

Marinated Kielbasa

The kielbasa may be marinated for up to two days before cooking.

    ⅓ pound gluten-free turkey kielbasa

    2 teaspoons honey

    1 teaspoon olive oil

    ½ teaspoon gluten-free soy sauce

    Dash powdered ginger

    Dash garlic powder

    ½ teaspoon gluten-free prepared mustard

Place the kielbasa in a sandwich-size, reclosable plastic bag. Stir together the honey, olive oil, soy sauce, ginger, garlic powder, and mustard. Spread the marinade over the kielbasa. Seal the bag and let the kielbasa marinate 30 minutes. Preheat the broiler. Remove the kielbasa from the bag, and set it on a broiler pan. Broil 10 minutes, turning frequently, till glazed. Slice into 8 pieces. *Makes 4 2-piece servings.*

One serving–Calories: 132; Total fat: 9.1 g; Saturated fat: 2.6 g; Cholesterol: 30 mg; Sodium: 154 mg; Carbohydrates: 1.4 g; Fiber: 0 g; Sugar: 2.6 g; Protein: 9.1 g

Omelet Brunch

Cheese Omelet

Eggs are most easily separated while they are still cold. Some manufacturers add a little flour to their grated cheese to keep the shreds from sticking together; you are safest buying a solid piece of gluten-free cheese and shredding your own.

3 eggs

2 egg whites

3 tablespoons warmed skim milk

⅛ teaspoon salt

⅛ teaspoon pepper

1 tablespoon corn oil

2 tablespoons grated gluten-free, reduced-fat cheddar cheese

Preheat oven to 350°F. Separate the eggs, combining the whites from the whole eggs with the additional 2 egg whites. Whip the egg whites until almost stiff. In a separate bowl, whip the egg yolks until slightly thickened and pale yellow; whip in the milk, salt, and pepper. Fold the yolk mixture into the egg whites. Heat the oil in a skillet or omelet pan. Spread the egg mixture evenly in the pan, and cook over low heat until it is puffy and light brown underneath. Put the skillet in the preheated oven, and bake 12 minutes or just until the top is dry to the touch. (Do not over-cook, or it will shrink and become tough.) Loosen the edges; cut most of the way through the center. Sprinkle with cheese, then fold the omelet in half, pressing slightly to help it stay in place. Cut the omelet into four wedges. *Makes 4 servings (wedges).*

One serving—Calories: 94; Total fat: 6.2 g; Saturated fat: 1.9 g; Cholesterol: 160 mg; Sodium: 209 mg; Carbohydrates: 1.4 g; Fiber: 0 g; Sugar: 0.4 g; Protein: 7.6 g

Shredded Hash Brown Potatoes

Use freshly cut onions and green bell pepper; frozen chopped onion or green bell pepper will make your potatoes too watery. The good news is that this recipe may also be made with frozen shredded hash brown potatoes. The bad news is that some commercial frozen hash browns are not gluten-free. You are always safe shredding your own potatoes.

3 medium russet potatoes
¼ cup minced onion
¼ cup minced green bell pepper
1 tablespoon corn oil
⅛ teaspoon black pepper
⅛ teaspoon salt

Preheat oven to 450°F. Peel and shred the potatoes. Rinse the potatoes, and drain well; pat dry with paper towels. In a large bowl, stir together the potatoes, onion, green bell pepper, corn oil, black pepper, and salt. Spray a cookie sheet with gluten-free nonstick spray. Spread the potatoes on the cookie sheet; bake 20 minutes, stirring occasionally. Lower heat to 350°F and continue to bake for 10 minutes, until the potatoes are crispy and golden. *Makes 4 ¾-cup servings.*

One serving–Calories: 160; Total fat: 3.6 g; Saturated fat: 0.5 g; Cholesterol: 0 mg; Sodium: 83 mg; Carbohydrates: 30 g; Fiber: 2.1 g; Sugar: 1 g; Protein: 3.5 g

Apple Spice Loaf

This spicy, moist quick bread may be served at room temperature, but it is really best when toasted. Make ahead of time to be served with brunch.

1½ cups Gluten-Free Flour Mixture (See the Hints chapter.)

¾ teaspoon baking soda

1¼ teaspoons gluten-free baking powder

¼ teaspoon salt

¾ teaspoon cinnamon

¼ teaspoon nutmeg

3 egg whites, beaten

⅔ cup light brown sugar

1¼ cups shredded, peeled
     McIntosh apple

3 tablespoons corn oil

½ teaspoon vanilla

1 tablespoon gluten-free, low-fat mayonnaise

3 tablespoons orange juice

⅓ cup chopped walnuts

Preheat oven to 350°F. Sift together the flour mixture, baking soda, baking powder, salt, cinnamon, and nutmeg. In a large bowl, whisk the egg whites until foamy; stir in the brown sugar, apple, corn oil, vanilla, mayonnaise, orange juice, and walnuts. Stir the dry ingredients into the apple mixture just till combined.

Spray a small tube pan (or an 8½″ × 4½″ × 2½″ loaf pan) with gluten-free nonstick spray. Pour the batter into the pan, and bake 45 to 50 minutes or until a toothpick inserted near the center comes out clean. Cool the bread in the pan for 10 minutes; remove from pan and cool thoroughly on a wire rack. *Makes 1 loaf (16 slices).*

One slice—Calories: 79; Total fat: 1.9 g; Saturated fat: 0.2 g; Cholesterol: 0 mg; Sodium: 54 mg; Carbohydrates: 13.4 g; Fiber: 0.6 g; Sugar: 5 g; Protein: 2.2 g

Mushroom Roulade Brunch

Mushroom Roulade

Before preparing the roulade, let the eggs come to room temperature. If you buy unsalted gluten-free margarine, read the label. Avoid any brands that contain coconut oil because they have up to four times more saturated fat than other margarines.

½ pound fresh mushrooms, chopped

¼ cup thinly sliced green onions

¾ teaspoon cornstarch

⅛ teaspoon plus ¼ teaspoon salt

¼ teaspoon dill weed

3 tablespoons plus ½ cup skim milk

3 tablespoons Gluten-Free Flour Mixture
(See the Hints chapter.)

⅛ teaspoon nutmeg

⅛ teaspoon pepper

3 tablespoons gluten-free margarine

5 eggs, separated

¼ teaspoon cream of tartar

2 tablespoons grated gluten-free Parmesan cheese

⅓ cup shredded gluten-free Swiss cheese

Preheat oven to 350°F. Spray a large skillet with gluten-free non-stick spray; sauté the mushrooms and green onions until the vegetables are tender and liquid is absorbed. Stir together the cornstarch, ⅛ teaspoon of the salt, and the dill. Stir 3 tablespoons of the milk into the cornstarch mixture until smooth, then add to the mushroom mixture; cook 1 minute, stirring constantly. Remove from heat, and set aside. Spray a 10″ × 15″ jelly roll pan with gluten-free nonstick spray; line with waxed paper, and spray the waxed paper with gluten-free nonstick spray. Sift together the flour mixture, remaining ¼ teaspoon of salt, and the nutmeg and pepper. Melt the margarine in a saucepan over low heat; stir in the dry ingredients. Cook 1 minute, stirring constantly. Gradually add ½ cup of the skim milk; cook, stirring constantly, until the mixture is very thick. In a mixer bowl, beat the egg yolks slightly. Very gradually, add the white sauce from the saucepan. Set aside. With clean, dry beaters, beat the egg whites until foamy. Add the cream of tartar, and continue beating until stiff peaks form. Stir a small amount of the beaten egg whites into the sauce; fold in the remaining whites. Spread the egg mixture evenly into the prepared pan. Bake 15 minutes or till puffy and firm in the center. Cover a baking sheet with foil, and spray the foil with gluten-free nonstick spray. Turn out the roulade onto the foil-lined pan. Carefully remove the waxed paper. Preheat the broiler. Spread the roulade with the mushroom filling, sprinkle with the Parmesan cheese and half of the Swiss cheese. Starting at one end (not a long side), roll up the roulade, ending with the seam side down. Sprinkle the remaining Swiss cheese over the top. Broil 4 inches from the heat 1 minute or until cheese melts. Cut into 6 slices. *Makes 6 servings (slices).*

One slice—Calories: 160; Total fat: 10.8 g; Saturated fat: 3.7 g; Cholesterol: 184 mg; Sodium: 125 mg; Carbohydrates: 6 g; Fiber: 0.4 g; Sugar: 1.4 g; Protein: 9.4 g

Apple Date Muffins

To dress up these muffins for company, drizzle the tops with a glaze made of sifted confectioner's sugar, skim milk, and vanilla.

½ cup peeled, cored, minced McIntosh apples

½ cup minced dates

⅔ cup skim milk

3 tablespoons light brown sugar

2 eggs

2 egg whites

3 tablespoons unsweetened applesauce

2 tablespoons corn oil

1 tablespoon gluten-free, reduced-fat mayonnaise

½ teaspoon vanilla

1½ cups Gluten-Free Flour Mixture (See the Hints chapter.)

1½ teaspoons gluten-free baking powder

1½ teaspoons baking soda

⅛ teaspoon salt

½ teaspoon cinnamon

¼ cup chopped walnuts

Topping

¼ cup Gluten-Free Flour Mixture (See the Hints chapter.)

¼ cup light brown sugar

½ teaspoon cinnamon

1 tablespoon gluten-free margarine

Preheat oven to 350°F. In a large bowl, mix the apples, dates, milk, sugar, eggs, egg whites, applesauce, corn oil, mayonnaise, and vanilla. Sift the flour mixture, baking powder, baking soda, salt, and cinnamon. Add the dry ingredients and the walnuts to the egg mixture; stir just until blended. Spoon the batter into muffin tins that have been sprayed with gluten-free nonstick spray. To make the topping, mix the flour mixture, sugar, cinnamon, and margarine in a small bowl with a fork until crumbly. Sprinkle over the muffin batter. Bake 15 minutes or until a toothpick inserted in the center of a muffin comes out clean. *Makes 18 muffins.*

One muffin—Calories: 96; Total fat: 3.3 g; Saturated fat: 0.6 g; Cholesterol: 24 mg; Sodium: 46 mg; Carbohydrates: 14.1 g; Fiber: 0.6 g; Sugar: 4.1 g; Protein: 2.7 g

Sausage Tart Brunch

Sausage Tarts

Make sure the eggs are fresh. Old eggs are smooth and shiny; fresh ones are rough and chalky by comparison. Set each sausage tart on a piece of red leaf lettuce. Garnish each tart with a fresh strawberry fan placed on top.

½ pound gluten-free turkey bulk sausage

1 tablespoon finely minced onion

½ cup gluten-free dried Corn Muffin crumbs (See Index.)

1 egg white plus 3 egg whites, divided

2 tablespoons skim milk

3 eggs

2 teaspoons gluten-free margarine

2 teaspoons minced green onion

2 tablespoons gluten-free light cream cheese, softened

2 teaspoons dill weed

⅛ teaspoon pepper

⅛ teaspoon salt

Preheat oven to 350°F. In a bowl, combine the sausage, 1 tablespoon of the onion, the corn bread crumbs, 1 egg white, and the milk. Divide the mixture evenly into six muffin cups. Press the mixture firmly around the bottom and sides to form hollow cups.

Bake 12 minutes or until cooked through. Remove the cups, and drain well on paper towels. Keep warm. With a whisk, beat the eggs and 3 egg whites. Melt the margarine in a skillet; add the eggs and stir as they start to cook. When the eggs are halfway cooked, stir in the green onions, cream cheese, dill, pepper, and salt. When the eggs are set, divide them among the sausage cups. Serve hot. *Makes 6 tarts.*

One tart–Calories: 110; Total fat: 6.3 g; Saturated fat: 3.2 g; Cholesterol: 122 mg; Sodium: 394 mg; Carbohydrates: 3.3 g; Fiber: 0 g; Sugar: 1.4 g; Protein: 9 g

Raspberry Almond Muffins

Muffins bake best in humid air. Before baking, fill any unused cups in the muffin tins with water.

> 1 cup Gluten-Free Flour Mixture (See the Hints chapter.)
> 1/3 cup sugar
> 1 1/4 teaspoons gluten-free baking powder
> 1/8 teaspoon salt
> 3 tablespoons ground almonds
> 1 tablespoon gluten-free margarine,
>   melted
> 2/3 cup skim milk
> 1 tablespoon gluten-free mayonnaise
> 2 egg whites
> 1/2 teaspoon vanilla
> 1/3 cup frozen raspberries, thawed (do not drain)

Preheat oven to 375°F. Sift the flour mixture, sugar, baking powder, and salt into a large bowl; stir in the almonds. In a small bowl, whisk together the margarine, milk, mayonnaise, egg whites, and vanilla. Stir the egg mixture into the flour mixture just till all ingredients are moistened; fold in the raspberries. Spray muffin tins with gluten-free nonstick spray. Spoon the batter into the muffin tins. Bake 15 minutes or till a toothpick inserted in the center of a muffin comes out clean. *Makes 15 muffins.*

One muffin—Calories: 42; Total fat: 1.2 g; Saturated fat: 0.2 g; Cholesterol: 0 mg; Sodium: 43 mg; Carbohydrates: 7.8 g; Fiber: 0.5 g; Sugar: 3.1 g; Protein: 1.6 g

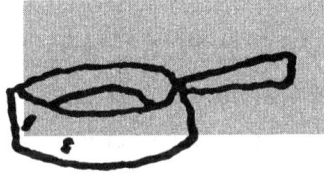

Spinach Casserole Brunch

Spinach Breakfast Casserole

This deceptively rich-tasting casserole may be assembled the day before, then covered and refrigerated until time to bake. This version of a much-loved recipe has far fewer calories than the traditional method of preparation.

  2 teaspoons olive oil
  4 green onions, sliced thin
  2 tablespoons cornstarch
  1 cup skim milk
  1 cup gluten-free, reduced-sodium chicken broth
  1/3 cup gluten-free dry sherry
  1/4 teaspoon salt
  1/4 teaspoon pepper
  1/4 teaspoon gluten-free prepared mustard
  1/4 teaspoon nutmeg
  2 ounces gluten-free, low-fat mozzarella cheese, shredded

1 10-ounce box frozen chopped spinach, thawed and
   squeezed dry

¼ cup gluten-free, low-fat sour cream

2 eggs, hard-boiled, peeled, and cut into ½-inch-thick slices

1 6-ounce can crabmeat, drained

¼ pound asparagus, trimmed and cut into ½-inch lengths

1 teaspoon grated gluten-free Parmesan cheese

Preheat oven to 350°F. In a large skillet, heat the olive oil 1 minute. Add the green onions, and sauté until soft and tender. Stir in the cornstarch, and whisk over low heat for 30 seconds. Slowly whisk in the milk, chicken broth, sherry, salt, and pepper. Bring to a boil, then reduce heat and cook, stirring constantly, until the sauce thickens. Whisk in the mustard, nutmeg, and mozzarella cheese. Remove from heat. In a bowl, stir together the spinach and sour cream. Place the spinach mixture in the bottom of four 4-ounce ramekins or custard cups that have been sprayed with gluten-free nonstick spray. Lay the sliced eggs on top of the spinach. Sprinkle the crabmeat on top of the eggs. Blanch the asparagus, then drain. Place the asparagus on top of the crabmeat. Spoon the sauce on top of the asparagus, then sprinkle with the Parmesan cheese. Bake 30 minutes or until hot. *Makes 4 individual casseroles.*

One casserole—Calories: 223; Total fat: 10.4 g; Saturated fat: 2.2 g; Cholesterol: 135 mg; Sodium: 714 mg; Carbohydrates: 13.4 g; Fiber: 2 g; Sugar: 4 g; Protein: 18.7 g

Strawberry Banana Muffins

This recipe uses frozen strawberries, because they contain more moisture than fresh strawberries, resulting in a moister muffin. Instead of strawberries, you can use a different fruit each time you prepare these muffins. Try either fresh diced or frozen (drained) blueberries, raspberries, peaches, or nectarines.

¾ cup Gluten-Free Flour Mixture (See the Hints chapter.)

¼ cup light brown sugar

1½ teaspoons gluten-free baking powder

¾ teaspoon baking soda

¼ teaspoon cinnamon

⅛ teaspoon salt

½ cup skim milk

⅓ cup frozen strawberries, drained and chopped

1 small, ripe banana, mashed

½ teaspoon vanilla

Preheat oven to 375°F. Sift together the flour mixture, sugar, baking powder, baking soda, cinnamon, and salt. Stir in the milk, strawberries, mashed banana, and vanilla just until combined. Spray muffin tins with gluten-free nonstick spray. Spoon the batter into the muffin tins. Bake 15 minutes or until a toothpick inserted in the center of a muffin comes out clean. *Makes 12 muffins.*

One muffin—Calories: 50; Total fat: 0.3 g; Saturated fat: 0 g; Cholesterol: 0 mg; Sodium: 91 mg; Carbohydrates: 11.7 g; Fiber: 0.6 g; Sugar: 3.2 g; Protein: 1.2 g

2

Lunches and Luncheons

Lunches are more casual, while luncheons tend to be a bit more formal. Either way, it's nice to make some effort to spruce up the table with flowers or a simple bowl of fruit.

Lentil Soup and Shrimp Salad

Lentil Soup

Lentils are rich in iron, fiber, and folic acid—one of the most healthful foods one can eat.

- ¼ pound lentils
- 1 tablespoon olive oil
- ½ cup chopped celery
- ¼ cup chopped carrot
- ½ cup chopped onion
- 1 clove garlic, minced
- 2 teaspoons tomato paste

    2 bay leaves

    1 teaspoon salt

    ½ teaspoon pepper

    2 teaspoons apple cider vinegar

Wash the lentils; cover with 1 quart of water in a large saucepan, and bring to a boil. When the water starts boiling, strain the lentils, and discard cooking water. Heat the olive oil in the same saucepan, and sauté the celery, carrot, onion, and garlic. Add the lentils and 6 to 7 cups of water. Bring to a boil, and simmer till the lentils are tender. Add the tomato paste, bay leaves, salt, pepper, and vinegar, and continue to simmer 30 minutes. Add more water as needed during cooking. *Makes 6 1-cup servings.*

One serving—Calories: 107; Total fat: 2.7 g; Saturated fat: 0.3 g; Cholesterol: 0 mg; Sodium: 243 mg; Carbohydrates: 15.7 g; Fiber: 5.8 g; Sugar: 2.2 g; Protein: 6.4 g

Shrimp Pasta Salad

Shrimp is very low in calories. Using only 4 shrimp per salad keeps cholesterol intake within safe levels.

    6 ounces gluten-free corn elbow
        or spiral macaroni
    9 tablespoons gluten-free,
        low-calorie Italian dressing
    ¼ teaspoon dill weed
    Dash coarsely ground pepper
    24 medium cooked shrimp
    3 tablespoons sliced black olives
    1 15-ounce can artichoke hearts,
        drained and cut in quarters
    1 small zucchini, sliced thin

Cook the macaroni according to package directions. Rinse with cold water, then drain. Spoon the macaroni into a large bowl, and

toss with the Italian dressing, dill, and pepper. Gently fold in the shrimp, olives, artichoke hearts, and zucchini. *Makes 6 1-cup servings.*

One serving—Calories: 229; Total fat: 2.3 g; Saturated fat: 0.4 g; Cholesterol: 116 mg; Sodium: 561 mg; Carbohydrates: 36.1 g; Fiber: 5.5 g; Sugar: 3.1 g; Protein: 17.3 g

Northern Bean Soup and California Salad

Northern Bean Soup

This soup holds several days in the refrigerator and freezes well.

1 15-ounce can Great Northern beans
½ tablespoon olive oil
¼ cup chopped celery
¼ cup chopped carrot
¼ cup chopped onion
½ cup tomato sauce
½ teaspoon salt
¼ teaspoon pepper
4 cups water

Wash the beans well in a strainer under cold running water; drain. Heat the olive oil in a large saucepan, and sauté the celery, carrot, and onion. Add the beans, tomato sauce, salt, pepper, and water. Bring to a boil, then simmer, covered, 30 minutes. Spoon half of the soup into a blender, and blend till pureed. Return the pureed soup to the saucepan. Simmer, covered, 20 minutes till soup is thickened. *Makes 4 1-cup servings.*

One serving—Calories: 209; Total fat: 4.2 g; Saturated fat: 0.5 g; Cholesterol: 0 mg; Sodium: 676 mg; Carbohydrates: 33.5 g; Fiber: 8.6 g; Protein: 11.1 g

California Salad

This salad uses a colorful mix of tender young greens known as *mesclun*, a salad mix available at many supermarkets and farmers' markets. If fresh strawberries are out of season, use kiwi (peeled and sliced) or fresh seedless grapes.

½ teaspoon gluten-free,
    low-calorie Italian dressing
Dash coarsely ground pepper
½ teaspoon gluten-free soy sauce
1 8-ounce chicken breast
4 cups mesclun greens
8 fresh strawberries
1 onion, sliced thin and separated into rings
1 tablespoon slivered almonds
2 tablespoons olive oil
3 tablespoons gluten-free balsamic vinegar

In a small bowl, mix the Italian dressing, pepper, and soy sauce. Marinate the chicken in this mixture for 30 minutes. While the chicken is marinating, preheat broiler or light grill. Remove the chicken from the marinade, and grill or broil just till cooked through. Meanwhile, divide mesclun greens among four salad plates. Arrange the strawberries, onion rings, and almonds on top of the lettuce. Combine the olive oil and vinegar, and sprinkle over the salads. Slice the hot chicken breast into thin slices, and place on top of the salads. *Makes 4 1½-cup servings.*

One serving—Calories: 187; Total fat: 10.1 g; Saturated fat: 1.5 g; Cholesterol: 48 mg; Sodium: 93 mg; Carbohydrates: 6.3 g; Fiber: 2.2 g; Sugar: 0.1 g; Protein: 19.4 g

Parmesan Chili with Veggies and Dip

Parmesan Chili

Chili is great topped with grated onions, a few tablespoons of cooked rice, or a dollop of gluten-free sour cream.

½ pound 93% lean ground beef

1 onion, chopped

¼ green bell pepper, chopped

1 15-ounce can diced tomatoes (with juice)

½ cup water

½ teaspoon gluten-free beef bouillon granules

Dash red pepper flakes

⅛ teaspoon garlic powder

⅛ teaspoon cumin

½ teaspoon gluten-free chili powder

1 10-ounce can undrained kidney beans

2 tablespoons grated gluten-free Parmesan cheese

In a large saucepan, brown the meat, onion, and green bell pepper; drain off any fat. Stir in the tomatoes with their juice, water, beef bouillon, red pepper flakes, garlic powder, cumin, chili powder, and kidney beans with their liquid. Reduce heat and simmer, uncovered, 20 minutes, stirring occasionally. Just before serving, stir in the cheese. *Makes 4 1-cup servings.*

One serving—Calories: 261; Total fat: 11.7 g; Saturated fat: 4.8 g; Cholesterol: 55 mg; Sodium: 685 mg; Carbohydrates: 4.7 g; Fiber: 7.1 g; Sugar: 1.6 g; Protein: 21.6 g

Veggies and Garlic Dip

To keep the garlic from sticking to your hands, rinse them frequently while pinching the cooked garlic cloves.

1 large bulb (entire head) garlic

1 cup gluten-free, low-fat cottage cheese

¼ teaspoon black pepper

⅛ teaspoon red pepper flakes

1 tablespoon minced fresh parsley

¼ teaspoon dill weed

¼ red bell pepper, finely diced

¼ green bell pepper, finely diced

Small carrots

Broccoli florets

Zucchini, sliced

Cauliflower florets

Red bell pepper, sliced

Hearts of celery, sliced into thin strips

Preheat oven to 375°F. Wrap the garlic in foil; set on a rack placed in middle of oven and bake for 1 hour. Remove the garlic from the foil, and let cool until easy to handle. Separate the garlic into cloves. Pinch each clove so the flesh of the garlic slips out of the skin. Put the cottage cheese into a blender; add the garlic, black pepper, red pepper flakes, parsley, and dill. Puree about 20 seconds. Spoon the dip into a bowl, stir in the red and green bell pepper, and set the bowl in the center of a serving dish. Surround the bowl of dip with freshly cut carrots, broccoli, zucchini slices, cauliflower, strips of red and green bell pepper, and celery. *Makes 4 3-tablespoon servings of dip.*

One serving (dip only)—Calories: 30; Total fat: 0.6 g; Saturated fat: 0.3 g; Cholesterol: 4 mg; Sodium: 100 mg; Carbohydrates: 2.7 g; Fiber: 0.1 g; Sugar: 1.8 g; Protein: 3.5 g

Parmesan Crackers

Don't place crackers too close together on the cookie sheet because they will spread a little.

¼ cup Gluten-Free Flour Mixture (See the Hints chapter.)

¼ teaspoon salt

¼ teaspoon pepper

½ teaspoon sugar

¼ cup grated gluten-free Parmesan cheese

3 teaspoons parsley flakes

¼ teaspoon oregano

2 egg whites

1 tablespoon corn oil

Preheat oven to 300°F. Sift together the flour mixture, salt, pepper, sugar, and cheese; stir in the parsley and oregano. In a small mixing bowl, beat the egg whites until foamy; add the corn oil, and beat until stiff. Fold in the dry ingredients. Spray a baking sheet with gluten-free nonstick spray. Drop the batter by level tablespoonfuls onto the baking sheet 1½ inches apart. Spread the batter slightly with the heel of the spoon to form 3½-inch circles. Bake 15 to 20 minutes or till golden. *Makes 20 2-cracker servings.*

One serving—Calories: 22; Total fat: 0.9 g; Saturated fat: 0.2 g; Cholesterol: 1 mg; Sodium: 49 mg; Carbohydrates: 1.2 g; Fiber: 0 g; Sugar: 0.1 g; Protein: 0.8 g

Thai Lunch

Thai Rice Ball Soup

For rice to go through a sieve easily, it must be hot and very soft.

6 cups water

2 cubes gluten-free chicken bouillon

1 green onion, sliced

½ carrot, thinly sliced on the diagonal

¼ cup sliced fresh mushrooms

1 tablespoon plus 1 teaspoon minced fresh parsley

⅛ teaspoon garlic powder

¾ cup cold cooked basmati rice

5 teaspoons Gluten-Free Flour Mixture
    (See the Hints chapter.)

1 egg white, slightly beaten

¼ teaspoon pepper

¼ teaspoon salt

¼ teaspoon dill weed

¾ teaspoon grated lemon zest

Bring the water to a boil; add the bouillon cubes, breaking them up with the back of a spoon. Add the green onion, carrot, mushrooms, 1 tablespoon of the parsley, and the garlic powder. Cover and simmer 10 minutes. In a small bowl, mix the rice, flour mixture, egg white, pepper, salt, dill, lemon zest, and remaining 1 teaspoon of parsley, and mix thoroughly. With hands, form into 12 balls. Drop the rice balls into the broth, and simmer until they become firm on the outside, about 10 minutes. *Makes 4 1½-cup servings.*

One serving—Calories: 60; Total fat: 0.3 g; Saturated fat: 0.1 g; Cholesterol: 0 mg; Sodium: 543 mg; Carbohydrates: 11.5 g; Fiber: 0.4 g; Sugar: 0.7 g; Protein: 2.5 g

Artichoke Crab Salad

Chopped pimiento may be added for additional color.

    2 15-ounce cans artichoke hearts, drained and cut in quarters
    1½ cups crabmeat pieces
    1 tablespoon sliced black olives
    3 tablespoons olive oil
    3 tablespoons lemon juice
    ⅛ teaspoon pepper
    ⅛ teaspoon salt
    2 green onions, sliced thin

Lay the artichoke hearts on four salad plates; top with the crab-meat pieces. In a bowl, mix together the olives, olive oil, lemon juice, pepper, salt, and green onions; sprinkle the dressing over the artichoke hearts and crabmeat. *Makes 4 ¾-cup servings.*

One serving—Calories: 121; Total fat: 1.9 g; Saturated fat: 0.3 g; Cholesterol: 45 mg; Sodium: 427 mg; Carbohydrates: 14.5 g; Fiber: 1.7 g; Sugar: 2 g; Protein: 14.4 g

South-of-the-Border Lunch

Taco Salad

Corn chips may be used in place of the tortillas; spoon the salad onto a serving dish, then sprinkle ⅓ cup of chips over each salad.

    4 6-inch gluten-free corn tortillas
    ½ pound lean ground beef
    1 onion, chopped
    1 clove garlic, minced
    ¾ cup kidney beans, rinsed and drained
    3 tablespoons tomato sauce

4 tablespoons water

1 tablespoon apple cider vinegar

½ teaspoon cumin

½ teaspoon gluten-free chili powder

¼ teaspoon crushed red pepper

4 cups shredded iceberg lettuce

4 cherry tomatoes, halved

½ cup chopped green bell pepper

¼ cup shredded gluten-free, low-fat cheddar cheese

4 tablespoons gluten-free, low-calorie Italian dressing

Preheat oven to 350°F. Wrap the tortillas in foil; bake for 10 minutes to soften. Spray four custard cups with gluten-free nonstick spray. Press one tortilla into each cup. Bake for 15 minutes till crisp. Cool; remove from custard cups. In a skillet, cook the beef, onion, and garlic till meat is browned; drain any fat. Stir in the beans, tomato sauce, water, vinegar, cumin, chili powder, and red pepper. Bring to a boil; reduce heat and simmer, uncovered, 10 minutes, stirring occasionally. Divide 2 cups of the lettuce among four serving plates. Put the tomatoes on the lettuce. Place a tortilla shell in center of each plate. Place the remaining 2 cups of the lettuce in the shells, topped by the meat mixture. Sprinkle each plate with the green bell pepper and cheese. Drizzle the dressing over the salads. *Makes 4 1½-cup servings.*

One serving—Calories: 312; Total fat: 14.4 g; Saturated fat: 4.6 g; Cholesterol: 49 mg; Sodium: 637 mg; Carbohydrates: 24.4 g; Fiber: 4.4 g; Sugar: 3.1 g; Protein: 21.7 g

Lite Lunch

Chinese Soup

The trick to this soup is not to overcook it; the vegetables need to be tender-crisp.

    6 cups water
    2 cubes gluten-free chicken bouillon
    1 cup thinly sliced bok choy
    ½ cup chopped green onion
    ½ cup julienned carrot
    ½ cup sliced celery
    ½ cup chopped spinach
    1 tablespoon gluten-free soy sauce
    2 tablespoons gluten-free dry sherry
    ¼ teaspoon pepper
    ¼ teaspoon salt

In a large saucepan, combine the water, bouillon, bok choy, green onion, carrot, celery, spinach, soy sauce, sherry, pepper, and salt. Bring to a boil. Reduce heat, cover, and simmer 10 minutes. *Makes 4 1¾-cup servings.*

One serving–Calories: 25; Total fat: 0.4 g; Saturated fat: 0.1 g; Cholesterol: 0 mg; Sodium: 798 mg; Carbohydrates: 4.3 g; Fiber: 1.4 g; Sugar: 1.6 g; Protein: 1.7 g

Turkey Roll-Ups

For variety, try using broccoli spears and gluten-free mozzarella cheese instead of the asparagus and cheddar cheese.

    8 stalks asparagus
    3 ounces cheddar cheese
    4 thin slices gluten-free turkey

Preheat oven to 350°F. In a skillet, simmer the asparagus in ¼ cup water 3 minutes to blanch, then drain. Cut the cheese into 4 thin slices. Lay two asparagus spears on each turkey slice; top with a cheese slice. Roll up the turkey and place it seam side down on a baking sheet. Cover with foil and bake about 5 minutes or just till heated through. *Makes 4 roll-ups.*

One roll-up—Calories: 81; Total fat: 2.2 g; Saturated fat: 1.1 g; Cholesterol: 19 mg; Sodium: 149 mg; Carbohydrates: 2.4 g; Fiber: 1 g; Sugar: 0 g; Protein: 12.5 g

Cheddar Soda Bread

Soda breads are light and airy with a texture similar to biscuits.

    1 cup Gluten-Free Flour Mixture (See the Hints chapter.)
    ¾ teaspoon gluten-free baking powder
    ½ teaspoon baking soda
    ⅛ teaspoon salt
    2 tablespoons gluten-free margarine
    ¼ teaspoon oregano
    1 tablespoon shredded gluten-free cheddar cheese
    1 slightly beaten egg white
    ⅓ cup buttermilk

Preheat oven to 375°F. Sift the flour mixture, baking powder, baking soda, and salt into a medium-size bowl. Cut in the margarine until the mixture resembles coarse crumbs. Mix in the oregano and cheese. In a small bowl, combine the egg white and buttermilk. Stir into the dry mixture just until moistened. Lightly sprinkle a cutting board with a little gluten-free flour; knead the dough on the board about 12 times till nearly smooth. Shape into a round loaf. Spray a baking sheet with gluten-free nonstick spray; place the loaf on the baking sheet. With a sharp knife, make two slashes in the top to form an X. Bake about 30 minutes, until golden. Cut the loaf into eight wedges; serve four sections with lunch, and freeze the remainder for use another day. *Makes 8 wedges.*

One wedge—Calories: 159; Total fat: 5.3 g; Saturated fat: 1.1 g; Cholesterol: 0 mg; Sodium: 193 mg; Carbohydrates: 23 g; Fiber: 1 g; Sugar: 1 g; Protein: 5.5 g

Baked Stuffed Tomato with Corn Muffins

Tuna-Stuffed Tomato

For a pretty presentation, put a few alfalfa sprouts on top just before serving.

    4 tomatoes
    1 6½-ounce can water-packed tuna, drained and flaked
    1 hard-boiled egg, diced
    ¼ teaspoon pepper
    ½ cup shredded gluten-free, low-fat cheddar cheese
    3 tablespoons thinly sliced celery
    1 tablespoon minced onion
    2 tablespoons gluten-free, reduced-fat mayonnaise
    ⅛ teaspoon gluten-free prepared mustard

Preheat oven to 350°F. Cut each tomato almost in half from stem to blossom end, without cutting all the way through. Rotate the tomato and cut in half again, from stem to blossom end, without cutting all the way through, making 4 equal sections. Carefully spread the sections open. Combine the tuna, egg, pepper, cheese, celery, onion, mayonnaise, and mustard in a bowl. Spoon one-fourth of the tuna filling into each of the tomatoes. Wrap each in foil, and place on a baking pan. Bake 20 minutes. If you prefer, you can wrap the tomatoes in waxed paper instead of foil, and heat in the microwave on High for 4 minutes. *Makes 4 stuffed tomatoes.*

One stuffed tomato—Calories: 151; Total fat: 4.9 g; Saturated fat: 1.6 g; Cholesterol: 64 mg; Sodium: 333 mg; Carbohydrates: 7.2 g; Fiber: 1.7 g; Sugar: 0.6 g; Protein: 18.3 g

Corn Muffins

This recipe is not "low calorie," but the original recipe was altered to create "reduced-calorie" muffins. You can crumble frozen muffins to make the corn muffin crumbs called for in several recipes throughout this cookbook.

    1 cup yellow cornmeal
    1 cup Gluten-Free Flour Mixture (See the Hints chapter.)
    ¼ cup sugar
    5 teaspoons gluten-free baking powder
    ¼ teaspoon salt
    1 cup skim milk
    2 tablespoons gluten-free, low-fat mayonnaise
    2 egg whites, slightly beaten
    1 egg, slightly beaten
    ¼ cup corn oil
    ½ teaspoon dill weed

Preheat oven to 400°F. Sift together the cornmeal, flour mixture, sugar, baking powder, and salt. In another bowl, stir together the milk, mayonnaise, egg whites, egg, corn oil, and dill; stir into the dry ingredients just till blended. Spray 8 muffin tins with gluten-free nonstick spray. Spoon the batter into the muffin tins. Let the muffins set for 5 minutes before baking. Bake for 15 to 20 minutes or until a toothpick inserted in the center of the muffins comes out clean (do not overbake—tops do not brown). *Makes 8 muffins.*

One muffin—Calories: 225; Total fat: 9 g; Saturated fat: 2 g; Cholesterol: 41 mg; Sodium: 210 mg; Carbohydrates: 45.2 g; Fiber: 2.6 g; Sugar: 11.5 g; Protein: 8.5 g

Beef Vegetable Soup and Tossed Tuna Salad

Beef Vegetable Soup

To remove fat from the soup, make the soup the day before, and refrigerate it. Before reheating, skim off all congealed fat.

¼ pound lean stewing beef, cut into ¼-inch cubes

6 cups water

¼ cup sliced carrot

¼ cup sliced celery

1 tablespoon diced green bell pepper

1 small onion, diced

2 sprigs parsley, chopped

¼ cup peas

¼ cup diced potatoes

1 8-ounce can tomato sauce

½ teaspoon salt

¼ teaspoon black pepper

1 bay leaf

Put the meat and water in a large saucepan; bring to a boil; skim off any brine. Lower heat, cover, and simmer 1½ hours or until meat is very tender. Add the carrot, celery, green bell pepper, onion, parsley, peas, potatoes, tomato sauce, salt, black pepper, and bay leaf. Simmer, covered, 30 minutes. Remove the bay leaf. *Makes 4 1½-cup servings.*

One serving—Calories: 100; Total fat: 2.2 g; Saturated fat: 0.7 g; Cholesterol: 25 mg; Sodium: 727 mg; Carbohydrates: 10.4 g; Fiber: 1.1 g; Sugar: 4.5 g; Protein: 10.6 g

Tossed Tuna Salad

For your convenience, grocery stores now carry shredded lettuce and shredded carrots.

    4 cups shredded iceberg lettuce
    1 3½-ounce can water-packed tuna, drained and flaked
    2 tablespoons shredded carrot
    2 tablespoons diced green bell pepper
    ¼ onion, minced
    4 tablespoons gluten-free, low-calorie Italian dressing

Toss the lettuce, tuna, carrot, green bell pepper, onion, and salad dressing together in a large bowl. Spoon onto four salad plates. *Makes 4 1¼-cup servings.*

One serving—Calories: 48; Total fat: 0.5 g; Saturated fat: 0.1 g; Cholesterol: 4 mg; Sodium: 297 mg; Carbohydrates: 3.8 g; Fiber: 1.1 g; Sugar: 1.4 g

Sesame Honey Crackers

In place of the oregano and basil, try seasoning with garlic and Parmesan cheese, or try finely minced green onion and dill.

    2 teaspoons sesame seeds
    ½ cup Gluten-Free Flour Mixture (See the Hints chapter.)
    ¼ teaspoon salt
    ¼ teaspoon pepper
    ¼ teaspoon gluten-free baking powder
    Dash dry mustard

⅛ teaspoon oregano

⅛ teaspoon basil

2 teaspoons gluten-free margarine

3 teaspoons skim milk

4 teaspoons honey

1½ teaspoons corn oil

In a skillet over medium heat, toast the sesame seeds until golden; remove from heat and set aside. Into a large bowl, sift the flour mixture, salt, pepper, baking powder, mustard, oregano, and basil. With two knives, cut in the margarine until the mixture resembles coarse meal. Stir in the sesame seeds, milk, honey, and corn oil until well blended. Roll into a long log; wrap in plastic wrap, and refrigerate 2 hours. Preheat oven to 350°F. Lightly spray a cookie sheet with gluten-free nonstick spray. Remove the plastic wrap from the log of cracker dough, and slice the roll into very thin rounds. Place the rounds on the cookie sheet. With a fork, poke two sets of holes through each round. Bake 10 minutes or until the crackers have set and are very lightly browned. *Makes 4 2-cracker servings.*

One serving—Calories: 110; Total fat: 3.9 g; Saturated fat: 0.7 g; Cholesterol: 0 mg; Sodium: 179 mg; Carbohydrates: 17.4 g; Fiber: 0.5 g; Sugar: 6.1 g; Protein: 2.2 g

Pork and Black Bean Salad with Peach Muffins

Pork and Black Bean Salad

If you freeze the pork for about a half hour, it will be much easier to slice into thin, even slices.

2 teaspoons plus 2 tablespoons olive oil

⅔ pound lean pork tenderloin, sliced thin

¼ pound fresh snow peas, halved crosswise

½ onion, sliced thin

1 head Bibb lettuce, torn into
   bite-sized pieces

¾ cup canned black beans,
   rinsed well and drained

1 cup bite-sized cubes of cantaloupe

1 cup halved cherry tomatoes

3 tablespoons gluten-free balsamic vinegar

¼ teaspoon gluten-free chili powder

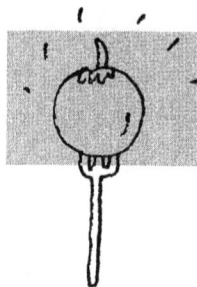

Put 2 teaspoons of the olive oil in a large skillet, and heat about 1 minute till the oil ripples. Add the pork slices; stir-fry 2 minutes. Add the snow peas; stir-fry until the pork is no longer pink and the peas are crisp-tender. In a large bowl, combine the pork mixture with the onion, lettuce, beans, cantaloupe, and tomatoes. In a small bowl, whisk together the vinegar, remaining 2 tablespoons of olive oil, and the chili powder. Pour the dressing over the salad. Toss until the dressing is evenly distributed. *Makes 4 1½-cup servings.*

One serving—Calories: 222; Total fat: 12.2 g; Saturated fat: 2.1 g; Cholesterol: 40 mg; Sodium: 255 mg; Carbohydrates: 13.8 g; Fiber: 4 g; Sugar: 2.8 g; Protein: 17.5 g

Peach Muffins

Orange juice and orange zest add flavor to these muffins, which have 90 percent less cholesterol than traditional muffins.

1½ cups Gluten-Free Flour Mixture (See the Hints chapter.)

⅓ cup plus 2 teaspoons sugar

2 teaspoons gluten-free baking powder

½ teaspoon baking soda

⅛ teaspoon salt

2 egg whites, slightly beaten

¾ cup skim milk

   3 tablespoons corn oil

   1 tablespoon orange juice

   ¾ teaspoon vanilla

   ¾ cup drained and finely chopped canned peaches (juice-packed)

   1 teaspoon finely grated orange zest

Preheat oven to 375°F. Sift the flour mixture, ⅓ cup of the sugar, and the baking powder, baking soda, and salt into a large bowl. In another bowl, whisk together the egg whites, milk, corn oil, orange juice, and vanilla. Stir the liquid ingredients into the dry ingredients just till blended. Gently fold in the peaches. Spray muffin cups with gluten-free nonstick spray. Spoon the batter into the muffin cups. Sprinkle the tops with the orange zest, then with the remaining 2 teaspoons of sugar. Bake 20 minutes. *Makes 18 muffins.*

One muffin—Calories: 176; Total fat: 10.2 g; Total fat: 1.2 g; Cholesterol: 4 mg; Sodium: 199 mg; Carbohydrates: 57.4 g; Fiber: 2.8 g; Sugar: 23.6 g; Protein: 12.9 g

Cabbage Soup and Pseudo Ham Sandwich

Cabbage Soup

This soup actually tastes better the second day, when the flavors have had a chance to blend.

   ½ tablespoon olive oil

   ½ onion, diced

   ¼ green bell pepper, diced

   ¼ cup diced celery

   ¼ cup diced carrot

   2 tablespoons parsley

   ½ cup tomato sauce

   3 cups water

½ teaspoon gluten-free beef bouillon granules

1½ cups chopped cabbage

¼ teaspoon black pepper

¼ teaspoon salt

1 small potato, peeled and diced

Heat the olive oil in a large saucepan. Sauté the onion, green bell pepper, celery, carrot, and parsley over medium heat till lightly browned, about 10 minutes. Stir in the tomato sauce, water, and bouillon granules until dissolved. Add the cabbage, black pepper, and salt. Cover and simmer 30 minutes. Add the potato; cover and continue to simmer for 25 minutes. *Makes 4 1½-cup servings.*

One serving—Calories: 108; Total fat: 4 g; Saturated fat: 0.5 g; Cholesterol: 0 mg; Sodium: 554 mg; Carbohydrates: 17 g; Fiber: 4.8 g; Sugar: 1.8 g; Protein: 2.8 g

Pseudo Ham Sandwich

If you are packing this pseudo sandwich for work, omit baking it; it is just as good eaten cold.

4 thin slices gluten-free ham

4 thin slices gluten-free,
    low-fat mozzarella cheese

8 thin slices tomato

Dash pepper

Preheat oven to 350°F. Lay the ham slices flat. Layer each with 1 cheese slice and 2 tomato slices. Sprinkle the tomato slices with pepper. Roll up each ham slice; lay the rolls on a baking sheet, seam side down; cover with foil. Bake 5 minutes or until warmed. *Makes 4 sandwich rolls.*

One sandwich roll—Calories: 51; Total fat: 2.1 g; Saturated fat: 1.2 g; Cholesterol: 10 mg; Sodium: 276 mg; Carbohydrates: 1.4 g; Fiber: 0.2 g; Sugar: 0 g; Protein: 6.4 g

Parmesan Dill Bread

Once you decide to make bread, it is just as easy to make several loaves at a time and freeze some for another day.

1 cup Gluten-Free Flour Mixture (See the Hints chapter.)

¾ teaspoon gluten-free baking powder

½ teaspoon baking soda

⅛ teaspoon salt

2 tablespoons gluten-free margarine

¼ teaspoon dill weed

1 tablespoon grated gluten-free Parmesan cheese

1 slightly beaten egg white

⅓ cup buttermilk

Preheat oven to 375°F. Sift the flour mixture, baking powder, baking soda, and salt into a large bowl. Cut in the margarine until the mixture resembles coarse crumbs. Mix in the dill and cheese. In a small bowl, combine the egg white and buttermilk. Stir the liquid ingredients into the dry ingredients just until moistened. Lightly sprinkle a cutting board with a little flour mixture; knead the dough on the board about 12 times till nearly smooth. Shape the dough into a round loaf. Spray a baking sheet with gluten-free nonstick spray; place the loaf on the baking sheet. With a sharp knife, make two slashes in the top to form an X. Bake about 30 minutes until golden. Cut the loaf into eight wedges; serve four sections with lunch, and freeze the other four sections for use another day. *Makes 8 wedges.*

One wedge—Calories: 79; Total fat: 2.6 g; Saturated fat: 1.2 g; Cholesterol: 1 mg; Sodium: 195 mg; Carbohydrates: 23 g; Fiber: 1 g; Sugar: 1 g; Protein: 5.2 g

Lobster Luncheon

Lobster Newburg

Use the most porous gluten-free bread available to make the toast baskets; these may be made well in advance. If you are boiling your own lobster, add a few drops of lemon juice to the water or poaching liquid to keep the meat white. If you prepare the Newburg sauce ahead of time, reheat it over *low* heat, stirring frequently, to prevent the sauce from turning watery; or warm in a double boiler over simmering water.

Toast Baskets

    4 slices gluten-free bread

    2 teaspoons soft gluten-free margarine

Sauce

    2 teaspoons gluten-free margarine

    ¼ red bell pepper, cut in half, then cut in thin strips

    ½ pound mushrooms, sliced

    1 tablespoon cornstarch

    ¼ teaspoon salt

    1½ cups 2% milk

    1 egg, beaten

    8 ounces cooked lobster, chopped

    1 tablespoon gluten-free dry sherry

    Dash red pepper flakes

    Dash black pepper

    ¼ teaspoon paprika

    Chopped fresh parsley for garnish

Preheat oven to 375°F. To make the toast baskets, remove the crusts from the bread. Spread ½ teaspoon of the margarine on one side of each slice of bread. Place the bread, buttered side down, into 4 cupcake tins, pressing firmly. Bake about 5 minutes till the edges of the toast baskets turn brown. To make the sauce, melt 2 teaspoons of margarine in a medium-size saucepan. Sauté the bell pepper strips and mushrooms. Stir in the cornstarch and salt. Cook and stir 1 minute. Add the milk; cook, stirring, until thickened, then 1 minute more. Slowly stir about half the hot mixture into the beaten egg. Return the egg and sauce to the saucepan. Cook and stir with a wire whisk until thickened, but do not boil. Stir in the lobster, sherry, red pepper flakes, black pepper, and paprika, and heat through. Spoon the sauce into the toast baskets. Sprinkle the top of each serving with the parsley. *Makes 4 baskets.*

One basket—Calories: 219; Total fat: 5.6 g; Saturated fat: 2.1 g; Cholesterol: 75 mg; Sodium: 597 mg; Carbohydrates: 22.1 g; Fiber: 0.8 g; Sugar: 6.6 g; Protein: 17.2 g

Marinated Vegetable Salad

Most of the ingredients in this salad come from your pantry shelf.

⅛ teaspoon salt

⅛ teaspoon pepper

⅛ teaspoon basil

¼ teaspoon dill weed

2 tablespoons olive oil

1 tablespoon gluten-free white wine vinegar

1 10-ounce can hearts of palm, drained, cut into ½-inch slices

1 10-ounce can artichoke hearts, drained, cut in half

1 10-ounce can small beets, drained

1 10-ounce can asparagus, drained

1 head Boston lettuce, torn into bite-sized pieces

Combine the salt, pepper, basil, dill, olive oil, and vinegar in a large bowl, and whisk till blended. Add the hearts of palm, artichoke hearts, beets, and asparagus; toss gently till evenly coated with dressing. Cover and refrigerate several hours. Divide the lettuce among four salad plates. Attractively arrange the vegetables over the lettuce. Drizzle any remaining dressing over the salads. *Makes 4 2-cup servings.*

One serving—Calories: 125; Total fat: 7.2 g; Saturated fat: 1.4 g; Cholesterol: 0 mg; Sodium: 320 mg; Carbohydrates: 13.9 g; Fiber: 3.1 g; Sugar: 4.5 g; Protein: 4.4 g

Broiled Tomatoes

Nestle each broiled tomato half in a piece of leaf lettuce for color appeal.

    2 large, ripe tomatoes
    1 teaspoon gluten-free, low-calorie Italian dressing
    ⅛ teaspoon garlic powder
    1 tablespoon minced fresh parsley
    ⅛ teaspoon pepper
    2 teaspoons grated gluten-free Parmesan cheese

Preheat broiler. Spray a baking sheet with gluten-free nonstick spray. Cut the tomatoes in half lengthwise (top to bottom); lay each half on the baking sheet. Sprinkle ¼ teaspoon of the Italian dressing on each tomato half. Stir together the garlic powder, parsley, pepper, and cheese; sprinkle over the tomatoes. Broil 3 minutes or until the cheese is golden. *Makes 4 tomato halves.*

One tomato half—Calories: 18; Total fat: 0.7 g; Saturated fat: 0.2 g; Cholesterol: 1 mg; Sodium: 42 mg; Carbohydrates: 4.3 g; Fiber: 1 g; Sugar: 0.1 g; Protein: 1.1 g

Chicken Crepe Luncheon

Chicken Spinach Crepes

These crepes may be made ahead, wrapped well, and frozen; thaw before baking.

1 egg

⅛ teaspoon salt

1 cup 1% milk

⅛ teaspoon vanilla

½ cup Gluten-Free Flour Mixture (See the Hints chapter.)

¼ teaspoon gluten-free baking powder

Olive oil to coat skillet

1½ cups sliced fresh mushrooms

⅓ cup sliced green onions

⅓ cup water

½ cup evaporated skim milk

1½ tablespoons cornstarch

⅛ teaspoon salt

⅛ teaspoon pepper

2 tablespoons gluten-free dry sherry

¾ cup shredded gluten-free cheddar cheese

1 10-ounce box frozen chopped spinach, thawed, drained, and squeezed dry

1¼ cups cooked chicken, finely chopped

Preheat oven to 400°F. Whisk together the egg, salt, milk, and vanilla in a large bowl. Sift the flour mixture and baking powder; beat the dry ingredients into the egg mixture. Add more milk, if needed, to make a thin batter. Brush a 6-inch skillet with olive oil; pour in 2 tablespoons of batter. Tilt the skillet to spread the batter. Brown one side of the crepe, then turn it, and lightly brown the other side. To remove the crepe, invert the skillet over paper towels. Repeat with the remaining batter. Simmer the mushrooms, green onions, and water in a saucepan, covered, for 5 minutes; do not drain. In a small bowl, combine the evaporated milk, cornstarch, salt, and pepper; stir into the vegetable mixture. Cook over low heat and stir until thickened. Stir in the sherry and ½ cup of the cheese till the cheese is melted. In a medium-size bowl, combine the spinach, chicken, and 1 cup of the cheese sauce. Spoon ¼ cup of this filling onto each crepe; roll up. Spray an 8″ × 12″ baking dish with gluten-free nonstick spray. Arrange the crepes, seam side down, in the baking dish. Spoon the remaining sauce over the crepes. Cover and bake 15 minutes or until hot. Sprinkle with the remaining ¼ cup of cheese. Bake, uncovered, 5 minutes to melt the cheese. *Makes 4 2-crepe servings.*

One serving—Calories: 329; Total fat: 11.2 g; Saturated fat: 5.7 g; Cholesterol: 127 mg; Sodium: 460 mg; Carbohydrates: 24.1 g; Fiber: 2 g; Sugar: 8 g; Protein: 32.5 g

Sweet Potato Fries

Fresh sweet potatoes are very hard and dense; you will need a butcher knife to slice them.

1 tablespoon olive oil

⅛ teaspoon salt

⅛ teaspoon black pepper

⅛ teaspoon paprika

⅛ teaspoon red pepper flakes

⅛ teaspoon gluten-free chili powder

2 sweet potatoes (about 1 pound total)

Preheat oven to 400°F. Combine the olive oil, salt, black pepper, paprika, red pepper flakes, and chili powder in a large bowl. Peel the sweet potatoes. Cut in half lengthwise. Cut each half into pencil-thin strips. Add the sweet potatoes to the oil mixture, and toss till evenly coated. Spray a baking sheet with gluten-free nonstick spray. Lay the sweet potatoes in a single layer on the baking sheet. Bake about 25 minutes, turning the sweet potatoes occasionally, until tender. *Makes 4 ¼-pound servings.*

One serving—Calories: 146; Total fat: 3.5 g; Saturated fat: 0.5 g; Cholesterol: 0 mg; Sodium: 85 mg; Carbohydrates: 27.5 g; Fiber: 3.5 g; Sugar: 0 g; Protein: 2 g

Asparagus Bundles

To serve, drape one strip of pimiento across the center of each bundle crosswise, and tuck the ends under the asparagus.

1½ pounds asparagus

1½ teaspoons gluten-free unsalted margarine

1 tablespoon sesame seeds

1 teaspoon gluten-free soy sauce

1 teaspoon sesame oil

⅛ teaspoon pepper

4 ounces canned pimientos, drained and sliced thin

In a 10-inch skillet, bring 1 inch of water to a boil. Add the asparagus; simmer for 3 minutes. Rinse under cold water, then drain. In the same skillet, melt the margarine. Add the sesame seeds; cook, stirring, till the seeds are golden. Add the soy sauce, sesame oil, and pepper. Return the asparagus to the pan. Cook 1 minute or until heated through. Lay the asparagus in a bundle along the side of each luncheon plate. Lay pimiento strips cross-wise across bundles. *Makes 4 bundles.*

One bundle—Calories: 55; Total fat: 0.8 g; Saturated fat: 0.6 g; Cholesterol: 0 mg; Sodium: 234 mg; Carbohydrates: 4.3 g; Fiber: 2 g; Sugar: 0 g; Protein: 2.9 g

Zucchini Tomato Salad

Vegetables may be sliced up to 2 hours ahead, wrapped in plastic wrap, and refrigerated.

4 lettuce leaves

2 large tomatoes, thinly sliced

2 small zucchini, thinly sliced

3 tablespoons green onions, sliced

4 tablespoons gluten-free, low-calorie Italian dressing

¼ teaspoon basil

2 tablespoons shredded gluten-free mozzarella cheese

Place the lettuce leaves on four salad plates. Layer the tomato and zucchini slices alternately on the lettuce. Sprinkle the green onions on top. Sprinkle with Italian dressing and basil. Sprinkle with cheese. *Makes 4 ¾-cup servings.*

One serving—Calories: 59; Total fat: 0.9 g; Saturated fat: 0.4 g; Cholesterol: 5 mg; Sodium: 236 mg; Carbohydrates: 4.2 g; Fiber: 1.8 g; Sugar: 1 g; Protein: 1.6 g

Cold Salmon Luncheon

Cold Poached Salmon

When cooking salmon, wash it well with cold water, then pat dry with paper towels. With a sharp knife, remove the skin from the fillets before cooking.

- 2 cups water
- 1 cup gluten-free white wine
- 2 tablespoons lemon juice
- 4 bay leaves
- ⅛ teaspoon salt
- ⅛ teaspoon pepper
- 4 4-ounce salmon fillets
- 4 teaspoons gluten-free, low-fat mayonnaise
- 12 capers

In a large skillet, combine the water, wine, lemon juice, bay leaves, salt, and pepper. Bring to a boil. Add the salmon fillets, and simmer gently about 15 minutes or till the fish is opaque and flakes easily with a fork. Drain the salmon, reserving the bay leaves, and cool. Spread 1 teaspoon of the mayonnaise on top of each fillet. To garnish, angle a bay leaf in the center; cluster 3 capers at the base of the leaf. *Makes 4 4-ounce servings.*

One serving—Calories: 248; Total fat: 15.1 g; Saturated fat: 3 g; Cholesterol: 68 mg; Sodium: 219 mg; Carbohydrates: 3.8 g; Fiber: 0 g; Sugar: 3.3 g; Protein: 23.5 g

Wild Rice Salad

This salad is perfect for picnics because it won't wilt. It tastes great cold if you have room to keep it in the cooler; if there isn't room, it may also be served at room temperature. Presoaking the rice shortens the cooking time and improves the final texture. Use natural wild rice; packaged wild rice mixes with added flavorings usually contain gluten. For a garnish at a luncheon, tuck a few sprigs of parsley into the side, and lay two mandarin orange sections on top.

1 cup wild rice

1 11-ounce can mandarin oranges

¼ cup yellow raisins

1 tablespoon pine nuts

2 green onions, finely chopped

½ cup chopped fresh parsley

2 tablespoons olive oil

1 tablespoon gluten-free balsamic vinegar

2 teaspoons lemon juice

⅛ teaspoon red pepper flakes

⅛ teaspoon salt

⅛ teaspoon black pepper

Rinse the rice thoroughly in cold water in a strainer. Transfer to a bowl, and cover with warm water; soak for 6 hours; drain. Place the rice in a large saucepan with 1½ cups of cold water. Bring to a boil; reduce heat, and simmer 20 minutes or till tender. Drain the oranges, reserving the juice. Soak the raisins in the mandarin orange juice 5 minutes, then remove raisins, reserving juice. Combine the rice, oranges, raisins, pine nuts, green onions, and parsley. Cover and refrigerate at least 1 hour. Whisk together the olive oil, vinegar, lemon juice, red pepper flakes, salt, black pepper, and 1 tablespoon of the reserved orange juice in a small bowl. Pour the dressing over the salad, and toss till well blended. *Makes 4 ¾-cup servings.*

One serving—Calories: 284; Total fat: 8.7 g; Saturated fat: 1.2 g; Cholesterol: 0 mg; Sodium: 85 mg; Carbohydrates: 48.2 g; Fiber: 3.8 g; Sugar: 16.2 g; Protein: 6.6 g

Julienned Vegetables

Lightly scrape the sides of the zucchini and yellow squash, leaving part of the skin.

- 1 zucchini
- 1 yellow squash
- 1 carrot
- 1 red bell pepper
- 2 teaspoons gluten-free white wine vinegar
- 1 tablespoon olive oil
- ¼ teaspoon dill weed
- ⅛ teaspoon salt
- ⅛ teaspoon black pepper

Cut the zucchini, yellow squash, carrot, and red pepper into thin strips, 2 inches long. In a medium-size salad bowl, mix the vinegar, olive oil, dill, salt, and black pepper. Toss the vegetables with the salad dressing. *Makes 4 ⅔-cup servings.*

One serving—Calories: 51; Total fat: 3.6 g; Saturated fat: 0.5 g; Cholesterol: 0 mg; Sodium: 87 mg; Carbohydrates: 4.8 g; Fiber: 1.6 g; Sugar: 1.2 g; Protein: 0.9 g

Melon Wine Mold

After unmolding the gelatin, tuck a lettuce leaf under the sides of the mold. Julienne leftover melon, and sprinkle it over the lettuce.

- 1 envelope (1 tablespoon) gluten-free unflavored gelatin
- ¼ cup cold water
- ¾ cup boiling water

¾ cup white grape juice

⅓ cup gluten-free white wine

⅛ teaspoon crushed dried mint

⅛ teaspoon cinnamon

1½ cups fresh or frozen melon balls

In a medium bowl, stir the gelatin into the cold water; let stand 3 minutes to soften. Pour the boiling water over the gelatin and stir to dissolve. Stir in the grape juice, wine, mint, and cinnamon. Spray four individual molds lightly with gluten-free nonstick spray. Pour the mixture into the molds. Cover and refrigerate until the gelatin is the consistency of unbeaten egg whites, about 40 minutes. Stir in the melon balls, dividing evenly among the four molds. Refrigerate at least 5 hours. To unmold, dip each mold quickly in warm water, immersing only ⅔ of the mold. Cover the mold with a salad plate, and invert; remove the gelatin from the pan. *Makes 4 ¾-cup servings.*

One serving—Calories: 57; Total fat: 0 g; Saturated fat: 0 g; Cholesterol: 0 mg; Sodium: 24 mg; Carbohydrates: 11.7 g; Fiber: 0 g; Sugar: 11 g; Protein: 2.2 g

Cranberry-Nut Bread

If you are using frozen cranberries, there is no need to thaw them first; just rinse them under cold water, drain, and proceed as directed in the recipe. If you are using dried cranberries, soak them first for 10 minutes in warm water, then drain well.

1½ cups Gluten-Free Flour Mixture (See the Hints chapter.)

½ cup sugar

¼ teaspoon baking soda

2 teaspoons gluten-free baking powder

⅛ teaspoon salt

¼ teaspoon cinnamon

1 egg white, slightly beaten

1 cup skim milk

2 tablespoons corn oil

1 tablespoon gluten-free, low-fat mayonnaise

1 teaspoon finely grated orange zest

½ cup coarsely chopped cranberries

¼ cup chopped walnuts

Preheat oven to 350°F. Sift the flour mixture, sugar, baking soda, baking powder, salt, and cinnamon into a large bowl. In another bowl, stir together the egg white, milk, corn oil, mayonnaise, and orange zest; add to the dry ingredients, stirring just until blended. Stir in the cranberries and walnuts. Spray a 4″ × 8″× 2″ loaf pan with gluten-free nonstick spray. Pour the batter into the pan. Bake 40 to 45 minutes or until a toothpick inserted in the center comes out clean. Cool on a wire rack 10 minutes, then remove the bread from the pan and cool completely. Wrap in foil and refrigerate for 2 hours before slicing. *Makes 1 loaf (10 slices).*

One slice—Calories: 138; Total fat: 4.4 g; Saturated fat: 1.3 g; Cholesterol: 0 mg; Sodium: 60 mg; Carbohydrates: 21.7 g; Fiber: 0.9 g; Sugar: 7.7 g; Protein: 3.4 g

Tropical Luncheon

Pineapple Chicken Salad

An impressive way to serve this salad is to cut a pineapple length-wise in quarters (without removing the crown). Hollow out the pineapple, and drain it upside down on paper towels for ½ hour. Spoon the salad into the shells to serve.

2 cups water

1 gluten-free chicken bouillon cube

2 whole skinless, boneless chicken breasts (6 ounces each)

¼ cup gluten-free, low-fat mayonnaise

½ onion, chopped

1 cup sliced celery

1 cup halved seedless grapes

¼ cup fresh pineapple tidbits, drained

2 tablespoons sliced almonds

¼ teaspoon pepper

4 large lettuce leaves

In a saucepan, heat the water to boiling. Add the bouillon cube, and press with the back of a spoon till dissolved. Add the chicken; reduce heat, cover, and simmer 12 minutes or till the chicken is tender. Remove from heat, and let the chicken stand in the broth 10 minutes; remove the chicken and let cool. Cut the chicken into bite-sized pieces. Place pineapple tidbits in a strainer to drain any collected juices. In a large bowl, combine the chicken pieces, mayonnaise, onion, celery, grapes, pineapple, almonds, and pepper; mix well. Serve on lettuce leaves. *Makes 4 1-cup servings.*

One serving—Calories: 227; Total fat: 9.5 g; Saturated fat: 2.1 g; Cholesterol: 72 mg; Sodium: 506 mg; Carbohydrates: 9.7 g; Fiber: 1.1 g; Sugar: 4.1 g; Protein: 27.7 g

Spinach Blankets

Rice paper is available at Asian groceries. It is very brittle and needs to be soaked in tepid water for 3 minutes before being used. Once it is soaked, it becomes quite pliable. Rice paper does not reheat well, so make only as much as you plan to eat.

1 tablespoon olive oil

1 onion, minced

3 green onions, minced

1 tablespoon dill weed

½ cup gluten-free, low-fat cottage cheese

1 egg

⅛ teaspoon salt

¼ teaspoon pepper

1 teaspoon lemon juice

1 10-ounce box frozen, chopped spinach, boiled and drained

3 tablespoons crumbled gluten-free feta cheese

2 teaspoons grated gluten-free Gruyère cheese

8 sheets gluten-free rice paper

Preheat oven to 350°F. Heat the olive oil in a small skillet. Sauté the onion and green onions over medium heat until tender but not browned, stirring occasionally. Transfer to a mixing bowl. Add the dill, cottage cheese, egg, salt, pepper, and lemon juice; blend well. Squeeze the spinach dry; add to the egg mixture, and beat until well blended. Stir in the feta and Gruyère cheeses. Soak the rice paper in a bowl of lukewarm water for 3 minutes. Working with just one sheet of rice paper at a time, lay a damp paper on a flat surface, and spray with gluten-free nonstick spray. Place 1 tablespoon of the cheese filling at one end of the paper. Roll the paper halfway, then fold in the sides; continue to roll. Spray a baking sheet with gluten-free nonstick spray. Place the rolled-up rice paper on the baking sheet, seam side down. Repeat filling and rolling with the other 7 rice papers. Spray the tops of the rolls with gluten-free nonstick spray. (The rolls may be covered and refrigerated at this point for up to 2 days.) Bake 20 minutes. Serve warm. *Makes 8 2-roll servings.*

One serving–Calories: 45; Total fat: 2.6 g; Saturated fat: 0.6 g; Cholesterol: 27 mg; Sodium: 114 mg; Carbohydrates: 1.9 g; Fiber: 0.6 g; Sugar: 0.5 g; Protein: 3.9 g

Orange Date Nut Bread

For ease in cutting the dates, dip scissors in hot water. Any sweet bread is much easier to slice if the bread is wrapped and frozen for an hour before cutting. Use a serrated knife.

1 medium navel orange

1 tablespoon grated orange zest

¾ cup finely chopped dates

2 tablespoons gluten-free margarine

1 egg

2 egg whites

1 teaspoon vanilla

1¾ cups Gluten-Free Flour Mixture (See the Hints chapter.)

¼ teaspoon salt

½ teaspoon baking soda

1¼ teaspoons gluten-free baking powder

1 cup sugar

½ cup coarsely chopped pecans

Preheat oven to 350°F. Cut the orange in half; squeeze its juice into a 1-cup measure; add boiling water to measure 1 cup. Transfer the juice and water to a large bowl, and add the orange zest, dates, and margarine. Stir until the margarine melts; let cool. In a small bowl, lightly whip egg and egg whites. Stir into juice mixture. Stir in vanilla. Sift the flour mixture, salt, baking soda, baking powder, and sugar. Add to the liquid mixture, and beat well.

Stir in the nuts. Spray a 9″ × 5″ loaf pan with gluten-free non-stick spray. Spoon the batter into the pan. Bake 45 minutes or until a toothpick inserted in the center comes out clean. Cool in pan 15 minutes; remove from pan, and finish cooling on a rack. *Makes 1 loaf (10 slices).*

One slice—Calories: 142; Total fat: 4.3 g; Saturated fat: 0.8 g; Cholesterol: 21 mg; Sodium: 112 mg; Carbohydrates: 24.2 g; Fiber: 1.3 g; Sugar: 13.4 g; Protein: 2.7 g

3

Family and Special-Occasion Dinners

For a quick centerpiece for a family dinner table, fill a large glass bowl with apples, oranges, or pears or a combination of all three. In the center, insert a 5-inch-wide candle. In the fall, fill the bowl with shelled nuts and the candle. In the summer, surround the candle with fresh flowers from the garden. This is a centerpiece for all seasons. For a more formal occasion, put fresh flowers around the candle.

Mexican Chicken Dinner

Mexican Chicken

If you enjoy really spicy foods, add more red pepper flakes to this dish.

1 2½- to 3-pound chicken, cut up and skinned
2 tablespoons olive oil
1 onion, minced
1 green bell pepper, minced
1 red bell pepper, minced
1 clove garlic, minced
2 teaspoons cornstarch
¼ teaspoon cumin
¼ teaspoon salt
1 14½-ounce can diced tomatoes with juice
1 tablespoon canned, chopped chili peppers
2 tablespoons chopped fresh parsley
⅛ teaspoon cayenne
Dash red pepper flakes

Preheat broiler. Spray a broiler pan with gluten-free nonstick spray. Lay the chicken pieces on the pan; broil 5 to 6 inches from the heat for 5 minutes. Turn the pieces, and broil 5 minutes longer or until the meat is no longer pink on the outside. In a large skillet, heat the olive oil for 1 minute. Add the onion, green and red bell peppers, and garlic; cook uncovered 5 minutes or until soft. Blend in the cornstarch, cumin, and salt. Cook, stirring constantly, for 1 minute. Stir in the tomatoes, chili peppers, parsley, cayenne, and red pepper flakes. Cook 5 minutes, stirring frequently. Add the chicken pieces, spooning the sauce over the chicken to cover. Simmer, covered, 30 minutes or until the chicken is fork-tender. Uncover and simmer 5 minutes more to thicken the sauce. *Makes 5 6-ounce servings.*

One serving—Calories: 321; Total fat: 20.8 g; Saturated fat: 4.7 g; Cholesterol: 80 mg; Sodium: 311 mg; Carbohydrates: 9.3 g; Fiber: 2.2 g; Sugar: 1.4 g; Protein: 26.7 g

Salsa Rice

After the rice has cooked, use a fork to fluff it up before serving.

1½ cups water

1½ cups gluten-free salsa

Dash red pepper flakes

3 tablespoons chopped fresh parsley

1¼ cups rice

Put the water, salsa, red pepper flakes, and parsley in a medium-size saucepan, and bring to a boil. Stir in the rice. Cover, lower heat, and simmer 20 minutes or until the rice is tender and the liquid has been absorbed. *Makes 5 ½-cup servings.*

One serving—Calories: 154; Total fat: 0.2 g; Saturated fat: 0.2 g; Cholesterol: 0 mg; Sodium: 794 mg; Carbohydrates: 33.2 g; Fiber: 0 g; Sugar: 3.4 g; Protein: 2.4 g

Market Salad

When marinating a salad in the refrigerator, stir it once or twice to redistribute the dressing.

1 cup small cauliflower florets

1 cup small broccoli florets

½ cup shredded gluten-free mozzarella cheese

1 carrot, julienned

1 8-ounce can garbanzo beans, well drained

⅓ cup red bell pepper, chopped

3 tablespoons gluten-free white wine vinegar

1 clove garlic, minced

½ teaspoon oregano

⅛ teaspoon salt

⅛ teaspoon black pepper

3 tablespoons olive oil

In a large bowl, combine the cauliflower, broccoli, cheese, carrot, garbanzo beans, and red pepper; set aside. In a small bowl, whisk together the vinegar, garlic, oregano, salt, black pepper, and olive oil until smooth and thickened. Pour the dressing over the vegetables, and toss to coat evenly. Cover and refrigerate several hours to blend flavors. *Makes 5 ¾-cup servings.*

One serving—Calories: 161; Total fat: 10.8 g; Saturated fat: 2.3 g; Cholesterol: 7 mg; Sodium: 260 mg; Carbohydrates: 13.8 g; Fiber: 3.7 g; Sugar: 2.8 g; Protein: 6.6 g

Raspberry Chicken Dinner

Browned-Onion Soup

If you are having trouble finding gluten-free beef broth, use 4 gluten-free beef bouillon cubes dissolved in 5 cups of boiling water.

1 teaspoon gluten-free margarine

2 teaspoons corn oil

2 large onions, sliced thin

⅛ teaspoon sugar

1 tablespoon cornstarch

5 cups hot gluten-free beef broth

2 tablespoons gluten-free white wine

¼ teaspoon salt

½ teaspoon pepper

1 tablespoon grated gluten-free Parmesan cheese

In a large saucepan, melt the margarine and heat the corn oil. Add the onions, and cook slowly for 15 minutes, stirring occasionally. Add the sugar and continue cooking, stirring frequently, for 20 minutes or until the mixture is golden. Sprinkle the cornstarch over the onion mixture. Slowly blend in the broth, wine, salt, and pepper. Cover the pan, and simmer 1 hour, stirring occasionally. Spoon the soup into bowls, and sprinkle with Parmesan cheese. *Makes 4 1½-cup servings.*

One serving–Calories: 78; Total fat: 3.7 g; Saturated fat: 0.9 g; Cholesterol: 1 mg; Sodium: 1,535 mg; Carbohydrates: 9.8 g; Fiber: 1.3 g; Sugar: 0.5 g; Protein: 1.9 g

Raspberry Chicken

For a little variety, try using orange marmalade or apricot or pineapple preserves in place of the raspberry preserves.

- 1 teaspoon olive oil
- ½ cup chopped onion
- ½ teaspoon thyme
- ½ teaspoon salt
- 4 4-ounce skinless, boneless chicken breast halves
- ¼ cup raspberry preserves
- 2 tablespoons gluten-free balsamic vinegar
- ¼ cup water
- ¼ teaspoon pepper

In a large nonstick skillet, heat the olive oil. Add the onion and sauté until soft, about 5 minutes. Sprinkle the chicken with the thyme and ¼ teaspoon of the salt. Add the chicken to the skillet, and sauté 6 minutes per side or until just cooked through. Remove the chicken and set aside. Reduce heat; add the remaining ¼ teaspoon of salt and the preserves, vinegar, water, and pepper. Cook, stirring constantly, until the preserves melt. Return the chicken to the pan, and baste with sauce. To serve, place the chicken on serving plates, and spoon the sauce over the meat. *Makes 4 half-breast servings (with 2 tablespoons sauce).*

One serving—Calories: 255; Total fat: 5.2 g; Saturated fat: 1.2 g; Cholesterol: 96 mg; Sodium: 380 mg; Carbohydrates: 15.2 g; Fiber: 0 g; Sugar: 12 g; Protein: 35.5 g

Sweet Potatoes with Apples

Even children who don't like sweet potatoes will love this side dish.

>   3 sweet potatoes (¾ pound total)
>   1 large Delicious apple, peeled, cored, sliced thin
>   3 tablespoons water
>   1 tablespoon light brown sugar
>   ¼ teaspoon cinnamon
>   1 tablespoon gluten-free margarine

Preheat oven to 375°F. Spray a 9-inch pie pan with gluten-free nonstick spray. Cut the sweet potatoes crosswise into ¼-inch slices. Lay the sweet potato and apple slices in the pan in a circle, alternating and overlapping slices. Sprinkle with the water. Mix the brown sugar and cinnamon in a small bowl; sprinkle over the sweet potatoes and apples. Dot with the margarine. Cover with foil. Bake 30 minutes. Uncover and bake 15 minutes more or until the sweet potatoes are tender. *Makes 4 3½-inch-thick slices.*

One slice—Calories: 135; Total fat: 2.5 g; Saturated fat: 0.5 g; Cholesterol: 0 mg; Sodium: 45 mg; Carbohydrates: 27.8 g; Fiber: 3.5 g; Sugar: 5.8 g; Protein: 1.5 g

Sugar Snap Peas

If fresh sugar snap peas are not available, use frozen, and proceed as directed.

    ¾ pound sugar snap peas, trimmed of any strings
    1 tablespoon gluten-free margarine
    ½ teaspoon freshly grated lemon zest
    1 tablespoon slivered almonds
    ⅛ teaspoon pepper
    ⅛ teaspoon salt

Place the peas in a large saucepan; add enough water to barely cover peas. Bring to a boil, and boil for 1 minute. Drain the peas, then plunge them into a bowl of ice and cold water to stop the cooking. Drain the peas well. In a large skillet, melt the margarine. Add the lemon zest and almonds, and cook over a medium-low heat until the almonds are browned. Add the peas, pepper, and salt; heat, stirring, until the peas are hot. *Makes 4 ½-cup servings.*

One serving—Calories: 56; Total fat: 3.1 g; Saturated fat: 0.5 g; Cholesterol: 0 mg; Sodium: 114 mg; Carbohydrates: 6.2 g; Fiber: 2.6 g; Sugar: 3.8 g; Protein: 3 g

Cranberry Mold

If fresh cranberries are not available, use frozen cranberries. There is no need to thaw frozen cranberries first.

    2 cups cranberry juice
    1 envelope gluten-free unflavored gelatin
    ¼ cup halved cranberries
    2 tablespoons sugar
    1 ripe pear, peeled, cored, and cut into ¼-inch cubes
    ½ cup diced celery
    1 tablespoon coarsely chopped pecans
    1 teaspoon grated orange zest

Pour 1 cup of the cranberry juice into a large bowl; sprinkle the gelatin over it, and let set for 3 minutes to soften. In a small bowl, toss the cranberries with 1 tablespoon of the sugar, and let set for 1 hour, tossing occasionally. While the cranberries set, pour the remaining 1 cup of juice and 1 tablespoon of sugar into a small saucepan, and bring to a boil. Stir the boiling juice into the gelatin mixture, stirring until the gelatin dissolves completely. Chill 1 hour until the mixture is the consistency of unbeaten egg whites. Fold the sugared cranberries, pear, celery, pecans, and orange zest into the gelatin. Spoon the mixture into a mold pan, and refrigerate 6 hours or until firm. Unmold onto a platter. *Makes 4 ¾-cup servings.*

One serving—Calories: 138; Total fat: 1.5 g; Saturated fat: 0.1 g; Cholesterol: 0 mg; Sodium: 57 mg; Carbohydrates: 29 g; Fiber: 1.7 g; Sugar: 20.8 g; Protein: 2.1 g

Chicken Marsala Dinner

Chicken Marsala

When a recipe calls for wine or sherry, use the real thing. Commercial "cooking wine" contains far more salt.

    4 4-ounce boneless chicken breast halves
    2 teaspoons gluten-free margarine
    1½ cups sliced fresh mushrooms
    2 tablespoons sliced green onion
    3 tablespoons water
    ¼ teaspoon salt
    ⅛ teaspoon pepper
    ⅛ teaspoon garlic powder
    ⅓ cup gluten-free dry marsala wine

Pound the chicken breasts to ¼-inch thickness. Spray a large skillet with gluten-free nonstick spray. Melt the margarine in the skillet. Add the chicken; cook over medium heat for 4 minutes per side or till cooked through. Remove the chicken breasts to a platter. Put the mushrooms, green onion, water, salt, pepper, and garlic powder in the same skillet. Cook for 3 minutes or until most of the liquid has evaporated. Add the wine, and heat through. Spoon the mushroom mixture over the chicken. *Makes 4 half-breast servings (with ½ cup sauce).*

One serving—Calories: 209; Total fat: 5.5 g; Saturated fat: 1.5 g; Cholesterol: 96 mg; Sodium: 303 mg; Carbohydrates: 1.5 g; Fiber: 0.2 g; Sugar: 0.8 g; Protein: 36 g

Vegetable Linguine

Most canned red roasted peppers are bathed in an olive-oil-based brine. Read the label to be sure they are gluten-free.

- ½ pound gluten-free corn linguine
- 2 tablespoons olive oil
- 1 onion, chopped
- 2 cloves garlic, minced
- 1 small zucchini, cubed
- 2 red roasted peppers (canned or jarred), diced
- 8 black olives, pitted and sliced
- ¼ teaspoon red pepper flakes
- ⅛ teaspoon salt
- ¼ teaspoon black pepper
- 3 tablespoons crumbled gluten-free feta cheese

Prepare the pasta according to the package directions; rinse with cold water, then drain. Heat the olive oil in a large skillet. Add the onion, garlic, and zucchini, and sauté until the zucchini is just barely tender. Stir in the red peppers, 2 tablespoons of the red pepper liquid from the can or jar, and the olives, red pepper flakes, salt, pepper, and pasta. Toss to blend well; heat till the linguine is heated through. Toss with the feta cheese. *Makes 4 1-cup servings.*

One serving—Calories: 311; Total fat: 10.7 g; Saturated fat: 1.7 g; Cholesterol: 13 mg; Sodium: 202 mg; Carbohydrates: 51.2 g; Fiber: 8.6 g; Sugar: 2.2 g; Protein: 5.4 g

Caesar Salad

Because of the risk of salmonella, no raw eggs are used in this dressing.

- 3 slices gluten-free bread
- ¼ teaspoon garlic powder
- ½ teaspoon plus 4 tablespoons grated gluten-free Parmesan cheese
- ½ teaspoon Italian seasoning
- ½ head romaine lettuce
- 1 head Boston lettuce
- 1 bunch watercress
- ¼ teaspoon dry mustard
- ¼ teaspoon pepper
- ⅛ teaspoon salt
- 1 clove garlic, minced
- 2 anchovy fillets
- 1 teaspoon gluten-free Worcestershire sauce
- 3 tablespoons gluten-free white wine vinegar
- 1 teaspoon freshly squeezed lemon juice
- ¼ cup olive oil

Preheat oven to 300°F. Cut bread into ½-inch squares and place in a medium-size bowl. In a small bowl, stir together garlic powder, ½ teaspoon Parmesan cheese, and Italian seasoning. Spray the bread cubes with gluten-free nonstick spray, tossing to coat evenly. Sprinkle cubes with Parmesan mixture, tossing again to distribute spices evenly. Spread cubes on a small baking sheet that has been sprayed with gluten-free nonstick spray. Bake bread cubes, stirring occasionally, for about 15 minutes or until bread cubes are dried and crispy. Remove from oven and cool completely.

Wash and dry the lettuce and watercress; tear into bite-sized pieces, and place in a large bowl. In a blender, combine the mustard, pepper, salt, garlic, anchovies, Worcestershire sauce, vinegar, and lemon juice; blend to mix. With the blender on the lowest setting, slowly add the olive oil; mix until well blended. Pour the dressing over the lettuce; add croutons, sprinkle with the cheese, and toss till the lettuce is evenly coated. *Makes 4 1¼-cup servings.*

One serving—Calories: 214; Total fat: 16.3 g; Saturated fat: 3.3 g; Cholesterol: 4 mg; Sodium: 378 mg; Carbohydrates: 13.1 g; Fiber: 1.9 g; Sugar: 1.9 g; Protein: 5.8 g

Dilled Flounder Dinner

Dilled Flounder

If you use a salt substitute, add it just before serving, since cooking may dull much of its flavor.

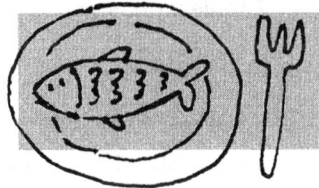

⅓ cup lemon juice

4 tablespoons olive oil

4 tablespoons chopped fresh dill

2 cloves garlic, minced

1½ tablespoons gluten-free
   prepared mustard

¼ teaspoon salt

¼ teaspoon pepper

5 flounder fillets (¼ pound each)

Whisk together the lemon juice, olive oil, dill, garlic, mustard, salt, and pepper. Pour the marinade over the fish; cover and refrigerate 2 hours. Preheat oven to 375°F. Remove the fish from the refrigerator, and allow to come to room temperature. Bake 10 minutes or until the fish flakes easily. *Makes 5 4-ounce servings.*

One serving—Calories: 219; Total fat: 11.7 g; Saturated fat: 1.7 g; Cholesterol: 73 mg; Sodium: 218 mg; Carbohydrates: 1.9 g; Fiber: 0.2 g; Sugar: 1.5 g; Protein: 26 g

Corn and Spinach Parmesan

Some brands of cream-style corn use wheat flour as a thickener, so read labels carefully.

2 teaspoons olive oil

¼ cup minced onion

1 14-ounce can gluten-free cream-style corn

1 teaspoon apple cider vinegar

2 10-ounce boxes frozen chopped spinach, thawed and squeezed dry

¼ teaspoon salt

¼ teaspoon pepper

¼ teaspoon dill weed

¼ teaspoon garlic powder

1 tablespoon gluten-free margarine

2 tablespoons grated gluten-free Parmesan cheese

Preheat oven to 375°F. In a small skillet, sauté the onion in oil until soft; spoon the onion into a bowl. Add the corn, vinegar, spinach, salt, pepper, dill, and garlic powder, mixing well. Spray a 1-quart baking dish with gluten-free nonstick spray. Spoon the

corn and spinach mixture into the baking dish. Melt the margarine. Sprinkle the top of the vegetable mixture with the Parmesan cheese; drizzle with the melted margarine. Bake 25 minutes. *Makes 5 ⅔-cup servings.*

One serving—Calories: 126; Total fat: 4.7 g; Saturated fat: 1.1 g; Cholesterol: 2 mg; Sodium: 479 mg; Carbohydrates: 19.1 g; Fiber: 3.4 g; Sugar: 5.4 g; Protein: 5.5 g

Marinated Tomato and Egg Salad

Tomatoes will ripen twice as quickly if you put them in a brown paper bag and close it tightly.

3 large ripe tomatoes, sliced

2 hard-boiled eggs, peeled and sliced

10 kalamata olives, pitted and sliced

2 tablespoons olive oil

⅛ teaspoon pepper

⅛ teaspoon oregano

Alternate the tomato and egg slices on four salad plates. Sprinkle with the olive slices; drizzle with the olive oil. Sprinkle with the pepper and oregano. *Makes 5 ¾-cup servings.*

One serving—Calories: 112; Total fat: 9 g; Saturated fat: 1.7 g; Cholesterol: 85 mg; Sodium: 111 mg; Carbohydrates: 6 g; Fiber: 1.5 g; Sugar: 0 g; Protein: 3.5 g

Asian Orange Roughy Dinner

Asian Orange Roughy

Do not let the fish overcook, or it will become tough.

1 pound orange roughy fillets

2 tablespoons lemon juice

¼ teaspoon salt

½ teaspoon black pepper

2 teaspoons olive oil

3 green onions, julienned

½ cup fresh bean sprouts

½ green bell pepper, julienned

1 clove garlic, minced

Dash red pepper flakes

¼ teaspoon powdered ginger

2 tablespoons gluten-free soy sauce

Sprinkle the fish fillets with the lemon juice, salt, and ¼ teaspoon of the black pepper. Heat the olive oil in a large nonstick skillet. Sauté the fish until it flakes easily with a fork; remove fish and keep warm. Stir the onion, bean sprouts, green bell pepper, and garlic into the same pan, and sauté 30 seconds on high heat. Stir in the red pepper flakes, remaining ¼ teaspoon of the black pepper, and the ginger and soy sauce; stir till heated through. Spoon the vegetables and sauce over the fish. *Makes 4 ¼-pound servings.*

One serving—Calories: 110; Total fat: 3 g; Saturated fat: 0.3 g; Cholesterol: 21 mg; Sodium: 672 mg; Carbohydrates: 3.6 g; Fiber: 0.3 g; Sugar: 0.4 g; Protein: 17.6 g

Cashew Lemon Rice

Washing the rice will rinse away some of the starch, preventing the rice from being sticky and clumping. When sautéing the nuts, watch closely so they brown lightly but do not burn.

1 cup basmati rice

1½ cups water

1 teaspoon gluten-free soy sauce

2 teaspoons olive oil

2 teaspoons fresh ginger

2 tablespoons coarsely chopped cashews

¼ teaspoon turmeric

⅛ teaspoon salt

⅛ teaspoon pepper

2 teaspoons freshly squeezed lemon juice

Wash the rice in several changes of water until the water runs clear; drain well. Put the rice, water, and soy sauce in a 1-quart saucepan, and bring to a boil. Lower heat, cover pan, and simmer 20 minutes until water is absorbed. Remove the pan from the heat, and let stand 10 minutes. Uncover and fluff the rice with a fork. Peel and then grate the ginger. Warm the olive oil in a large skillet 1 minute; stir in the ginger and cashews. Sauté over medium-low heat 3 minutes or till nuts just begin to brown. Add the rice, turmeric, salt, and pepper, stirring till well mixed. Remove from heat; stir in the lemon juice. *Makes 4 ½-cup servings.*

One serving—Calories: 212; Total fat: 4.4 g; Saturated fat: 1.1 g; Cholesterol: 0 mg; Sodium: 158 mg; Carbohydrates: 38.3 g; Fiber: 0.7 g; Sugar: 0 g; Protein: 1.2 g

Bamboo Shoots and Peas

The drier mushrooms are kept, the fresher they will remain. Never wash mushrooms until just before using.

2 teaspoons gluten-free margarine

3 green onions, sliced

¼ pound fresh mushrooms, sliced

⅛ pound fresh bamboo shoots

1 8-ounce can sliced water chestnuts, drained

¼ teaspoon gluten-free chicken bouillon granules

1 teaspoon gluten-free soy sauce

3 cups frozen peas

⅛ teaspoon salt

⅛ teaspoon pepper

Melt the margarine in a large skillet. Add the green onions and mushrooms, and sauté over high heat until the mushrooms begin to brown. Add the bamboo shoots, water chestnuts, chicken bouillon, and soy sauce, stirring until blended. Add the peas, salt, and pepper. Heat, stirring, about 1 minute or until the peas are heated through. *Makes 4 1-cup servings.*

One serving—Calories: 130; Total fat: 2 g; Saturated fat: 0.5 g; Cholesterol: 0 mg; Sodium: 135 mg; Carbohydrates: 21.1 g; Fiber: 3.7 g; Sugar: 9.5 g; Protein: 7.1 g

South-of-the-Border Pork Chop Dinner

South-of-the-Border Pork Chops

If available, buy Lean Generation pork, which has much less fat than traditional pork.

    4 pork chops (¼ pound each)
    2 teaspoons olive oil
    1 large onion, sliced thin
    1 green bell pepper, chopped
    1 16-ounce can chopped tomatoes, drained
    1 cup frozen corn, thawed

Preheat broiler. Lay the pork chops on a broiler pan, and broil 4 inches from the heat about 3 minutes per side or until the chops are browned and their juices are sealed inside. In a large skillet over medium heat, sauté the onion and green bell pepper in oil for 5 minutes. Add the tomatoes and corn; raise heat to high, and cook 5 minutes more. Spray a 1½-quart casserole with gluten-free nonstick spray. Transfer the vegetable mixture to the casserole. Preheat oven to 400°F. Lay the pork chops on top of the vegetable mixture. Cover and bake 35 minutes or until the chops are cooked through and fork-tender. *Makes 4 1-pork chop servings (with 1 cup sauce).*

One serving—Calories: 250; Total fat: 9.9 g; Saturated fat: 2.3 g; Cholesterol: 54 mg; Sodium: 243 mg; Carbohydrates: 15.4 g; Fiber: 3.2 g; Sugar: 3 g; Protein: 23.2 g

Potato Skins

By eliminating the traditional method of deep-frying the potato skins, this recipe cuts down significantly on calories. Cover and refrigerate the potato scooped out of the skins to make mashed potatoes or potato pancakes later in the week.

- 2 large baking potatoes
- 1 tablespoon minced green onion
- 2 tablespoons shredded gluten-free cheddar cheese
- Dash garlic powder
- 4 tablespoons gluten-free salsa

Preheat oven to 400°F. Prick the potatoes with a fork; bake 55 minutes or till tender. Cut the potatoes in half lengthwise, then lengthwise into quarters. Scoop out the insides, leaving a ½-inch shell. Place the shells, skin side up, on a baking sheet; spray the potatoes evenly with gluten-free nonstick spray. Bake, uncovered, 20 minutes or until crisp. Turn potatoes skin side down. Toss together the green onion, cheese, and garlic powder; sprinkle over potatoes. Bake 2 minutes to melt the cheese. Place the skins on a platter, and spoon the salsa over the top. *Makes 4 2-piece servings.*

One serving—Calories: 45; Total fat: 2.3 g; Saturated fat: 1.5 g; Cholesterol: 7 mg; Sodium: 161 mg; Carbohydrates: 3.6 g; Fiber: 0.5 g; Sugar: 0.2 g; Protein: 2.2 g

Citrus Salad

Garnish this salad with slivered orange zest or coarsely chopped pecans, almonds, or walnuts.

- 1 pink grapefruit, peeled and cut into sections
- 1 navel orange, peeled and sectioned
- 1 tangerine, peeled and sectioned
- 1 bunch watercress, rinsed and dried
- 3 tablespoons orange juice

1 tablespoon gluten-free balsamic vinegar

⅛ teaspoon salt

⅛ teaspoon pepper

¼ teaspoon poppy seeds

1 tablespoon olive oil

4 large red lettuce leaves

Combine the grapefruit, orange, and tangerine sections in a bowl. Add the watercress, and toss. In a small bowl, whisk together the juice, vinegar, salt, pepper, poppy seeds, and olive oil. Add the dressing to the fruits, and toss. Serve on dishes lined with red lettuce leaves. *Makes 4 1¼-cup servings.*

One serving—Calories: 105; Total fat: 3.7 g; Saturated fat: 0.5 g; Cholesterol: 0 mg; Sodium: 83 mg; Carbohydrates: 18.6 g; Fiber: 1.8 g; Sugar: 17.4 g; Protein: 1.6 g

Pork Chops and Beans Dinner

Pork Chops and Beans

Do not use a skillet with nonstick coating. In an uncoated skillet, the browning chops leave bits stuck to the bottom of the pan. These bits of meat, when scraped up into the beans, give this dish its unique flavor.

4 lean 5-ounce pork chops

⅛ teaspoon salt

¼ teaspoon pepper

2 tablespoons paprika

1 tablespoon gluten-free margarine

1 large onion, chopped

1 16-ounce jar gluten-free pork and beans

Sprinkle both sides of the pork chops with the salt, pepper, and paprika. Melt the margarine in a large skillet; add the chops, and brown quickly on both sides. Remove the chops; add the onion to the pan, and brown, stirring often. Add 2 cups of water; scrape up the browned bits from the bottom of the pan. Return the chops to the pan; lower heat. Cover and simmer slowly, adding ¼ cup of water as needed to keep a little moisture in the bottom of the pan, for 1½ hours or until the chops are very tender. Remove the chops to a serving plate. Stir the beans into the pan, and heat through, stirring up browned bits from the bottom of the pan. Spoon the beans over the chops. *Makes 4 1-pork chop servings (with ½ cup beans).*

One serving–Calories: 289; Total fat: 11 g; Saturated fat: 3.8 g; Cholesterol: 59 mg; Sodium: 482 mg; Carbohydrates: 203 g; Fiber: 5 g; Sugar: 5.2 g; Protein: 25.4 g

Hot Beet and Chard Salad

Peel the beets over the sink; the beet juice may stain kitchen counters.

    1 bunch fresh beets with greens
    1 small bunch Swiss chard
    ⅛ teaspoon salt
    ⅛ teaspoon pepper
    1 tablespoon apple cider vinegar
    4 tablespoons olive oil

Cut greens off beets. Wash the beets, beet greens, and Swiss chard well; drain. Cut the beet and chard greens into shorter sections. Put the greens in a large pot, and fill the pot with water to cover the vegetables. Bring to a boil, lower heat, cover, and simmer 20 minutes or until the greens are fork-tender. Remove from heat and drain. Put the beets in a medium-size saucepan, cover with water, and bring to a boil. Reduce heat and simmer for 45 minutes or until tender. Remove from heat and drain. When cool enough to handle, peel the beets, cutting off both stem and root ends. Cut the beets into small wedges, and return the beets and greens to the medium-size pot. Add the salt, pepper, vinegar, and olive oil; toss to coat evenly. Serve warm. *Makes 4 1-cup servings.*

One serving–Calories: 164; Total fat: 13.7 g; Saturated fat: 1.7 g; Cholesterol: 0 mg; Sodium: 275 mg; Carbohydrates: 10 g; Fiber: 2 g; Sugar: 5 g; Protein: 2.5 g

Sausage and Pepper Dinner

Sausage with Peppers and Onions

The secret to this dish is to keep the pan uncovered so the onion and peppers don't get steamed and are able to remain a little crisp.

    1½ pounds gluten-free turkey sausage links
    4 teaspoons olive oil
    4 cloves garlic, minced
    4 onions, sliced thin
    2 red bell peppers, cut in strips
    3 green bell peppers, cut in strips
    2 tablespoons minced dried parsley
    ¾ teaspoon oregano

Place the sausage in a large skillet with 3 teaspoons of the olive oil; brown over medium heat, turning occasionally. Add the remaining 1 teaspoon of olive oil and the garlic, onions, red and green bell peppers, parsley, and oregano; continue cooking until the vegetables are lightly browned. *Makes 6 ¼-pound sausage servings (with ½ cup vegetables).*

One serving–Calories: 188; Total fat: 9.3 g; Saturated fat: 2 g; Cholesterol: 37 mg; Sodium: 535 mg; Carbohydrates: 20 g; Fiber: 3.6 g; Sugar: 2.7 g; Protein: 10.5 g

Cornflake Potatoes

Do not use a dark, nonstick pan, or the bottoms of the potato slices will burn before the potatoes are cooked through.

¾ cup gluten-free cornflake crumbs

½ teaspoon salt

¼ teaspoon pepper

1 ½ tablespoons paprika

4 baking potatoes, sliced

2 tablespoons olive oil

Preheat oven to 375°F. In a small bowl, mix together the cornflake crumbs, salt, pepper, and paprika. Brush the potato slices with olive oil, then coat the slices with the crumbs. Spray a baking sheet with gluten-free nonstick spray. Arrange the potato slices in a single layer on the baking sheet. Bake 1 hour or until the potatoes are tender. *Makes 6 ⅔-cup servings.*

One serving—Calories: 109; Total fat: 0.1 g; Saturated fat: 0 g; Cholesterol: 0 mg; Sodium: 124 mg; Carbohydrates: 25.1 g; Fiber: 1.9 g; Sugar: 2 g; Protein: 2.3 g

Eggplant Oregano

Sprinkle a bit of shredded gluten-free cheddar cheese on top of the Eggplant Oregano just before serving.

1 tablespoon olive oil

1 medium eggplant, peeled and cubed

1 14-ounce can sliced mushrooms, drained

2 onions, sliced

3 ribs celery, sliced

1 green bell pepper, chopped

1 8-ounce jar gluten-free spaghetti sauce

2 teaspoons oregano

¾ teaspoon basil

2 tablespoons chopped fresh parsley

⅛ teaspoon red pepper flakes

3 tablespoons shredded gluten-free cheddar cheese

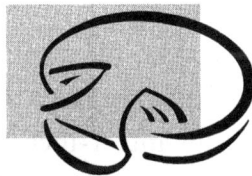

Preheat oven to 375°F. Heat the olive oil in a large nonstick pan. Add the eggplant, mushrooms, onions, celery, and green bell pepper; sauté on high heat until browned. Stir in the spaghetti sauce, oregano, basil, parsley, and red pepper flakes. Spray a shallow 2-quart casserole with gluten-free nonstick spray. Transfer the vegetables to the casserole dish. Sprinkle cheese over the vegetables. Bake 35 minutes. *Makes 6 ¾-cup servings.*

One serving—Calories: 112; Total fat: 7.4 g; Saturated fat: 2.2 g; Cholesterol: 7 mg; Sodium: 499 mg; Carbohydrates: 21.9 g; Fiber: 6.5 g; Sugar: 0.4 g; Protein: 5.7 g

Broccoli Salad

Sesame oil has a distinctive taste that cannot be duplicated by substituting olive oil.

    1½ pounds broccoli
    ¼ teaspoon gluten-free soy sauce
    1 teaspoon sugar
    2 tablespoons rice vinegar
    2 tablespoons sesame oil
    1 tablespoon minced garlic
    ¼ teaspoon powdered ginger
    ¼ teaspoon red pepper flakes
    ½ teaspoon sesame seeds

Peel away the tough, outer skin from the stem of the broccoli. Cut off the florets, cutting up larger clusters on the diagonal. Cut the stems into 1-inch sections. Combine the soy sauce, sugar, and vinegar in a bowl, stirring until the sugar has dissolved. Heat 1½ inches of water in a large saucepan until boiling; add the broccoli. Return to a boil, and cook until the stems and florets are barely tender. Rinse under cold running water to cool. Drain the broccoli, and place it in a mixing bowl. Heat the sesame oil in a wok or skillet over high heat; add the garlic, ginger, red pepper flakes, and sesame seeds; stir-fry 10 seconds until fragrant. Add the soy sauce mixture; cook 30 seconds, stirring constantly. Add the broccoli, tossing to coat. Transfer to a bowl; cover with plastic wrap, and chill several hours before serving. Serve cold or at room temperature. *Makes 6 ⅔-cup servings.*

One serving—Calories: 77; Total fat: 3.2 g; Saturated fat: 0.8 g; Cholesterol: 0 mg; Sodium: 51 mg; Carbohydrates: 9.4 g; Fiber: 3.8 g; Sugar: 2.4 g; Protein: 4.2 g

Marvelous Meat Loaf Dinner

Marvelous Meat Loaf

Leftover meat loaf makes marvelous cold sandwiches for lunch the next day.

- 2 slices gluten-free bread
- ¼ cup water
- 1 egg
- 3 tablespoons gluten-free ketchup
- 1 pound 93% lean ground beef
- 1 small onion, minced
- ¼ green bell pepper, minced
- 1 clove garlic, minced
- 1 carrot, shredded
- 1 tablespoon gluten-free Worcestershire sauce
- ¼ teaspoon black pepper
- ¼ teaspoon salt
- 1 teaspoon gluten-free beef bouillon granules
- 2 tablespoons minced fresh parsley

Preheat oven to 350°F. Crumble the bread into a large bowl; pour the water over the bread. Add the egg, ketchup, ground beef, onion, green bell pepper, garlic, carrot, Worcestershire sauce, black pepper, salt, beef bouillon, and parsley; mix well with hands. Spray a 9″ × 5″ loaf pan with gluten-free nonstick spray. Spoon the meat mixture into the pan; bake 50 minutes or till cooked through. *Makes 4 2-slice servings.*

One serving—Calories: 228; Total fat: 7.5 g; Saturated fat: 2.8 g; Cholesterol: 123 mg; Sodium: 724 mg; Carbohydrates: 11.5 g; Fiber: 1.7 g; Sugar: 5.1 g; Protein: 25.8 g

Rice-Stuffed Tomatoes

You can also stuff green bell peppers. Follow the same recipe, but substitute green bell peppers for the tomatoes and fresh or canned tomatoes for the tomato pulp.

4 small tomatoes
2 tablespoons olive oil
½ onion, chopped
2 cloves garlic, minced
⅓ cup rice
⅓ cup boiling water
2 tablespoons dill weed
¼ teaspoon salt
¼ teaspoon pepper
2 tablespoons chopped fresh parsley
¼ teaspoon cinnamon
1 teaspoon mint

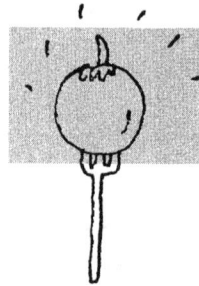

Preheat oven to 350°F. Slice the tops from the tomatoes; scoop the centers (and juices) into a medium-size bowl. Chop the tomato pulp; set aside. Place the tomato shells in a baking pan. Heat the olive oil in a small skillet; add the onion and garlic. Brown slowly, then set aside. Add the rice and chopped tomato pulp to the boiling water in a saucepan; cover and simmer 5 minutes or until all the water has been absorbed. Stir in the onion, garlic, dill, salt, pepper, parsley, cinnamon, and mint. Spoon the rice mixture into the tomato shells. Pour enough boiling water around the tomatoes to cover the bottom of the pan. Cover and bake 45 minutes or until the rice is cooked through and the tomatoes still hold their shape. *Makes 4 tomatoes.*

One tomato—Calories: 142; Total fat: 7.2 g; Saturated fat: 1 g; Cholesterol: 0 mg; Sodium: 154 mg; Carbohydrates: 18.3 g; Fiber: 1.4 g; Sugar: 0.5 g; Protein: 2.1 g

Pineapple Acorn Squash

In place of the pineapple, try using gluten-free cranberry sauce or diced canned peaches.

1 acorn squash, cut into quarters
1½ tablespoons gluten-free dry sherry
1½ tablespoons gluten-free margarine, melted
¼ cup canned crushed pineapple, drained
1½ tablespoons light brown sugar
¼ teaspoon nutmeg
¼ teaspoon cinnamon
⅛ teaspoon pepper
¼ teaspoon salt

Preheat oven to 350°F. Remove the seeds from the squash; place the squash, cut side up, in a shallow baking pan. Add boiling water to a depth of ½ inch. Cover and bake 45 minutes or until the squash is tender. In a bowl, stir together the sherry, margarine, pineapple, brown sugar, nutmeg, cinnamon, pepper, and salt; spoon into squash cavities. Bake an additional 10 minutes or until lightly browned. *Makes 4 ¼-squash servings.*

One serving—Calories: 87; Total fat: 3.1 g; Saturated fat: 0.8 g; Cholesterol: 0 mg; Sodium: 199 mg; Carbohydrates: 15.2 g; Fiber: 1.7 g; Sugar: 5.7 g; Protein: 0.9 g

Mexican Pot Pie Dinner

Mexican Pot Pie

This hearty casserole needs only a salad to make a complete meal.

¾ cup chopped onion

⅓ cup chopped green bell pepper

½ pound 95% lean ground beef

1 15½-ounce can pinto beans

2 tablespoons chopped green chilies

1 14½-ounce can no-salt-added diced tomatoes

¼ cup gluten-free salsa

⅛ teaspoon red pepper flakes

¾ cup Gluten-Free Flour Mixture (See the Hints chapter.)

1 tablespoon sugar

3 teaspoons gluten-free baking powder

½ teaspoon paprika

1 tablespoon minced fresh parsley

¼ teaspoon salt

¼ teaspoon black pepper

¼ teaspoon cumin

½ cup skim milk

2 teaspoons gluten-free margarine, melted

2 eggs, lightly beaten

Preheat oven to 375°F. Brown the onion, bell pepper, and ground beef in a skillet, breaking up the meat with a fork. Drain the beans; stir into meat mixture. Stir in the chilies, tomatoes, salsa, and red pepper flakes. Cook 5 minutes, stirring frequently. Spray a 2-quart casserole with gluten-free nonstick spray. Spoon the beef mixture into the casserole. Sift together into a medium-size bowl the flour mixture, sugar, baking powder, paprika, parsley, salt, black pepper, and cumin. Add the milk, margarine, and eggs, stirring till blended. Spoon the batter over the beef mixture;

spread evenly. Bake 35 minutes or until the crust is golden. *Makes 4 1¼-cup servings.*

One serving—Calories: 295; Total fat: 7.4 g; Saturated fat: 2.5 g; Cholesterol: 141 mg; Sodium: 476 mg; Carbohydrates: 36.8 g; Fiber: 4.5 g; Sugar: 4.5 g; Protein: 13.4 g

Mexican Cobb Salad

Assemble this salad at the last minute; the tortilla chips stay crunchy for only about 10 minutes, once the dressing is added.

½ head iceberg lettuce

2 tomatoes, cut in wedges

¼ avocado, peeled and diced

1 moderately hot red chili pepper, minced

2 ounces sharp cheddar cheese, diced

8 gluten-free tortilla chips

3 tablespoons gluten-free, low-fat mayonnaise

1 tablespoon gluten-free sour cream

⅛ teaspoon cumin

Pinch cinnamon

¼ cup gluten-free salsa

Tear the lettuce into bite-sized pieces; arrange on four salad dishes. Top each salad with the tomatoes, avocado, pepper, and cheese. Crumble 2 tortilla chips on top of each salad. Stir together the mayonnaise, sour cream, cumin, cinnamon, and salsa; drizzle over the salads. *Makes 4 ¾-cup servings.*

One serving—Calories: 166; Total fat: 12 g; Saturated fat: 4.3 g; Cholesterol: 16 mg; Sodium: 333 mg; Carbohydrates: 10.8 g; Fiber: 2.2 g; Sugar: 1.5 g; Protein: 5.3 g

Greek Casserole Dinner

Greek Casserole (Moussaka)

Lean ground beef may be substituted for the ground lamb. Three zucchini may be used in place of the eggplant. This casserole may be made ahead, covered, and refrigerated overnight or covered with foil and frozen before baking; thaw in the refrigerator completely before baking.

    1 large eggplant, peeled
    2 teaspoons olive oil
    1 large onion, chopped
    ½ pound lean ground lamb
    5 teaspoons tomato paste
    ¼ cup gluten-free white wine
    ¼ cup chopped fresh parsley
    ⅛ teaspoon cinnamon
    ⅛ teaspoon salt
    ⅛ teaspoon pepper
    1 tablespoon gluten-free margarine
    1½ tablespoons cornstarch
    1 cup scalded 1% milk
    1 egg, beaten until frothy
    ⅛ teaspoon nutmeg
    ½ cup gluten-free, low-fat cottage cheese
    ⅓ cup dried Corn Muffin crumbs (See Index.)
    ⅓ cup grated gluten-free Parmesan cheese

Preheat broiler. Peel the eggplant; cut lengthwise into ½-inch-thick slices. Spray both sides of the eggplant slices with gluten-free nonstick spray; set on a broiler pan and broil, until browned, turning once. Preheat oven to 350°F. Heat the olive oil in a skillet; add the onion, and sauté until lightly browned. Add the lamb and cook, breaking meat up with a fork, for 10 minutes or until the meat is browned. In a small bowl, stir together the tomato paste, wine, parsley, cinnamon, salt, and pepper; add to the meat, and simmer, stirring frequently, until all liquid has been absorbed. Remove from heat. Melt the margarine in a medium-size saucepan; blend in the cornstarch with a whisk. Slowly stir the hot milk into the cornstarch; cook over medium heat, stirring constantly, until thickened. Cool slightly, then stir in the beaten egg, nutmeg, and cottage cheese. Spray a 9-inch square pan with gluten-free nonstick spray. Sprinkle the bottom lightly with 2 tablespoons of the Corn Muffin crumbs. Arrange alternate layers of eggplant slices and meat mixture in the pan. Sprinkle each meat layer with the Parmesan cheese and remaining Corn Muffin crumbs. Pour the cottage cheese mixture over the top. Bake 45 minutes or until the top is golden. Cool slightly before cutting. *Makes 6 4½- by 3-inch servings.*

One serving—Calories: 307; Total fat: 14.8 g; Saturated fat: 5.9 g; Cholesterol: 69 mg; Sodium: 531 mg; Carbohydrates: 15.8 g; Fiber: 3.5 g; Sugar: 3.3 g; Protein: 14.8 g

Milk-Roasted Potatoes

Do not presoak the sliced potatoes; the starch will help thicken the mixture.

    1½ pounds red-skinned potatoes
    2 tablespoons chopped fresh parsley
    1 cup gluten-free chicken broth

½ cup 1% milk

2 cloves garlic, minced

¼ teaspoon salt

¼ teaspoon pepper

2 cups sliced mushrooms

1½ tablespoons gluten-free margarine, melted

Paprika

Preheat oven to 350°F. Scrub but do not peel the potatoes. Slice the potatoes ¼-inch thick. In a medium saucepan, place the potatoes, parsley, and chicken broth. Bring to a boil; reduce heat to low, cover, and simmer for 15 minutes or until the potatoes are partially cooked, stirring occasionally. Add the milk, garlic, salt, and pepper. Increase heat to medium-high. Bring to a boil, and boil 2 minutes, stirring occasionally. Remove from heat. Spray a 9-inch square baking dish with gluten-free nonstick spray. Spread half of the mushrooms on the bottom of the baking dish; top with half of the potatoes with half of the milk sauce. Repeat the layers of mushrooms and potatoes. Drizzle with the margarine. Sprinkle the top generously with paprika. Cover the pan with foil, and bake 30 minutes. Uncover and bake 20 more minutes or until the potatoes are tender. *Makes 6 4½- by 3-inch servings.*

One serving—Calories: 116; Total fat: 3 g; Saturated fat: 0.2 g; Cholesterol: 1 mg; Sodium: 410 mg; Carbohydrates: 19.9 g; Fiber: 2.2 g; Sugar: 4 g; Protein: 5.3 g

Feta Mayonnaise Salad

While most feta cheeses are gluten-free, a few brands are not. Check with the vendor before purchasing.

1 head romaine lettuce, torn into bite-sized pieces

2 ribs celery, chopped

½ cup frozen peas, thawed

1 small onion, sliced thin

1 large, ripe tomato, cut in half, then into wedges

4 ounces gluten-free feta cheese, crumbled

¼ teaspoon pepper

3 tablespoons gluten-free, low-fat mayonnaise

3 tablespoons gluten-free, fat-free Italian dressing

In a large bowl, toss together the romaine, celery, peas, onion, and tomato. Divide the salad among four salad plates. In a blender, whip together the cheese, pepper, mayonnaise, and Italian dressing; drizzle the dressing over the salads. *Makes 6 1¼-cup servings.*

One serving—Calories: 106; Total fat: 6.8 g; Saturated fat: 3.3 g; Cholesterol: 17 mg; Sodium: 432 mg; Carbohydrates: 7.3 g; Fiber: 1.7 g; Sugar: 2.2 g; Protein: 4.4 g

Veal Piccata Dinner

Veal Piccata

Chicken breasts, sliced into thin cutlets, may be substituted for the veal.

3 tablespoons Gluten-Free Flour Mixture (See the Hints chapter.)

¼ teaspoon pepper

1 tablespoon minced fresh parsley

1 pound thin boneless veal slices

2 tablespoons gluten-free margarine

½ pound fresh mushrooms, sliced

½ lemon

½ cup gluten-free dry white wine

2 tablespoons capers

Sift together the flour mixture and pepper; stir in the parsley. Place the seasoned flour mixture on a plate; coat the veal pieces with the seasoned flour mixture. Melt the margarine in a large

skillet. Add the veal, and cook over high heat until browned on both sides. Add the mushrooms, and sauté till browned. Squeeze the lemon over the veal. Add the wine and capers; cook 1 minute more. *Makes 4 ¼-pound servings.*

One serving—Calories: 257; Total fat: 14.7 g; Saturated fat: 5.4 g; Cholesterol: 90 mg; Sodium: 309 mg; Carbohydrates: 8.7 g; Fiber: 0.4 g; Sugar: 1.6 g; Protein: 22.7 g

Garlic Potato Gratin

Roasting the onions and garlic before adding them to the other ingredients gives a unique, added depth of flavor.

1 whole head garlic

1 onion

2 large baked potatoes, peeled

¼ teaspoon salt

¼ teaspoon pepper

3 tablespoons skim milk

2 tablespoons grated gluten-free Parmesan cheese

Preheat oven to 425°F. Wrap the garlic head in foil. Put the onion on a double sheet of foil, but do not wrap. Bake the onion and garlic 1 hour or until the onion is very soft (almost collapsed). Lower the oven temperature to 350°F. Unwrap garlic; separate the cloves. Squeeze the softened garlic out so it pops into a bowl. Discard the stem and root ends of the onion and the first layer of skin. Mince the onion; add to garlic in bowl. Rice the potatoes. Beat together the onion, garlic, potatoes, salt, and pepper. Beat in 1 tablespoon of the milk. Scrape the mixture into a buttered pan; smooth the top, and sprinkle with the cheese. Drizzle the remaining 2 tablespoons of milk over the top of the potatoes. Bake uncovered 35 minutes, or until the top is lightly browned. *Makes 4 ⅔-cup servings.*

One serving—Calories: 107; Total fat: 1.2 g; Saturated fat: 0.5 g; Cholesterol: 2 mg; Sodium: 222 mg; Carbohydrates: 22.6 g; Fiber: 1 g; Sugar: 6.9 g; Protein: 4.4 g

Marinated Zucchini Salad

Make this salad ahead, then cover and refrigerate until serving time, up to 6 hours. Serve cold.

2 small zucchini

1 tablespoon olive oil

1 clove garlic, minced

¼ red bell pepper, sliced thin

¼ pound mushrooms, sliced

2 green onions, sliced

2 plum tomatoes, quartered

¼ teaspoon sage

¼ teaspoon dill weed

¼ teaspoon mint

¼ teaspoon salt

⅛ teaspoon black pepper

Cut the zucchini in half crosswise, then cut into thin matchstick-sized strips. In a skillet, heat the olive oil; add the garlic, and sauté 1 minute. Add the zucchini, red pepper, mushrooms, and green onions. Sauté over low heat 30 seconds, stirring, to barely wilt the vegetables; remove from heat. Stir in the tomatoes, and sprinkle with the sage, dill, mint, salt, and black pepper. Toss to coat evenly. Transfer to a medium-size bowl, cover, and refrigerate. *Makes 4 ½-cup servings.*

One serving—Calories: 54; Total fat: 3.7 g; Saturated fat: 0.5 g; Cholesterol: 0 mg; Sodium: 154 mg; Carbohydrates: 5 g; Fiber: 1.7 g; Sugar: 0.6 g; Protein: 1.6 g

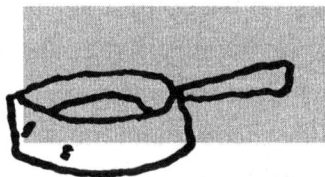

Potato Lasagna Dinner

Potato Lasagna

When you cut potatoes in advance, soak the slices in a bowl of cold water to prevent them from turning brown.

  1 teaspoon olive oil

  1 cup chopped onion

  1 clove garlic, minced

  ½ pound gluten-free bulk hot turkey sausage

  1 28-ounce jar gluten-free spaghetti sauce

  ¼ teaspoon pepper

  2 tablespoons chopped fresh parsley

  ½ teaspoon oregano

  ½ teaspoon basil

  ¾ cup gluten-free, low-fat cottage cheese

  4 tablespoons grated gluten-free Parmesan cheese

  3 egg whites, slightly beaten

  4 medium russet potatoes, peeled and thinly sliced

  2 ounces cheddar cheese, shredded

  3 ounces gluten-free mozzarella cheese, shredded

Preheat oven to 350°F. Warm the olive oil in a large skillet. Add the onion, garlic, and sausage; sauté, breaking up the meat with a fork, until the meat is brown. Stir in the spaghetti sauce, pepper, parsley, oregano, and basil. Lower heat; cover and simmer 8 minutes. In a small bowl, mix the cottage cheese, 2 tablespoons of the Parmesan cheese, and the egg whites. Spread a little spaghetti sauce on the bottom of a 9-inch glass pan. Place half of the potatoes, overlapping, in the pan; spread with half of the meat sauce. Spoon half of the cottage cheese mix over the meat sauce, then half of the cheddar and mozzarella cheeses. Repeat the layers. Sprinkle 2 tablespoons of Parmesan cheese on top. Cover the pan with foil that has been sprayed with gluten-free nonstick spray. Bake 1 hour or till potatoes are cooked through. Remove foil, and bake 10 more minutes till the top is browned. Let stand 10 minutes before cutting. *Makes 6 4½- by 3-inch servings.*

One serving—Calories: 378; Total fat: 13.8 g; Saturated fat: 4.8 g; Cholesterol: 35 mg; Sodium: 1,147 mg; Carbohydrates: 37.9 g; Fiber: 4.6 g; Sugar: 7.3 g; Protein: 23.3 g

Lemon Broccoli

Broccoli should be bright green when served; overcooking will cause the color to fade.

- 1 large bunch broccoli
- ⅛ teaspoon salt
- ⅛ teaspoon pepper
- 3 tablespoons olive oil
- 4 teaspoons lemon juice

Put the broccoli in a saucepan with 1 inch of water. Bring the water to a boil; reduce heat, cover pan, and steam for 3 minutes or till tender-crisp. Drain well. Sprinkle with the salt and pepper, then drizzle the olive oil and lemon juice over the top. *Makes 6 ⅔-cup servings.*

One serving—Calories: 76; Total fat: 6.7 g; Saturated fat: 0.8 g; Cholesterol: 0 mg; Sodium: 66 mg; Carbohydrates: 3.5 g; Fiber: 1.7 g; Sugar: 1.3 g; Protein: 2 g

Spaghetti Dinner

Spaghetti with Meat Sauce

To serve, sprinkle each serving with freshly grated gluten-free Romano cheese.

- 2 tablespoons olive oil
- 1 onion, chopped
- 1 carrot, finely minced
- 2 cloves garlic, minced
- 1 28-ounce can diced tomatoes
- 1 8-ounce can tomato sauce
- 1/4 teaspoon sugar
- 1/2 teaspoon salt
- 3/4 teaspoon pepper
- 3/4 teaspoon oregano
- 2 tablespoons minced fresh parsley
- 1/2 pound lean ground beef
- 8 mushrooms, diced
- 1/2 pound gluten-free corn spaghetti

In a medium-size saucepan, heat the olive oil for 1 minute. Add the onion, carrot, and garlic; brown lightly. Stir in the tomatoes (with juice), tomato sauce, sugar, salt, pepper, oregano, and parsley. Cover and simmer gently for 30 minutes. Brown the ground beef and mushrooms in a skillet over medium-high heat, breaking up the meat with a fork. Drain off any fat. Add the meat and mushrooms to the tomato mixture, and simmer another 20 minutes. Cook the spaghetti according to the package directions. Drain well. Spoon the spaghetti onto individual dinner plates; spoon the sauce over the top. *Makes 6 ¾-cup pasta servings (with 1¼ cups sauce).*

One serving—Calories: 344; Total fat: 18.7 g; Saturated fat: 10.5 g; Cholesterol: 56 mg; Sodium: 701 mg; Carbohydrates: 24.8 g; Fiber: 3.3 g; Sugar: 3.4 g; Protein: 18.4 g

Breaded Brussels Sprouts

This is equally good when made with cauliflower or broccoli in place of the brussels sprouts.

- 2 10-ounce boxes frozen brussels sprouts
- 3 tablespoons gluten-free margarine, melted
- 3 tablespoons grated gluten-free Parmesan cheese
- 1 tablespoon minced fresh parsley
- 3 tablespoons gluten-free Corn Muffin crumbs (See Index.)
- ¼ teaspoon dill weed
- ⅛ teaspoon garlic powder
- ⅛ teaspoon pepper
- ⅛ teaspoon salt
- ¼ teaspoon paprika

Preheat broiler. In a medium-size saucepan, cover the brussels sprouts with water; bring to a boil. Reduce heat, and simmer until tender. Drain. Place the brussels sprouts in a small casserole dish; stir in 2 tablespoons of the margarine; toss to coat. Combine the Parmesan cheese, parsley, corn bread crumbs, dill, garlic powder, pepper, salt, and paprika in a small bowl; blend in the remaining 1 tablespoon of margarine. Sprinkle the crumb mixture over the brussels sprouts. Place under the broiler for 5 minutes till top is lightly browned. *Makes 6 ½-cup servings.*

One serving—Calories: 76; Total fat: 5.4 g; Saturated fat: 1.7 g; Cholesterol: 2 mg; Sodium: 197 mg; Carbohydrates: 5.7 g; Fiber: 2.2 g; Sugar: 3.5 g; Protein: 2.4 g

Tossed Bean Salad

Almost any beans may be added to this salad but it is especially good with black beans and garbanzo beans.

- ½ cup wax beans
- ½ cup green beans
- ½ cup kidney beans

2 cups leaf lettuce torn into bite-sized pieces

1 cup Bibb lettuce torn into bite-sized pieces

3 green onions, sliced

1 tomato, diced

¼ green bell pepper, chopped

3 fresh basil leaves, sliced thin

3 tablespoons olive oil

2 tablespoons gluten-free white wine vinegar

¼ teaspoon dill weed

⅛ teaspoon salt

¼ teaspoon black pepper

Rinse the beans under cold running water; drain. In a large bowl, toss together the beans, lettuces, green onions, tomato, green bell pepper, and basil leaves. In a smaller bowl, whisk together the olive oil, vinegar, dill, salt, and black pepper. Pour the dressing over the salad, and toss. *Makes 6 1-cup servings.*

One serving—Calories: 96; Total fat: 7.1 g; Saturated fat: 0.9 g; Cholesterol: 0 mg; Sodium: 41 mg; Carbohydrates: 7.2 g; Fiber: 2.5 g; Sugar: 1.2 g; Protein: 2.3 g

Broiled Vegetable Dinner

Broiled Vegetables and Rice

Other vegetables may be added. Try asparagus, broccoli, eggplant, or artichoke hearts.

2½ cups gluten-free chicken broth

1 cup rice

2 tablespoons chopped fresh parsley

2 medium zucchini, julienned

1 medium yellow squash, julienned

2 portobello mushrooms, sliced thin

½ green bell pepper, julienned

½ red bell pepper, julienned

1 large tomato, cut into 12 wedges

1 onion, sliced thin

3 tablespoons olive oil

2 tablespoons gluten-free balsamic vinegar

1 tablespoon gluten-free soy sauce

¼ teaspoon salt

¼ teaspoon black pepper

¼ teaspoon garlic powder

½ teaspoon dill weed

Bring the chicken broth to a boil in a 1-quart saucepan. Stir in the rice and parsley; lower heat, cover, and cook 20 minutes or until moisture is absorbed. Preheat broiler. Spray a baking sheet with gluten-free nonstick spray. Spread out the vegetables on the baking sheet. In a small bowl, whisk together the olive oil, vinegar, soy sauce, salt, black pepper, garlic powder, and dill. Drizzle the sauce over the vegetables. Broil the vegetables 3 inches from the heat for 4 minutes. Turn the vegetables, and continue to broil until the vegetables are browned but still slightly crisp. To serve, spoon the vegetables over hot rice. *Makes 6 1-cup vegetable servings (with ½ cup rice).*

One serving—Calories: 243; Total fat: 8.4 g; Saturated fat: 1.2 g; Cholesterol: 1 mg; Sodium: 910 mg; Carbohydrates: 33.4 g; Fiber: 2.6 g; Sugar: 0.3 g; Protein: 8.3 g

Toasted-Almond Salad

Watch the almonds closely when toasting. Once they start to brown, they may burn quickly.

½ cup whole almonds

2 teaspoons sugar

¼ teaspoon cinnamon

Dash paprika

Dash cayenne

Dash ground cloves

2 tablespoons honey

1 head red leaf lettuce, torn into bite-sized pieces

3 green onions, sliced

6 green olives, pitted and sliced

¼ teaspoon black pepper

3 tablespoons olive oil

2 tablespoons gluten-free balsamic vinegar

4 tablespoons grated gluten-free Parmesan cheese

Preheat oven to 400°F. Roast the almonds in a baking pan for 30 minutes or until golden, tossing every 10 minutes. Remove from oven, and let cool to room temperature. In a small bowl, combine the sugar, cinnamon, paprika, cayenne, and cloves. When the nuts are cooled, drizzle lightly with honey, and toss. Sprinkle the spice mixture on the nuts; toss again until the nuts are covered evenly. Return to oven for 6 minutes. Remove from oven, and let cool. In a large bowl, mix the lettuce, green onions, olives, black pepper, and cooled almonds. Add the olive oil, vinegar, and cheese; toss to coat evenly. *Makes 6 ⅔-cup servings.*

One serving—Calories: 186; Total fat: 14.8 g; Saturated fat: 2 g; Cholesterol: 3 mg; Sodium: 127 mg; Carbohydrates: 12.1 g; Fiber: 1.7 g; Sugar: 8.8 g; Protein: 2.6 g

Cornish Game Hen Dinner

This dinner is great for themes such as an "Academy Awards" dinner. Wrap film around the napkins as napkin rings. Buy some inexpensive black sunglasses to use as place cards; paint a guest's name on each pair.

Glazed Shrimp Appetizer

The shrimp may be coated early in the day, then covered and refrigerated until close to serving time. Cook just before serving.

⅓ cup freshly squeezed tangerine juice (2 small tangerines)

2 tablespoons plus 2 teaspoons freshly squeezed lemon juice

2 tablespoons gluten-free chicken broth

1 clove garlic, minced

1 tablespoon light corn syrup

2 teaspoons sugar

⅛ teaspoon plus ¼ teaspoon black pepper

¼ teaspoon salt

Dash cayenne

1 egg white

½ teaspoon paprika

12 large uncooked shrimp, peeled and deveined

¼ cup sesame seeds

2 tablespoons olive oil

Put the tangerine juice, 2 tablespoons of lemon juice, chicken broth, garlic, corn syrup, sugar, ⅛ teaspoon of black pepper, ⅛ teaspoon of the salt, and cayenne in a small saucepan; bring to a boil. Reduce heat, and simmer about 10 minutes until reduced to 1 cup, stirring occasionally. In a medium-size bowl, whisk together the egg white, 2 teaspoons of lemon juice, the paprika, ⅛ teaspoon of salt, and ¼ teaspoon of black pepper until well blended. Add the shrimp, and toss to coat evenly. Spread the sesame seeds in a flat dish. Dip the shrimp into the sesame seeds, coating both sides, and set shrimp on a sheet of waxed paper. Heat the olive oil in a nonstick skillet over medium-high heat. Add the shrimp, and sauté about 2 minutes per side or until golden and opaque. To serve, drizzle the glaze over the shrimp, or place the glaze in a bowl for dipping. *Makes 4 3-shrimp servings.*

One serving—Calories: 161; Total fat: 11.7 g; Saturated fat: 1.7 g; Cholesterol: 55 mg; Sodium: 252 mg; Carbohydrates: 8.8 g; Fiber: 0 g; Sugar: 3.6 g; Protein: 9 g

Herbed Cornish Game Hens

Marinating helps keep these hens moist during cooking. If you prefer, they may be grilled with the cover down, or covered with heavy-duty foil on an open grill.

2 Cornish game hens, cut in half
1 cube gluten-free chicken bouillon
1 cup hot water
1 tablespoon olive oil
¼ cup gluten-free white wine
¼ teaspoon pepper
½ teaspoon salt
2 cloves garlic, minced
¼ teaspoon sage
½ teaspoon dill weed
⅛ teaspoon cinnamon

Spray a shallow glass baking dish with gluten-free nonstick spray. Place the hens, skin side up, in the dish. In a medium-size bowl, dissolve the bouillon cube in hot water; whisk in the olive oil, wine, pepper, salt, garlic, sage, dill, and cinnamon. Pour half of the marinade over the hens. Turn the hens over, and pour on the remaining marinade. Cover and refrigerate for 6 hours. Preheat oven to 400°F. Uncover the hens, and bake 30 minutes; turn the hens skin side up, and bake another 45 minutes or until fork-tender. *Makes 4 ½-hen servings.*

One serving—Calories: 278; Total fat: 17.6 g; Saturated fat: 0.5 g; Cholesterol: 75 mg; Sodium: 598 mg; Carbohydrates: 1.4 g; Fiber: 0 g; Sugar: 1 g; Protein: 28.3 g

Sweet Potato in Orange Shells

Canned yams may be used in place of raw sweet potatoes. Drain them thoroughly, then mash well with a fork before adding to the reduced orange juice mixture.

2 large navel oranges

1 cinnamon stick

1 pound sweet potatoes, cut in half lengthwise

¼ teaspoon salt

2 teaspoons honey

¼ teaspoon ground ginger

¼ teaspoon cinnamon

3 teaspoons gluten-free margarine

2 teaspoons light brown sugar

Preheat oven to 400°F. Cut the oranges in half; cut out the pulp, reserving the shells. Squeeze the juice from the orange pulp into a medium-size saucepan. Add the cinnamon stick, and bring to a boil. Continue to cook at a high simmer until juice is reduced to about 2 teaspoons; remove the cinnamon stick. Boil the sweet potatoes in enough water to cover them in a medium-size saucepan until fork-tender; peel, then rice them. (If you don't have a ricer, mash the potatoes.) Stir the sweet potatoes into the reduced orange juice mixture. Add the salt, honey, ginger, cinnamon, and 2 teaspoons of the margarine. Spray an 8-inch square baking pan with gluten-free nonstick spray. Fill the orange shells with the sweet potato mixture, and place them in the baking pan. Dot the tops with the remaining 1 teaspoon of margarine, and sprinkle with the brown sugar. Bake 15 minutes or until nicely browned. *Makes 4 1–half orange servings.*

One serving—Calories: 183; Total fat: 2.5 g; Saturated fat: 0.5 g; Cholesterol: 0 mg; Sodium: 195 mg; Carbohydrates: 39.2 g; Fiber: 5 g; Sugar: 11.4 g; Protein: 2.5 g

Spinach Squares

These squares can be served with grated gluten-free white cheddar cheese on top.

　2 eggs
　1 egg white
　1/3 cup Gluten-Free Flour Mixture (See the Hints chapter.)
　1/4 teaspoon salt
　1/4 teaspoon pepper
　1/2 teaspoon dill
　1/2 teaspoon gluten-free baking powder
　1/3 cup 1% milk
　1/3 cup grated gluten-free, white sharp cheddar cheese
　1 10-ounce box frozen chopped spinach, thawed and
　　squeezed dry

Preheat oven to 350°F. Whisk the eggs and egg white in a large bowl till fluffy. Whisk in the flour mixture, salt, pepper, dill, baking powder, and milk. Stir in the cheese and spinach till well blended. Spray an 8-inch square pan well with gluten-free nonstick spray. Spoon the spinach mixture into the pan. Bake 20 minutes or till a knife inserted near the center comes out clean. *Makes 9 3-inch-square servings.*

One serving—Calories: 81; Total fat: 4.3 g; Saturated fat: 2.4 g; Cholesterol: 57 mg; Sodium: 169 mg; Carbohydrates: 4.9 g; Fiber: 0.8 g; Sugar: 0.6 g; Protein: 5.7 g

Kiwi Salad

Add a colorful accent to this salad by scattering a few well-washed petunia flower heads on it.

2 teaspoons sesame seeds
4 tablespoons olive oil
2 teaspoons gluten-free soy sauce
3 tablespoons gluten-free white wine vinegar
¼ teaspoon salt
Dash paprika
4 cups fresh spinach in bite-sized pieces
3 kiwis, peeled and sliced
1 small red onion, sliced
¼ cup sliced almonds

In a small skillet, stir the sesame seeds over medium-high heat until golden. (Watch carefully so the seeds don't burn.) In a small container with a tight-fitting lid, combine the olive oil, soy sauce, vinegar, salt, and paprika. Add the sesame seeds. Refrigerate up to 24 hours before serving. Divide the spinach among four salad plates. Place the kiwi and onion slices on top. Sprinkle with almonds. Shake the salad dressing well, and pour over the salads. *Makes 4 1⅓-cup servings.*

One serving—Calories: 218; Total fat: 18.3 g; Saturated fat: 2.2 g; Cholesterol: 0 mg; Sodium: 175 mg; Carbohydrates: 13 g; Fiber: 3.9 g; Sugar: 0.2 g; Protein: 3.4 g

Halibut with Pine Nut Crust Dinner

A variety of gluten-free breads make a nice centerpiece with this meal.

Spinach-Stuffed Mushrooms

If the mushrooms leave stains on your hands, you can remove the stains by rubbing your hands with a slice of lemon. Peel the onion under cold running water to help keep your eyes from tearing.

> 12 large mushrooms
> 1 tablespoon gluten-free margarine
> 1 small onion, minced fine
> 1 10-ounce box frozen chopped spinach
> 1 egg, slightly beaten
> 2 tablespoons grated gluten-free Parmesan cheese
> ½ teaspoon nutmeg
> ⅛ teaspoon salt
> ⅛ teaspoon pepper

Rinse off the mushrooms, and pat them dry. Remove the stems from the mushrooms, and chop fine. Melt the margarine in a medium-size skillet; add the mushroom stems and onion, and sauté. Cook the spinach according to the package directions; drain thoroughly, then squeeze dry. Add the spinach, egg, and cheese to the onion mixture. Stir in the nutmeg, salt, and pepper; mix well. Preheat broiler. Stuff the mushroom caps with the spinach mixture. Spray an 8″ × 12″ baking dish with gluten-free nonstick spray. Place the mushroom caps in the baking dish. Broil about 5 minutes. Serve hot. *Makes 6 2-mushroom servings.*

One serving—Calories: 45; Total fat: 1.6 g; Saturated fat: 0.7 g; Cholesterol: 37 mg; Sodium: 29 mg; Carbohydrates: 1 g; Fiber: 0.4 g; Sugar: 0 g; Protein: 1 g

Halibut with Pine Nut Crust

To serve, lay the halibut on a dish that has been drizzled with basil-flavored olive oil.

6 tablespoons finely chopped pine nuts

3 tablespoons grated gluten-free Parmesan cheese

½ teaspoon minced garlic

½ teaspoon chopped fresh basil

1¼ teaspoons chopped fresh mint

½ teaspoon chopped fresh sage

⅛ teaspoon cayenne

¼ teaspoon salt

6 teaspoons olive oil

6 halibut fillets (4 ounces each)

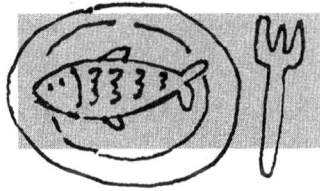

Preheat oven to 400°F. In a small bowl, mix together the pine nuts, Parmesan cheese, garlic, basil, mint, sage, cayenne, salt, and olive oil. Spray a 9″ × 13″ pan with gluten-free nonstick spray. Set the fish in the pan. Carefully pat the nut topping over the surface of each fillet, pressing lightly so it sticks. Bake 20 minutes or until fish flakes easily. *Makes 6 4-ounce servings.*

One serving—Calories: 260; Total fat: 13 g; Saturated fat: 2.3 g; Cholesterol: 48 mg; Sodium: 272 mg; Carbohydrates: 1.7 g; Fiber: 0.4 g; Sugar: 0.2 g; Protein: 33.4 g

Herb Risotto

You may have to go to a specialty grocery store to find the saffron threads. They are usually sold in a small jar in the spice section.

3 teaspoons olive oil

1 onion, minced

2 cloves garlic, minced

1½ cups basmati rice

¾ cup gluten-free dry white wine

¼ teaspoon pepper

3 teaspoons minced fresh parsley

5 cups water

1 gluten-free chicken bouillon cube

¼ teaspoon saffron threads

3 tablespoons grated gluten-free Parmesan cheese

Heat the olive oil in a 2-quart saucepan. Add the onion and garlic; sauté 4 minutes or until the onion is soft but not browned. Stir in the rice, and cook for 1 minute or until all the grains are shiny. Add the wine, and bring to a boil, stirring constantly. When all the wine has been absorbed, add the pepper, parsley, ½ cup of the water, and the bouillon cube, pressing the cube with the back of a spoon until it has dissolved. When most of the liquid is absorbed, add another ½ cup of water. Continue adding water, ½ cup at a time, until all the water has been added. If the rice is still hard, add an additional ¼ cup of water. Soak the saffron in 1 tablespoon of warm water for 3 minutes, add the saffron and soaking water to the rice. Continue cooking the rice for another 3 minutes, stirring. Remove the pan from the heat, and stir in the cheese. *Makes 6 ¾-cup servings.*

One serving—Calories: 112; Total fat: 3.2 g; Saturated fat: 0.9 g; Cholesterol: 2 mg; Sodium: 335 mg; Carbohydrates: 16.5 g; Fiber: 0.3 g; Sugar: 1.5 g; Protein: 2.3 g

Artichokes with Lima Beans

When serving this dish for company, place a large portobello mushroom cap on each plate after lightly brushing them with olive oil. Spoon the artichokes and lima beans into the mushroom caps and garnish with a sprig of fresh dill.

1 14-ounce can small green lima beans, drained

2 14-ounce cans artichoke hearts, drained

Juice of 1 lemon

3 tablespoons olive oil

⅛ teaspoon salt

⅛ teaspoon pepper

2 teaspoons minced fresh parsley

2 teaspoons dill weed

Preheat oven to 400°F. Spray a small casserole with gluten-free nonstick spray. Spoon the lima beans into the casserole. Cut the artichoke hearts in half, then lay them on top of the beans. In a small bowl, combine the lemon juice, olive oil, salt, pepper, parsley, and dill; sprinkle on top of the vegetables. Cover the casserole, and bake 15 to 20 minutes or till heated through. *Makes 6 ½-cup servings.*

One serving–Calories: 122; Total fat: 7 g; Saturated fat: 1 g; Cholesterol: 0 mg; Sodium: 238 mg; Carbohydrates: 13 g; Fiber: 0.4 g; Sugar: 1.3 g; Protein: 4 g

Roasted Mini Pumpkins

Roasted pumpkin is similar in taste to sweet potatoes. The taste and presentation will impress your guests. This recipe uses decorative mini pumpkins, which are surprisingly tender and sweet.

6 mini pumpkins

1½ tablespoons gluten-free margarine, melted

¼ teaspoon salt

¼ teaspoon pepper

¼ teaspoon cinnamon

¾ teaspoon chopped fresh parsley

¼ teaspoon thyme

Preheat oven to 400°F. Cut the tops off of the pumpkins and reserve. Scrape out the seeds and stringy pulp with a spoon. Lightly brush the pumpkins inside and out with the melted margarine. Sprinkle the inside of the pumpkins with the salt, pepper, cinnamon, parsley, and thyme. Spray an 8″ × 12″ baking dish with gluten-free nonstick spray. Replace the lids of the pumpkins, and place in the baking dish. Bake about 30 minutes or until tender. *Makes 6 mini pumpkins.*

One mini pumpkin—Calories: 60; Total fat: 2.2 g; Saturated fat: 0.7 g; Cholesterol: 0 mg; Sodium: 42 mg; Carbohydrates: 10 g; Fiber: 3 g; Sugar: 4 g; Protein: 1 g

Cranberry Salad with Balsamic Dressing

Mesclun greens are readily available in prepackaged bags at most grocery stores. The traditional mixture includes various wild and cultivated greens including chervil, arugula, lettuce, purslane, chicory, cresses, and endives. For extra flavor, lightly drizzle honey over the nuts, then toast them in the oven before adding them to the salad.

　　6 cups mesclun greens
　　3 tablespoons dried cranberries
　　3 tablespoons coarsely chopped walnuts
　　1 onion, sliced
　　3 tablespoons virgin olive oil
　　1½ tablespoons gluten-free balsamic vinegar
　　1½ teaspoons dill weed
　　⅛ teaspoon pepper
　　¼ teaspoon salt

In a large bowl, toss the greens, cranberries, walnuts, and onion. In a small bowl, whisk together the olive oil, vinegar, dill, pepper, and salt. Pour the dressing over the salad, and toss. *Makes 6 1¼-cup servings.*

One serving—Calories: 140; Total fat: 11.3 g; Saturated fat: 1.2 g; Cholesterol: 0 mg; Sodium: 81 mg; Carbohydrates: 9.2 g; Fiber: 2 g; Sugar: 3.7 g; Protein: 2.4 g

Basil Breadsticks

Spraying breadsticks with gluten-free nonstick spray before baking helps the crust get nice and crispy. The longer you bake these, the harder and crisper they get, so bake according to your taste. Before baking, you may wish to sprinkle the tops with poppy or sesame seeds. Make the breadsticks the day you plan to serve them.

  4½ tablespoons ½% milk

  1½ tablespoons finely minced green onion

  1½ teaspoons gluten-free baking powder

  ¼ teaspoon basil

  ¼ teaspoon oregano

  ¼ teaspoon salt

  ⅛ teaspoon pepper

  ¾ cup Gluten-Free Flour Mixture (See the Hints chapter.)

Preheat oven to 375°F. In a small bowl, mix together the milk, green onion, baking powder, basil, oregano, salt, and pepper. Sift the flour mixture into a medium-size bowl. Stir the milk mixture into the flour, 1 tablespoon at a time, until blended. Turn the dough onto a surface sprinkled with a little flour mixture, and knead about 4 minutes or until the dough is smooth and elastic, adding a little more flour mixture if the dough is too sticky. Let stand 30 minutes at room temperature. Spray a baking sheet with gluten-free nonstick spray. Divide the dough into four equal balls. Roll each ball into a thin rope, and place on the baking sheet. Lightly spray the tops of the breadsticks with the nonstick spray. Bake about 12 minutes or until the bottoms are golden brown. Turn the breadsticks over, and bake 10 minutes more or until the other side is browned. *Makes 6 breadsticks.*

One breadstick—Calories: 67; Total fat: 0 g; Saturated fat: 0 g; Cholesterol: 1 mg; Sodium: 172 mg; Carbohydrates: 13.4 g; Fiber: 0.5 g; Sugar: 2.7 g; Protein: 0.7 g

Seafood Dinner

Carry out the sea theme in the table setting, as well as in the foods served. Serve small foods out of clamshells. If you have any seashells, use them as the centerpiece.

Crab-Stuffed Mushrooms

To attractively display this appetizer, nestle the stuffed mushrooms inside Belgium endive leaves. The endive leaves are boat-shaped and form a natural container for appetizers, dips, peas, and even melon balls.

    12 large mushrooms
    1 tablespoon gluten-free margarine
    2 green onions
    ½ small red bell pepper, minced
    1 6½-ounce can crabmeat, drained
    ¼ cup chopped blanched almonds
    1 teaspoon lemon juice
    2 tablespoons gluten-free mayonnaise
    1 tablespoon gluten-free dry sherry
    Dash salt
    Paprika
    6 small leaves Belgian endive

Preheat oven to 350°F. Remove the stems from mushrooms; chop fine. Melt the margarine in a large skillet. Add the green onions, red pepper, and mushroom stems; sauté until mushroom stems are golden. Stir in the crabmeat, almonds, lemon juice, mayonnaise, sherry, and salt. Fill the mushroom caps with the crabmeat mixture. Sprinkle the tops with paprika. Spray an 8″ × 12″ baking pan with gluten-free nonstick spray. Place the filled mushroom caps in the baking pan. Bake 15 minutes. Place the endive leaves in a circular pattern on a serving plate. Nestle two hot mushrooms caps in each endive leaf, and serve. *Makes 6 2-mushroom servings.*

One serving—Calories: 93; Total fat: 6.1 g; Saturated fat: 0.9 g; Cholesterol: 19 mg; Sodium: 148 mg; Carbohydrates: 4 g; Fiber: 1.3 g; Sugar: 0.5 g; Protein: 6.7 g

Broiled Lobster Tails

For an attractive presentation, decorate the rim of each plate with a sprinkling of minced parsley and paprika.

    6 lobster tails (5 ounces each)
    2 tablespoons lemon juice
    1 tablespoon gluten-free margarine, melted
    Paprika
    2 tablespoons sliced almonds

Thaw the lobster tails if frozen. Preheat broiler. Butterfly each tail by using kitchen shears to cut lengthwise through the center of the hard top shell and the meat; use your fingers to slightly spread the halves apart. Place the tails, meat side up, on a broiler pan. In a small bowl, combine the lemon juice and margarine. Brush the mixture over the top of the lobster meat. Sprinkle lightly with paprika. Broil 4 inches from the heat for 8 to 10 minutes or until nearly done. Sprinkle with the almonds, and broil 1 to 2 minutes more or till lobster meat is opaque and almonds are lightly toasted. *Makes 6 lobster tails.*

One lobster tail—Calories: 156; Total fat: 4 g; Saturated fat: 0.7 g; Cholesterol: 135 mg; Sodium: 444 mg; Carbohydrates: 1.4 g; Fiber: 0.2 g; Sugar: 0.1 g; Protein: 27.1 g

Linguine with Clam Sauce

Adding a few drops of corn oil to the boiling water will help keep the pasta from sticking together; a little salt in the boiling water will raise the temperature and cook the pasta more quickly. To keep the clams tender, add the sauce 5 minutes before serving.

3 tablespoons olive oil

4 cloves garlic, minced

⅓ cup chopped green onion

1 7-ounce can mushrooms, drained

1 8-ounce bottle clam juice

Juice of ½ lemon

⅓ cup gluten-free dry white wine

1 teaspoon oregano

3 tablespoons minced fresh parsley

Dash red pepper flakes

8 ounces gluten-free corn linguine

2 6½-ounce cans minced clams

Heat the olive oil in a large saucepan. Add the garlic, green onion, and mushrooms; sauté slowly until golden brown. Add the clam juice, lemon juice, wine, oregano, parsley, and red pepper flakes. Warm over medium heat 15 minutes. Meanwhile, cook the pasta according to package directions. Five minutes before serving, add the clams to the garlic mixture, and simmer. Drain the pasta; add to the sauce, and toss to mix. *Makes 6 ¾-cup servings.*

One serving—Calories: 174; Total fat: 8.1 g; Saturated fat: 1.2 g; Cholesterol: 0 mg; Sodium: 543 mg; Carbohydrates: 12.7 g; Fiber: 1.4 g; Sugar: 1.7 g; Protein: 11.4 g

Shrimp Feta Salad

French or Bulgarian feta cheese may be difficult to find, but the search is worth it in flavor.

¾ pound shrimp, shelled and deveined

3 green onions, sliced thin

1 cucumber, diced

½ cup chopped green bell pepper

2 tablespoons snipped fresh dill

1 tablespoon minced fresh parsley

¼ cup crumbled gluten-free feta cheese

2 tablespoons lemon juice

3 tablespoons olive oil

1 tablespoon gluten-free white wine vinegar

1 clove garlic, minced

¼ teaspoon black pepper

In a small saucepan, bring 1 quart of water to a boil. Add the shrimp, and cook just until firm and pink, about 2 minutes. Rinse in a colander under cold running water; drain. Place the shrimp in a large bowl. Add the green onions, cucumber, green bell pepper, dill, parsley, and cheese. In a small bowl, whisk together the lemon juice, olive oil, vinegar, garlic, and black pepper. Pour the dressing over the shrimp mixture, and toss gently to mix. *Makes 6 ½-cup servings.*

One serving—Calories: 166; Total fat: 10.5 g; Saturated fat: 3.2 g; Cholesterol: 123 mg; Sodium: 288 mg; Carbohydrates: 3.7 g; Fiber: 0.7 g; Sugar: 0.2 g; Protein: 14.5 g

Artichokes with Dipping Sauce

Before working with artichokes, rub your hands with lemon juice, then squeeze the lemon into a bowl of water; add the artichokes to the bowl. The lemon juice will prevent the artichokes from turning dark and keep them from staining your hands. Do not cook artichokes in a corrosive metal pan (aluminum), or they may turn an unappetizing gray; use a stainless steel, enamel, or flameproof glass pan.

6 artichokes

1 lemon, sliced

2 tablespoons gluten-free margarine

1 clove garlic, minced

2 tablespoons minced fresh parsley

¼ teaspoon salt

¼ teaspoon paprika

½ cup freshly squeezed lemon juice

2 tablespoons gluten-free white wine vinegar

Using kitchen shears, cut the sharp tips from the outer leaves of the artichokes. Cut off the stem ends so the artichokes stand level. Cut off the top inch of the tightly closed inner leaves. Separate the inner leaves enough to insert a spoon; use the spoon to remove the choke from the center. Pour water into a 4-quart pot until half full. Bring the water to a boil over high heat. Add the lemon and trimmed artichokes; cover. When the water returns to a boil, reduce heat until water barely simmers. Simmer 20 to 30 minutes until the artichokes are tender when pierced with a fork at the stem ends. Drain the artichokes; place upside down on paper towels to drain. In a small saucepan, melt the margarine. Add the garlic and parsley; sauté 1 minute. Add the salt, paprika, lemon juice, and vinegar. Stir over medium heat 1 minute. Spoon 3 teaspoons of the warm sauce into each of six individual serving cups. Serve the artichokes with the sauce. *Makes 6 artichokes (with 3 teaspoons sauce).*

One artichoke—Calories: 96; Total fat: 3.2 g; Saturated fat: 0.7 g; Cholesterol: 0 mg; Sodium: 261 mg; Carbohydrates: 16.6 g; Fiber: 0 g; Sugar: 2.3 g; Protein: 4.4 g

Leg of Lamb Dinner

For a light, spring look, instead of using a tablecloth, place one long table runner lengthwise down the center of the table and two shorter table runners crosswise across the table. Set each place setting on a runner.

Creamed Salmon Slices

Nestle a fresh sprig of parsley or dill into the creamed salmon before serving. Canned salmon that has been drained may be substituted for the smoked salmon, but there will be a difference in taste.

1 ounce smoked salmon, broken into small pieces

2 tablespoons gluten-free sour cream

½ teaspoon chopped fresh dill

¼ teaspoon freshly squeezed lemon juice

¼ teaspoon finely chopped capers

Dash salt

Dash pepper

1 cucumber, sliced into 16 ¼-inch slices

Combine the smoked salmon, sour cream, dill, lemon juice, capers, salt, and pepper in a small bowl. Cover and refrigerate 2 hours. Just before serving, slice the cucumbers; place on a platter. Put a dollop of the creamed salmon on top of each cucumber slice. *Makes 8 2-piece servings.*

One serving—Calories: 15; Total fat: 0.8 g; Saturated fat: 0.4 g; Cholesterol: 2 mg; Sodium: 73 mg; Carbohydrates: 1.2 g; Fiber: 0.2 g; Sugar: 0.1 g; Protein: 1 g

Roast Leg of Lamb

Marinating the meat for 2 days before cooking fully develops the flavors. Baking the meat in a 500°F oven for 15 minutes sears the outside of the roast, sealing in the natural juices.

1 whole head of garlic

1 3-pound leg of lamb

2 tablespoons olive oil

3 tablespoons
   freshly squeezed
   lemon juice

¼ cup gluten-free white wine

1 teaspoon oregano

½ teaspoon salt

½ teaspoon pepper

Preheat oven to 500°F. Peel the garlic cloves; cut each clove in half (small cloves) or thirds (large cloves). Remove all visible fat from the lamb. Cut thin slits all over the lamb, approximately 1 inch deep. Insert a garlic sliver into each slit. Place the lamb in a roasting pan; rub the meat all over with the olive oil. Stir together the lemon juice, wine, oregano, salt, and pepper; drizzle over the roast. Add 2 cups of water to the pan; roast 15 minutes. Lower the oven temperature to 350°F, and bake 1 hour, basting frequently with pan juices, or until the meat is well browned. Cover with foil, and continue to bake another 35 minutes or until the meat is very tender but not dry. Add more water during cooking if needed. *Makes 8 ¼-pound servings.*

One serving—Calories: 320; Total fat: 20 g; Saturated fat: 4.5 g; Cholesterol: 133 mg; Sodium: 274 mg; Carbohydrates: 1.7 g; Fiber: 0.1 g; Sugar: 1.2 g; Protein: 42.4 g

Grecian Roasted Potatoes

Cubing the potatoes gives the illusion of a larger portion, so fewer potatoes are needed, saving on calories.

6 large baking potatoes, cut into 1-inch cubes

3 tablespoons lemon juice

¼ cup water

4 tablespoons olive oil

¼ teaspoon salt

¼ teaspoon pepper

½ teaspoon garlic powder

¾ teaspoon oregano

¾ teaspoon dill weed

Preheat oven to 350°F. Spray a casserole dish with gluten-free nonstick spray. Put the potatoes in the baking dish. In a small saucepan, combine the lemon juice, water, olive oil, salt, pepper, garlic powder, oregano, and dill. Bring to a boil; pour the sauce over the potatoes. Bake 50 minutes, stirring occasionally and adding a little more water if needed. *Makes 8 1¼-cup servings.*

One serving—Calories: 126; Total fat: 6.8 g; Saturated fat: 1 g; Cholesterol: 0 mg; Sodium: 153 mg; Carbohydrates: 15.6 g; Fiber: 0.3 g; Sugar: 0.1 g; Protein: 1.3 g

Spinach Rice Tomatoes

Freeze the pulp from the tomatoes to use in soups or stews.

8 medium tomatoes

4 tablespoons olive oil

2 onions, chopped

¼ cup shredded carrot

1 tablespoon chopped fresh parsley

1 tablespoon chopped fresh dill

1 10-ounce box frozen chopped spinach, thawed

¼ cup rice

⅛ teaspoon pepper

⅛ teaspoon salt

3 tablespoons tomato sauce

¾ cup water

Preheat oven to 350°F. Cut a slice off the stem end of each tomato; remove the pulp. Cut a small X on the bottom of each tomato; place in a 9″ × 13″ baking pan. Pour ½ inch of water in the pan; cover and bake 15 minutes till the tomatoes are barely soft.

Remove the tomatoes with a spatula; drain water from pan. Spray the pan with gluten-free nonstick spray; return tomatoes to pan. Heat the olive oil in a medium-size saucepan. Add the onion and carrot; sauté until golden brown, stirring frequently. Stir in the parsley, dill, spinach, rice, pepper, salt, tomato sauce, and water. Simmer, covered, 15 minutes till moisture is absorbed. Fill the tomato cavities with the spinach mixture. Cover and bake 15 minutes. *Makes 8 tomatoes.*

One tomato—Calories: 57; Total fat: 0.6 g; Saturated fat: 0.1 g; Cholesterol: 0 mg; Sodium: 101 mg; Carbohydrates: 12.1 g; Fiber: 3.4 g; Sugar: 0.9 g; Protein: 3 g

Shredded Salad

To shred the lettuce, cut the head in quarters lengthwise. Slice each quarter crosswise into thin strips.

½ teaspoon oregano

¼ teaspoon dill weed

¼ teaspoon mint, crushed

¼ teaspoon salt

¼ teaspoon pepper

¼ teaspoon garlic powder

2 tablespoons chopped fresh parsley

¼ cup olive oil

2 tablespoons apple cider vinegar

½ cup small cubes gluten-free feta cheese

½ cup kalamata olives

1 head iceberg lettuce, shredded

12 cherry tomatoes, cut in half

1 cucumber, cut in half lengthwise, then sliced

1 onion, sliced thin

¼ cup canned garbanzo beans, rinsed then drained

6 artichoke hearts, cut in half

In a medium-size bowl, whisk together the oregano, dill, mint, salt, pepper, garlic powder, parsley, olive oil, and vinegar. Stir in the cheese and olives. Cover and refrigerate at least 2 hours. In a large salad bowl, toss together the lettuce, tomatoes, cucumber, onion, garbanzo beans, and artichoke hearts. Add the cheese and olives with the marinade, and toss to coat evenly. *Makes 8 1-cup servings.*

One serving–Calories: 141; Total fat: 11.1 g; Saturated fat: 3.3 g; Cholesterol: 13 mg; Sodium: 349 mg; Carbohydrates: 8.4 g; Fiber: 2.2 g; Sugar: 0.4 g; Protein: 4 g

Onion Brown Bread

If you make the bread the day before you serve it, wrap it in plastic wrap, then in foil, and refrigerate.

1 teaspoon corn oil

1 onion, minced

1 ¼ cups Gluten-Free Flour Mixture (See the Hints chapter.)

1 ½ teaspoons gluten-free baking powder

1 teaspoon baking soda

¼ teaspoon salt

¼ cup cornmeal

2 eggs

2 egg whites

¼ cup unsulfured molasses

1 ½ tablespoons sugar

1 tablespoon olive oil

1 cup buttermilk

Preheat oven to 350°F. Spray a small skillet with gluten-free non-stick spray. Heat the corn oil in the skillet. Add the onion, and sauté till soft but not browned; set aside. Sift together the flour mixture, baking powder, baking soda, salt, and cornmeal on to a sheet of waxed paper, then resift into a medium-size bowl. In a large bowl, whisk the eggs, egg whites, molasses, sugar, and olive oil. Add the dry ingredients alternately with the buttermilk. Beat at medium speed till blended. Add the onions; beat 30 seconds more to blend. Spray a 5″ × 9″ loaf pan with gluten-free nonstick spray. Spoon the dough into the pan. Bake 45 to 50 minutes or until a toothpick inserted in the center comes out clean. *Makes 1 loaf (10 slices).*

One slice—Calories: 136; Total fat: 3.4 g; Saturated fat: 0.6 g; Cholesterol: 42 mg; Sodium: 100 mg; Carbohydrates: 22 g; Fiber: 0.8 g; Sugar: 6.2 g; Protein: 4.6 g

4

Buffet Dinners

I f you are entertaining a large group, consider hiring someone
to help out. Set your table several days in advance, and prepare
whatever foods you can ahead of time so you won't feel rushed
on the day of the dinner.

Italian Buffet

You will be relaxed when your guests arrive because much of this
dinner may be prepared ahead of time. In keeping with the Italian theme, you may want to serve wine with dinner; serve a
domestic wine, because many imported wines are not gluten-free.

Spaghetti Pie

This may be prepared the day ahead, covered with foil, and refrigerated before baking. Do not overcook pasta; gluten-free pastas tend to get mushy and fall apart if they are overcooked.

    8 ounces gluten-free corn spaghetti
    1 tablespoon olive oil
    1 onion, minced
    3 cloves garlic, minced
    ¼ cup minced fresh parsley
    1 tablespoon lemon juice
    1½ teaspoons oregano
    1 teaspoon basil
    ¼ teaspoon pepper
    ½ cup gluten-free, low-fat cottage cheese
    1 large egg white
    ¼ cup grated gluten-free Parmesan cheese
    2 tomatoes, sliced thin
    ¼ cup shredded gluten-free mozzarella cheese

Preheat oven to 350°F. Cook the spaghetti al dente according to package directions but omitting any salt. Rinse well under cold water; drain. Return to cooking pot. Heat the olive oil in a skillet for 1 minute. Add the onion and garlic, and cook until the onion is soft, about 5 minutes. Add to the spaghetti along with the parsley, lemon juice, 1 teaspoon of oregano, ½ teaspoon of basil, and the pepper. Toss well. In a small bowl, combine the cottage cheese, egg white, 2 tablespoons of the Parmesan cheese, and the remaining ½ teaspoon of oregano and ½ teaspoon of basil. Add the cheese mixture to the spaghetti, and toss well. Spray an 8-inch springform pan with gluten-free nonstick spray. Spoon half of the spaghetti mixture into the pan, and press lightly over the bottom.

Arrange half of the tomato slices on top, and sprinkle with half of the mozzarella cheese. Repeat the layers. Sprinkle the remaining 2 tablespoons of Parmesan cheese on top. Cover with foil, and bake 55 minutes or until set. Remove the foil, and bake 5 minutes longer. Cool 10 minutes, then gently loosen the pie around the edges with a thin-bladed knife. Remove the sides from the springform pan. Cut the pie into 8 wedges. *Makes 8 1-wedge servings.*

One serving—Calories: 150; Total fat: 4.7 g; Saturated fat: 0.8 g; Cholesterol: 2 mg; Sodium: 530 mg; Carbohydrates: 19.2 g; Fiber: 0.5 g; Sugar: 1 g; Protein: 7.6 g

Sherried Steak

Do not use a nonstick skillet to cook the steaks. Use an uncoated skillet, so you have enough burnt-on bits for the sauce.

    2 teaspoons olive oil
    8 ½-inch-thick beef tenderloin steaks (4 ounces each)
    ½ cup gluten-free dry sherry
    ½ teaspoon salt
    ½ teaspoon cracked pepper
    4 tablespoons snipped fresh parsley

Spray a cold skillet with gluten-free nonstick spray; add the olive oil. Heat the skillet over medium-high heat. Add the steaks, and cook for 3 minutes on each side or to desired doneness; transfer to serving platter. Slowly add the sherry to the skillet, then add the salt and pepper. Cook, stirring, for 2 minutes, scraping any browned bits from the bottom of the pan. Drizzle the sauce over the steaks, and sprinkle with the parsley. *Makes 8 4-ounce servings.*

One serving—Calories: 235; Total fat: 11.6 g; Saturated fat: 4.2 g; Cholesterol: 89 mg; Sodium: 262 mg; Carbohydrates: 0.4 g; Fiber: 0 g; Sugar: 0.4 g; Protein: 30 g

Basil Roulades

The roulades may be assembled up to 6 hours before serving; cover tightly with plastic wrap, and refrigerate. Rice paper circles may be found at most Asian grocery stores. To serve, nestle the logs in a bed of alfalfa sprouts.

> 4 rice paper circles
> 1 ounce gluten-free cream cheese, softened
> 1 ounce gluten-free feta cheese, crumbled
> ½ tablespoon minced kalamata olives
> 1 tablespoon minced green bell pepper
> ⅛ teaspoon oregano
> Dash basil
> 1 clove garlic, minced
> Dash salt
> Dash black pepper
> 1 tablespoon grated gluten-free Parmesan cheese
> 1 tablespoon chopped walnuts, toasted
> Olive oil

Soak the rice paper in water 5 minutes to soften. Pat dry. Whip together the cream cheese, feta cheese, olives, green bell pepper, oregano, basil, garlic, salt, black pepper, and Parmesan cheese. Add the walnuts and mix just until the nuts are mixed through-out. Spread the cheese mixture on the rice paper circles. Fold two sides of a rice paper toward the center, then continue to roll to form a log shape. Brush all sides with olive oil. Repeat with the other rice paper circles. Wrap the logs in plastic wrap, and chill for 3 hours, or up to 2 days. To serve, slice into ¾-inch rolls (4 slices per roll). *Makes 8 2-slice servings.*

One serving—Calories: 68; Total fat: 3.5 g; Saturated fat: 1.5 g; Cholesterol: 7 mg; Sodium: 93 mg; Carbohydrates: 7.2 g; Fiber: 0.2 g; Sugar: 0.6 g; Protein: 2.5 g

Eggplant Rolls

The rolls may be assembled the day before serving if covered and refrigerated.

- 1 large eggplant, peeled
- 2 eggs, beaten
- ¼ cup Gluten-Free Flour Mixture (See the Hints chapter.)
- 1 tablespoon olive oil
- 8 1-ounce slices gluten-free, low-fat mozzarella cheese
- 16 ounces gluten-free cottage cheese
- 2 tablespoons chopped fresh parsley
- ¼ teaspoon oregano
- ⅛ teaspoon pepper
- 2 cups gluten-free spaghetti sauce

Preheat oven to 350°F. Cut eight thin, lengthwise slices from the eggplant. Dip the slices in the beaten eggs, then dredge in the flour mixture. Spray a skillet with gluten-free nonstick spray; add the olive oil and warm 1 minute. Fry the eggplant until golden, turning once. Pat the slices dry with paper towels. Place a slice of mozzarella in the middle of each eggplant slice. In a bowl, stir together the cottage cheese, parsley, oregano, and pepper; put a spoonful of cheese filling on top of the cheese in the middle of each eggplant slice. Roll up the slices and place, seam side down, in an

8″ × 12″ baking pan that has been sprayed with gluten-free non-stick spray. Spoon the spaghetti sauce over the top. Bake 20 minutes. *Makes 8 rolls.*

One roll—Calories: 152; Total fat: 5.2 g; Saturated fat: 1.6 g; Cholesterol: 57 mg; Sodium: 541 mg; Carbohydrates: 13.7 g; Fiber: 3.3 g; Sugar: 5.6 g; Protein: 13.4 g

Mixed-Greens Salad

Roses are edible if untreated with pesticides. For a dramatic effect, tuck in a few well-washed red rosebuds on the top of the salad for color.

2 bags mixed salad greens

6 radishes, sliced

3 green onions, sliced thin

¼ cup olive oil

2 tablespoons lemon juice

1 teaspoon lemon zest

½ teaspoon salt

½ teaspoon oregano

½ teaspoon coarsely ground pepper

1 clove garlic, minced

¼ teaspoon basil

1 tablespoon chopped fresh parsley

4 tablespoons grated gluten-free Parmesan cheese

Wash the greens well; put on paper toweling to absorb most of the moisture. Put the greens, radishes, and green onions in a salad bowl. Whisk together the olive oil, lemon juice, lemon zest, salt, oregano, pepper, garlic, basil, parsley, and Parmesan cheese. Pour the dressing over the salad, and toss. *Makes 8 1-cup servings.*

One serving—Calories: 80; Total fat: 7.7 g; Saturated fat: 1.4 g; Cholesterol: 2 mg; Sodium: 200 mg; Carbohydrates: 1.9 g; Fiber: 1 g; Sugar: 0.2 g; Protein: 1.8 g

Turkey Tenderloin Buffet

For an elegant touch, intersperse lit votive candles among the various platters.

Lemon Turkey with Capers

Garnish Lemon Turkey with very thin slices of spiraled lemon zest.

½ cup Gluten-Free Flour Mixture (See the Hints chapter.)

½ teaspoon pepper

1 teaspoon paprika

8 5-ounce slices turkey tenderloin

3 tablespoons olive oil

1 cube gluten-free chicken bouillon

½ cup water

4 tablespoons freshly squeezed lemon juice

2 tablespoons capers

Sift together the flour mixture, pepper, and paprika on a plate. Press the turkey slices into the flour mixture to coat them evenly, shaking off the excess. Heat the olive oil 1 minute in a skillet over medium-high heat. Add the turkey, and cook about 3 minutes on each side. (Do not overcook.) Transfer the turkey slices to a heated serving platter. Put the bouillon cube and water in the same skillet; press on the cube with the back of a spoon till dissolved. Scrape up any browned bits on the bottom of the pan. Stir in the lemon juice and capers, and heat through. Pour the sauce over the turkey. *Makes 8 5-ounce servings.*

One serving—Calories: 250; Total fat: 8.8 g; Saturated fat: 1.9 g; Cholesterol: 78 mg; Sodium: 167 mg; Carbohydrates: 6.1 g; Fiber: 0.2 g; Sugar: 0.2 g; Protein: 34.8 g

Spinach Rice Timbales

For an attractive presentation, sprinkle finely chopped parsley around the edge of the Timbale platter. These may also be baked in cupcake tins.

> 3 teaspoons gluten-free margarine
>
> ½ cup minced green onion
>
> 1¼ cups rice
>
> 1 10-ounce box frozen chopped spinach, thawed
>
> 2½ cups water
>
> 2 cubes gluten-free chicken bouillon
>
> ¼ teaspoon pepper
>
> 5 tablespoons grated gluten-free Parmesan cheese
>
> ½ teaspoon grated lemon zest

Heat the margarine in a medium-size saucepan. Add the onion, and sauté, stirring occasionally, for 3 minutes or till softened. Add the rice; cook, stirring, for 1 minute. Squeeze the spinach dry; add to the rice along with the water, bouillon cubes, and pepper. Press on the bouillon cube to dissolve. Cover and simmer till liquid has been absorbed. Stir in the cheese and lemon zest, mixing well. Spray eight custard cups (or a muffin tin) with gluten-free non-stick spray. Spoon the spinach-rice mixture into the custard cups, packing it lightly. Invert onto a platter. *Makes 8 ⅔-cup servings.*

One serving—Calories: 142; Total fat: 2.5 g; Saturated fat: 1 g; Cholesterol: 2.3 mg; Sodium: 288 mg; Carbohydrates: 25 g; Fiber: 1.2 g; Sugar: 0 g; Protein: 4.6 g

Baked Stuffed Zucchini

The stuffed zucchini may be assembled ahead of time and frozen without the cheese topping. Thaw before baking.

> 4 small zucchini
>
> 2 teaspoons gluten-free margarine
>
> 2 onions, minced

½ pound lean ground round

2 tablespoons chopped fresh parsley

¼ teaspoon plus dash salt

⅛ teaspoon plus dash pepper

¼ teaspoon mint

¼ cup gluten-free spaghetti sauce

1 egg, beaten

¼ cup grated gluten-free Parmesan cheese

1 teaspoon 1% milk

Paprika

Preheat oven to 350°F. Cut each zucchini in half lengthwise; scoop out the pulp, leaving the shell intact. Chop the pulp. Melt the margarine in a 10-inch skillet. Add the onion and ground beef; sauté, breaking up the meat with a fork. When the meat is browned, drain off any fat. Stir in the zucchini pulp, parsley, ¼ teaspoon of salt, ¼ teaspoon of pepper, the mint, and spaghetti sauce; simmer 5 minutes. Spoon the filling into the shells. Bake 35 minutes. Preheat broiler. Mix the eggs, cheese, milk, and dash of salt and pepper; spread on top of the stuffed zucchini. Sprinkle each with paprika. Place under the broiler 3 minutes to brown. *Makes 8 stuffed zucchini.*

One stuffed zucchini—Calories: 122; Total fat: 7.9 g; Saturated fat: 3.2 g; Cholesterol: 54 mg; Sodium: 213 mg; Carbohydrates: 2.8 g; Fiber: 0.6 g; Sugar: 0.4 g; Protein: 9.4 g

Baked Broccoli with Crabmeat

Use real crabmeat. The artificial seafood blends often contain gluten.

2 10-ounce boxes frozen cut broccoli

2 ounces crabmeat pieces

2 tablespoons gluten-free margarine

4 cups sliced mushrooms

2 cloves garlic, minced

3 tablespoons cornstarch

¼ teaspoon pepper

1½ cups skim milk

½ cup (2 ounces) shredded gluten-free, low-fat sharp
cheddar cheese

4 tablespoons grated gluten-free Parmesan cheese

Preheat oven to 350°F. Cook the broccoli according to the package directions; drain. Spray a 9-inch square pan with gluten-free nonstick spray. Arrange the broccoli in the baking dish. Sprinkle the crabmeat over the broccoli. Melt the margarine in a medium saucepan. Add the mushrooms and garlic; sauté over high heat for 4 minutes or till mushrooms are tender, stirring frequently. Stir in the cornstarch and pepper; slowly stir in the milk. Continue to cook, stirring, till the sauce thickens; remove from heat. Stir in the cheddar cheese till melted. Spoon the sauce on top of the crabmeat. Bake, covered, 20 minutes or until bubbly. Sprinkle with the Parmesan cheese just before serving. *Makes 8 ¾-cup servings.*

One serving—Calories: 152; Total fat: 4.2 g; Saturated fat: 1.2 g; Cholesterol: 34 mg; Sodium: 291 mg; Carbohydrates: 11.8 g; Fiber: 2 g; Sugar: 5.2 g; Protein: 16.4 g

Raspberry Tossed Salad

For variety, you may substitute strawberries for the raspberries and strawberry jam for the raspberry preserves.

2 cups spinach

2 cups endive

2 cups red leaf lettuce

2 small onions, sliced

1 cup fresh red raspberries

½ cup gluten-free Italian dressing

¼ teaspoon pepper

2 tablespoons all-fruit raspberry preserves

2 tablespoons dried sunflower seeds

Tear the spinach, endive, and lettuce leaves into bite-sized pieces; place in a large bowl. Add the onions and raspberries; toss well. Whisk together the Italian dressing, pepper, raspberry preserves, and sunflower seeds; pour over the salad. Toss to coat evenly. Transfer to a serving bowl. *Makes 8 1-cup servings.*

One serving—Calories: 53; Total fat: 1.2 g; Saturated fat: 0.2 g; Cholesterol: 1 mg; Sodium: 255 mg; Carbohydrates: 9.1 g; Fiber: 2.4 g; Sugar: 3.5 g; Protein: 1.7 g

Irish Potato Bread

For muffins, pinch off pieces of dough and place in mini-muffin tins; reduce baking time to 15 minutes.

3 medium golden potatoes, peeled and cubed

3 tablespoons gluten-free margarine, melted

½ cup 1% milk

½ teaspoon salt

3 tablespoons grated gluten-free Parmesan cheese

1 cup Gluten-Free Flour Mixture (See the Hints chapter.)

1½ teaspoons gluten-free baking powder

Preheat oven to 350°F. Boil the potatoes till tender; drain well. Whip the potatoes, margarine, milk, and salt until smooth and fluffy. Stir in the cheese. Sift together the flour mixture and baking powder; stir into the whipped potatoes. Spread the dough into a 10-inch circle on an ungreased baking sheet. Bake 30 minutes or until lightly browned. Cut bread into 10 wedges after cooling. *Makes 10 wedges.*

One wedge—Calories: 121; Total fat: 3.2 g; Saturated fat: 1 g; Cholesterol: 2mg; Sodium: 199 mg; Carbohydrates: 19.6 g; Fiber: 1.3 g; Sugar: 1.7 g; Protein: 3.8 g

Fall Buffet

For a fall centerpiece, pile mini pumpkins, dried corn, and small gourds on a flat pedestal dish. Between these, tuck in bunches of kale, chrysanthemums, and colorful dried or silk leaves.

Pork with Apricot Stuffing

This pork roast will definitely impress your guests. To assure the roast is juicy and tender, do not overcook. Pitted prunes may be used in place of, or in addition to, the apricots.

¼ cup light brown sugar
2 cloves garlic, minced
1 teaspoon ground ginger
⅛ teaspoon salt
¼ teaspoon pepper
⅛ teaspoon cinnamon
Dash ground cloves
2 pounds lean pork tenderloin
4 dried apricots, cut in quarters
1 tablespoon gluten-free soy sauce

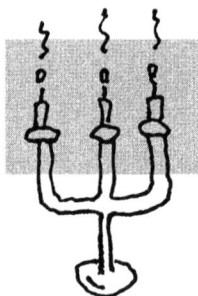

In a small bowl, combine the brown sugar, garlic, ginger, salt, pepper, cinnamon, and cloves to form a seasoning rub. Slice the meat down the center lengthwise, and insert the apricots. Tie the roast together in several places with string. Brush the soy sauce over the surface of the meat; rub the seasoning mixture onto the top of the meat. Insert a meat thermometer near the center of the roast. Spray a grill with gluten-free nonstick spray and preheat the grill to medium setting, or, if using charcoal, cook meat on a piece of heavy-duty foil that has been sprayed with gluten-free nonstick spray. Place the meat on the grate; cover and grill 20 minutes, turning frequently. (If you don't have a grill, place the meat in a roasting pan that has been sprayed with gluten-free nonstick spray, and broil about 20 minutes, turning the meat once.) Slice the meat. *Makes 8 ¼-pound servings.*

One serving–Calories: 249; Total fat: 7.5 g; Saturated fat: 2.6 g; Cholesterol: 110 mg; Sodium: 226 mg; Carbohydrates: 7.2 g; Fiber: 0.4 g; Sugar: 6.6 g; Protein: 36.1 g

Wild Rice Dressing

Use plain wild rice, not the seasoned packages found at the grocery store.

3 teaspoons olive oil

2 cups chopped onion

4½ cups water

1 cup brown rice

½ cup wild rice

3 cubes gluten-free chicken bouillon

¼ teaspoon pepper

4 cups sliced mushrooms

1 cup chopped celery

¼ cup pine nuts

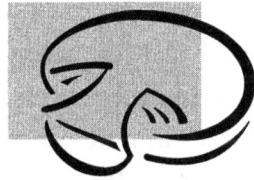

Heat 1 teaspoon of the olive oil in a 2-quart saucepan. Add the onion, and sauté till softened and lightly browned. Add the water, brown rice, wild rice, bouillon, and pepper. Bring to a boil; reduce heat, and simmer, covered, 20 minutes. In a large skillet, heat the remaining 2 teaspoons of oil; add the mushrooms, celery, and pine nuts. Sauté till mushrooms are golden; stir into rice mixture. Continue simmering, covered, until all the moisture has been absorbed, about 10 minutes. *Makes 8 ¾-cup servings.*

One serving–Calories: 136; Total fat: 4.5 g; Saturated fat: 0.7 g; Cholesterol: 0 mg; Sodium: 300 mg; Carbohydrates: 20.1 g; Fiber: 2.8 g; Sugar: 0.6 g; Protein: 4.9 g

Maple Acorn Squash

Acorn squash is a very firm vegetable. To slice it raw, use a butcher's knife.

   2 large acorn squash
   1 tablespoon gluten-free margarine
   2 tablespoons maple syrup
   8 teaspoons gluten-free Parmesan cheese

Preheat oven to 400°F. Cut the squash in half crosswise, and scoop out the seeds with a spoon. Slice the squash into rounds ½-inch thick (8 slices per squash). Spray a baking sheet with gluten-free nonstick spray. Place the squash rounds in a single layer on the baking sheet. Bake 10 minutes; turn and bake 10 more minutes. Remove from oven and let cool. Reduce oven temperature to 350°F. Melt the margarine; stir in the maple syrup. Drizzle the syrup mixture evenly over the squash. Sprinkle with the cheese. Bake 15 minutes or until the squash is tender and golden brown. For added effect, scatter acorns around the outside base of the dish. *Makes 8 2-piece servings.*

One serving—Calories: 58; Total fat: 1.6 g; Saturated fat: 0.7 g; Cholesterol: 1 mg; Sodium: 50 mg; Carbohydrates: 9.5 g; Fiber: 2 g; Sugar: 3.2 g; Protein: 1.3 g

Avocado Salad

If necessary, place the avocado in a paper bag and leave it on the counter for several days to ripen.

   2 tablespoons apple cider vinegar
   2 tablespoons freshly squeezed orange juice
   ¼ teaspoon dry mustard
   1 teaspoon lemon juice
   ½ teaspoon salt

½ teaspoon black pepper

3 tablespoons olive oil

Dash red pepper flakes

1 Bermuda onion, sliced thin and separated into rings

1 avocado, peeled, seed removed, and sliced thin

1 large head leaf lettuce, torn into pieces

In a medium bowl, whisk together the vinegar, orange juice, mustard, lemon juice, salt, black pepper, olive oil, and red pepper flakes. Stir in the onion rings and avocado slices. Cover and chill for 3 to 6 hours. To serve, add the lettuce to the bowl, and toss to coat. *Makes 8 1-cup servings.*

One serving—Calories: 63; Total fat: 9.1 g; Saturated fat: 1.2 g; Cholesterol: 0 mg; Sodium: 155 mg; Carbohydrates: 5 g; Fiber: 2.2 g; Sugar: 0.6 g; Protein: 1.1 g

Braised Beef Buffet

For an eye-catching centerpiece, pile artichokes pyramid style in a shallow bowl. Fill in the gaps with fresh lemons and leafy sprigs.

Braised Beef

Warm the olive oil in a pan before adding meat for browning to help prevent the meat from sticking to the pan.

2 tablespoons olive oil

1 2½-pound lean beef roast, tied into a compact shape

2 large onions, chopped

3 carrots, peeled and chopped

2 ribs celery, chopped

4 cloves garlic, cut into slivers

2 15-ounce cans diced tomatoes

1 3-inch strip lemon zest

1 cinnamon stick

4 whole cloves

½ teaspoon salt

½ teaspoon pepper

2 cups gluten-free white wine

⅓ cup gluten-free brandy

Warm the olive oil in a large pot or Dutch oven over high heat. Reduce the heat to medium-high and add the roast, and brown well on all sides. Add the onion, carrot, celery, and garlic; cook 2 more minutes, browning and stirring the vegetables. Add the tomatoes, lemon zest, cinnamon stick, cloves, salt, and pepper. Pour in the wine and brandy to cover the roast (adding some water if necessary). Bring to a boil; reduce heat to medium-low, and simmer slowly for 2½ hours until the meat is very tender and the pan juices are thickened. Remove the roast to a cutting board, and let it set for 10 minutes. Slice the meat thinly, against the grain; place on a serving platter. Strain the juices from the pan over the meat. *Makes 8 ¼-pound servings.*

One serving—Calories: 315; Total fat: 10.7 g; Saturated fat: 2.9 g; Cholesterol: 83 mg; Sodium: 770 mg; Carbohydrates: 19.1 g; Fiber: 5 g; Sugar: 5.2 g; Protein: 32.2 g

Dilled Green Beans

Watch the browning margarine closely so it does not burn.

3 9-ounce boxes frozen whole green beans

1 cup boiling water

3 tablespoons gluten-free margarine

½ pound sliced mushrooms

3 tablespoons sliced almonds

1 tablespoon minced fresh parsley

¼ teaspoon salt

¼ teaspoon pepper

1 tablespoon dried dill weed

Place the green beans in a saucepan with the boiling water. Cover; return to a boil. Separate the beans with a fork. Reduce heat, and simmer 10 minutes or till tender-crisp; drain. Melt the margarine in a saucepan over medium-low heat just until it begins to brown. Stir in the mushrooms and almonds; cook, stirring, 4 minutes or until mushrooms begin to brown. Stir in the parsley, salt, pepper, and dill. Stir in the beans, tossing gently until evenly coated. *Makes 8 ½-cup servings.*

One serving—Calories: 43; Total fat: 4.3 g; Saturated fat: 0.8 g; Cholesterol: 0 mg; Sodium: 305 mg; Carbohydrates: 3.7 g; Fiber: 1.6 g; Sugar: 1.7 g; Protein: 1.4 g

Cheese-Stuffed Tomatoes

If the tomatoes don't sit upright in the pan, cut a thin slice off the bottom of each tomato to level it.

¾ teaspoon gluten-free beef bouillon granules

½ cup gluten-free, low-fat cottage cheese

4 tablespoons grated gluten-free Parmesan cheese

2 egg whites

4 medium tomatoes

1 tablespoon olive oil

¼ teaspoon oregano

¼ teaspoon basil

1 teaspoon minced fresh parsley

¼ teaspoon pepper

Preheat oven to 350°F. Combine the bouillon granules and cottage cheese; let stand 5 minutes. Stir in the Parmesan cheese. Beat the egg whites till soft peaks form. Fold into the cottage cheese mixture. Cut the tomatoes in half; place them cut side up in a 9″ × 13″ baking pan. Drizzle the olive oil over the tomatoes; sprinkle with the oregano, basil, parsley, and pepper. Cover and bake 5 minutes. Preheat broiler. Spoon the cottage cheese mixture over the cut surface of the tomatoes. Broil 5 inches from the heat for 4 minutes till nicely browned. *Makes 8 tomato halves.*

One tomato half—Calories: 56; Total fat: 2.8 g; Saturated fat: 0.8 g; Cholesterol: 2 mg; Sodium: 206 mg; Carbohydrates: 3.6 g; Fiber: 0.7 g; Sugar: 0.5 g; Protein: 4.5 g

Pomegranate Caesar Salad

When removing the seeds from pomegranates, wear plastic gloves to prevent the fruit from staining your fingers red.

    1 head romaine lettuce
    1 head Boston lettuce
    2 tablespoons apple cider vinegar
    2 teaspoons minced anchovies
    ¼ teaspoon dry mustard
    1 teaspoon minced garlic
    ¼ teaspoon pepper
    ⅓ cup virgin olive oil
    2 teaspoons freshly squeezed lemon juice
    ⅛ teaspoon gluten-free Worcestershire sauce
    1 large onion, sliced
    1 cup pomegranate seeds
    ¼ cup grated gluten-free Romano cheese
    1 hard-boiled egg, shelled and sieved

Remove the coarse outer leaves of the romaine. Tear the remaining leaves into 2-inch pieces; tear the Boston lettuce into bite-sized pieces. Place the lettuces in a colander; wash with cold water, then drain. Place several sheets of paper toweling in the bottom of a plastic bag; add the greens, and chill several hours to crisp. In a bowl, whisk together the vinegar, anchovies, mustard, garlic, and pepper. Slowly whisk in the olive oil, then the lemon juice and Worcestershire sauce. Place the greens, onion, pomegranate seeds, and cheese in a large bowl. Toss with the dressing until evenly coated. Sprinkle the top with the sieved egg. *Makes 8 1-cup servings.*

One serving–Calories: 118; Total fat: 10.2 g; Saturated fat: 1.9 g; Cholesterol: 29 mg; Sodium: 104 mg; Carbohydrates: 4.7 g; Fiber: 1 g; Sugar: 0.4 g; Protein: 3.3 g

Parmesan Salmon Buffet

Complement this dinner with a vase brimming with fresh flowers—they will add color to your table, and the scent of fresh flowers will permeate the room.

Parmesan Baked Salmon

If a piece of fish is thick on one side and narrow on the other, fold the narrow side under partway before placing the fish in the baking pan. This gives the fish a uniform thickness so it will cook evenly.

    6 4-ounce salmon fillets
    ⅓ cup gluten-free, low-fat mayonnaise
    3 tablespoons grated gluten-free Parmesan cheese
    3 tablespoons sliced green onion
    1 teaspoon gluten-free white wine Worcestershire sauce

Preheat oven to 400°F. Rinse the fish, and pat it dry with paper towels. Spray a baking dish with gluten-free nonstick spray. Place the fish in the baking dish. In a small bowl, whisk together the mayonnaise, Parmesan cheese, green onion, and white wine Worcestershire sauce; spread on top of the fish fillets. Bake, uncovered, 15 minutes or until the fish flakes easily with a fork. *Makes 6 4-ounce servings.*

One serving—Calories: 281; Total fat: 19 g; Saturated fat: 4 g; Cholesterol: 70 mg; Sodium: 231 mg; Carbohydrates: 1.2 g; Fiber: 0 g; Sugar: 1 g; Protein: 24.5 g

Potato Spinach Casserole

This side dish also makes an excellent vegetarian entree.

    6 cups gluten-free beef broth
    ¾ cup gluten-free white wine
    1 teaspoon tarragon
    3 bay leaves
    ⅔ cup minced fresh parsley
    4 cloves garlic
    2 pounds red potatoes, sliced thin
    3 tablespoons gluten-free margarine
    ½ teaspoon salt
    ½ teaspoon pepper
    2 10-ounce boxes frozen chopped spinach,
        thawed and squeezed dry
    ¼ cup gluten-free sour cream
    ¼ cup grated gluten-free Parmesan cheese
    4 green onions, minced
    ½ cup minced fresh dill
    1½ tablespoons minced kalamata olives
    1 egg
    ¼ teaspoon nutmeg

Preheat oven to 400°F. In a large pot, bring the broth and wine to a boil. Stir in the tarragon, bay leaves, parsley, garlic cloves, and potatoes; simmer 10 minutes until potatoes are almost tender. Remove the potatoes with a slotted spoon, and transfer to a large bowl. Gently toss the potatoes with 1½ tablespoons of the margarine, ¼ teaspoon of the salt, and ¼ teaspoon of the pepper. Place half of the potatoes in a 9-inch square pan that has been sprayed with gluten-free nonstick spray. In a medium-size bowl, whisk together the spinach, sour cream, 2 tablespoons of the Parmesan cheese, and the green onions, dill, olives, egg, nutmeg, and remaining ¼ teaspoon each of salt and pepper. Place the spinach mixture on top of the potatoes in the baking dish. Top with the remaining potatoes. Ladle 1 cup of the broth over the potatoes. Sprinkle with the remaining 2 tablespoons of Parmesan cheese. Dot with the remaining 1½ tablespoons of margarine. Bake 45 minutes or until the potatoes are browned and tender. *Makes 6 4½- by 3-inch servings.*

One serving—Calories: 188; Total fat: 9 g; Saturated fat: 3.3 g; Cholesterol: 41 mg; Sodium: 920 mg; Carbohydrates: 22.2 g; Fiber: 2 g; Sugar: 3.3 g; Protein: 16.3 g

Ratatouille

If you love okra, include eight pods in this recipe. The secret to keeping okra from getting slimy is to use a wooden spoon when stirring and a glass or stainless steel pan for cooking; never let okra touch aluminum.

> 2 tablespoons olive oil
> 1 onion, chopped
> 2 cloves garlic, minced
> 2 zucchini, sliced
> 1 eggplant, peeled and cubed
> 1 yellow squash, sliced
> 2 ribs celery, sliced

2 carrots, sliced

½ green bell pepper, chopped

½ red bell pepper, chopped

8 mushrooms, sliced

3 tablespoons Gluten-Free Flour Mixture
(See the Hints chapter.)

1 28-ounce can crushed tomatoes

½ teaspoon freshly ground black pepper

4 teaspoons chopped fresh parsley

1 teaspoon oregano

1 teaspoon basil

¼ cup shredded gluten-free mozzarella cheese

In a large skillet, heat the olive oil 1 minute. Add the onion and garlic, and sauté till soft. Place the zucchini, eggplant, yellow squash, celery, carrots, green and red pepper, and mushrooms in a large bowl. Sprinkle with the flour mixture, and toss to coat the vegetables evenly. Add the vegetables and the tomatoes, black pepper, parsley, oregano, and basil to the skillet. Cover and cook over medium heat 30 minutes. Lower heat, stir, cover, and simmer gently 1 hour, stirring occasionally. Stir in the cheese just before serving. *Makes 6 1¼-cup servings.*

One serving—Calories: 178; Total fat: 7 g; Saturated fat: 0.7 g; Cholesterol: 0 mg; Sodium: 298 mg; Carbohydrates: 23 g; Fiber: 5.1 g; Sugar: 2.4 g; Protein: 6.3 g

Zesty Spinach Salad

To garnish the salad, cut two thin slices from a fresh orange. Dip one side of each slice into sesame seeds, and lay the slices in the center of the salad.

Juice of 1 lemon

¼ teaspoon grated lemon zest

1 clove garlic, crushed

½ teaspoon grated fresh ginger

¾ teaspoon gluten-free soy sauce

½ teaspoon orange juice

¾ teaspoon cayenne

2 tablespoons sesame oil

1 tablespoon olive oil

1 tablespoon sesame seeds

5 cups spinach leaves torn into bite-sized pieces

½ cup fresh bean sprouts

½ cup sliced mushrooms

2 green onions, sliced

In a large bowl, mix together the lemon juice, lemon zest, garlic, ginger, soy sauce, orange juice, and cayenne. Slowly whisk in the sesame and olive oils until thoroughly blended. Add the sesame seeds, spinach, bean sprouts, mushrooms, and green onions; toss until evenly coated. *Makes 6 ¾-cup servings.*

One serving—Calories: 82; Total fat: 7.7 g; Saturated fat: 1.2 g; Cholesterol: 0 mg; Sodium: 158 mg; Carbohydrates: 2.9 g; Fiber: 1 g; Sugar: 0.2 g; Protein: 1.7 g

5

Ethnic Dinners

The following recipes are authentic ethnic dishes, sure to enhance the ambience of your gathering. When entertaining, it's fun to carry over the theme from an ethnic dinner to the invitations, music, table setting, and food garnishes. Use your imagination and have fun setting the scene.

Mexican Dinner

Mexico is synonymous with color—bright reds, oranges, yellows, lime greens . . . colors that explode with vitality. Drape three different vibrantly colored pieces of material, overlapping at an angle, across your table. An ideal centerpiece would be small cactus plants set in a dish of sand.

Taco Bean Dip

Use a small, colorful bowl for this dip; set it on a large colorful platter, and surround the dip with tortilla chips. The two dishes do not have to match so long as both have vibrant colors. An alternative container for the chips would be a basket lined with multicolored napkins; serve the dip in a hollowed-out fresh artichoke.

> 2 6-inch gluten-free corn tortillas
> 4 ounces pinto beans, rinsed and drained
> 1 tablespoon gluten-free salsa
> 1 teaspoon canned green chilies
> ⅛ teaspoon cumin
> 1 green onion, sliced thin
> 1 tablespoon minced fresh parsley
> 2 tablespoons shredded gluten-free cheddar cheese

Preheat oven to 400°F. Cut each tortilla into 6 wedges; place in a single layer on an ungreased baking sheet. Bake 8 minutes or till the tortilla wedges are crisp. In a blender, process the beans, salsa, chilies, and cumin until fairly smooth; transfer to a saucepan. Stir in the onion and parsley. Blend in all but 1 teaspoon of the cheese. Cook over medium heat until hot, stirring constantly. Place in a serving bowl; sprinkle with the remaining 1 teaspoon of cheese. Serve warm with the tortilla chips. *Makes 4 servings (3 tablespoons dip plus 3 chips).*

One serving—Calories: 213; Total fat: 11.2 g; Saturated fat: 3.7 g; Cholesterol: 15 mg; Sodium: 434 mg; Carbohydrates: 24.7 g; Fiber: 3.5 g; Sugar: 0.5 g; Protein: 8 g

Cheese Enchiladas

To serve, lay the enchiladas on a bed of Spanish Rice (recipe follows), and drizzle with a little gluten-free salsa. Seasoned, cooked ground beef or chicken may also be added for heartier appetites.

¾ cup water

1 gluten-free chicken bouillon cube

¾ cup tomato sauce

1 ½ tablespoons cornstarch

2 teaspoons gluten-free chili powder

½ teaspoon cumin

1 large onion, chopped

½ green bell pepper, minced

2 teaspoons olive oil

1 4-ounce can whole green chilies, drained

3 ounces gluten-free mozzarella cheese

4 6-ounce gluten-free corn tortillas

2 ounces sharp cheddar cheese, grated (½ cup)

Preheat oven to 350°F. In a saucepan, combine ½ cup water and the bouillon cube. Bring to a boil; reduce heat until water barely simmers. Crush the bouillon cube with the back of a spoon, and stir until completely dissolved. Stir in the tomato sauce. In a bowl, blend the cornstarch, chili powder, and cumin; slowly stir in ¼ cup of water. Pour the cornstarch mixture into the bouillon mixture; cook until slightly thickened, stirring constantly. Remove from heat. In a small skillet, sauté onion and green bell pepper in oil until barely limp. Remove from heat. Cut the chilies in half lengthwise; discard the seeds. Cut each half into two lengthwise strips. Cut the mozzarella into 4 long sticks. Spray an 8″ × 12″ baking dish with gluten-free nonstick spray. Dip a tortilla into the warm sauce, coating both sides; place in baking dish. Down the center of the tortilla, lay 1 cheese stick, 2 chili strips, and ¼ of the onions and green bell peppers. Roll up the tortilla seam down. Repeat with the remaining tortillas. Pour the remaining hot sauce over the enchiladas. Bake 10 minutes. Sprinkle the cheddar cheese over the top, and bake 5 minutes longer. *Makes 4 enchiladas.*

One enchilada–Calories: 229; Total fat: 13.5 g; Saturated fat: 3.6; Cholesterol: 15 mg; Sodium: 708 mg; Carbohydrates: 16 g; Fiber: 2.2 g; Sugar: 1.5 g; Protein: 10.8 g

Spanish Rice

For garnish, cut an orange in half, and cut each of the halves into 4 slices (discard the end pieces). Dip one side of each orange slice in minced fresh parsley. Cut through each slice just to the rind, leaving the rind intact. Twist each slice to form an S (one side with parsley, one side without). Lay two slices on each plate beside the rice.

    1 cup water
    ¾ cup chopped green bell pepper
    ½ cup chopped onion
    ½ cup thinly sliced celery
    ¼ teaspoon salt
    ⅛ teaspoon black pepper
    1 14½-ounce can diced tomatoes, undrained
    Dash red pepper flakes
    ⅔ cup rice
    1 clove garlic, minced
    1 teaspoon gluten-free chili powder

In a saucepan, combine the water, green bell pepper, onion, celery, salt, and black pepper. Bring to a boil. Reduce heat; cover and simmer 5 minutes. Stir in the tomatoes with their juice, red pepper flakes, rice, garlic, and chili powder. Cover and simmer 20 minutes till liquid is absorbed. *Makes 4 ½-cup servings.*

One serving–Calories: 158; Total fat: 0.4 g; Saturated fat: 0.1 g; Cholesterol: 0 mg; Sodium: 409 mg; Carbohydrates: 32.9 g; Fiber: 2.4 g; Sugar: 0.6 g; Protein: 3.8 g

South-of-the-Border Salad

For a garnish, top each salad with a spiral of lime zest.

¼ cup gluten-free dry white wine

2 tablespoons lime juice

1 tablespoon chopped fresh parsley

2 tablespoons plus 1 teaspoon olive oil

⅛ teaspoon salt

16 medium raw shrimp, peeled and deveined

1 clove garlic, minced

2 tablespoons chopped green onion

4 cups shredded iceberg lettuce

In a bowl, whisk the wine, lime juice, parsley, 2 tablespoons of the olive oil, and the salt; set aside. Rinse the shrimp under cold water; drain on paper towels. Spray a medium-size skillet with gluten-free nonstick spray, then brush with the remaining 1 teaspoon of olive oil. Add the shrimp, garlic, and green onion; sauté, stirring constantly, until the shrimp turn pink. Cool to room temperature; transfer to a small bowl. Pour the lime juice marinade over the shrimp, cover and refrigerate 2 to 8 hours. Divide the lettuce among four salad plates; top with shrimp. Drizzle with marinade. *Makes 4 1¼-cup servings.*

One serving—Calories: 113; Total fat: 8.2 g; Saturated fat: 1.2 g; Cholesterol: 55 mg; Sodium: 189 mg; Carbohydrates: 5.1 g; Fiber: 0.6 g; Sugar: 3.6 g; Protein: 6.6 g

Mexican "Fried" Ice Cream

Mexican cooking features "fried" ice cream. This low-calorie version tastes just as good as the original recipe!

1½ cups gluten-free frozen vanilla yogurt

½ cup coconut

⅛ teaspoon cinnamon

Divide the yogurt into four equal sections; form each into a ball. Place the balls on a plate lined with waxed paper; cover with heavy-duty foil, and freeze about 1 hour until firm. Preheat oven to 375°F. Mix the coconut with the cinnamon; spread out on a cookie sheet, and bake it until lightly browned, stirring frequently. Cool coconut. To serve, place a yogurt ball in a serving bowl, and sprinkle with coconut. *Makes 4 ⅓-cup servings.*

One serving—Calories: 132; Total fat: 6 g; Saturated fat: 4.5 g; Cholesterol: 1 mg; Sodium: 71 mg; Carbohydrates: 17.5 g; Fiber: 0.8 g; Sugar: 15 g; Protein: 2.5 g

Spanish Dinner

This menu begins with a Spanish tradition, *tapas*—small selections of a variety of appetizers, often including fish—followed by paella for the main course. (Many Spaniards dine on tapas alone.) Red is the color of Spain—drape your table with a red tablecloth, and set a large, colorful ornamental fan surrounded by red and gold flowers in the center of your table. If you have any thin, black, lacy material, drape it over one edge of the table.

Aubergine Salad

Aubergine is the British and French name for eggplant. Select tender, baby eggplants, approximately 5 inches long and 1½ inches wide, for this dish. Garnish it with diced Spanish olives.

- 2 baby eggplants
- ½ small onion
- 1 clove garlic, crushed
- ½ tomato, peeled and diced
- 3 tablespoons olive oil
- ½ tablespoon apple cider vinegar

⅛ teaspoon salt

⅛ teaspoon pepper

Juice of ¼ fresh lemon

Preheat oven to 350°F. Place the eggplants in a baking pan; bake 1 hour or until soft. Allow the skin to turn black; this gives the salad a smoky flavor. Skin the eggplants while they are still hot; chop into small pieces; put in a bowl. Add the onion, garlic, tomato, olive oil, vinegar, salt, pepper, and lemon juice; blend well. Cover and refrigerate for 4 hours to allow flavors to blend. *Makes 4 ½-cup servings.*

One serving–Calories: 111; Total fat: 10.4 g; Saturated fat: 1.3 g; Cholesterol: 0 mg; Sodium: 77 mg; Carbohydrates: 5.3 g; Fiber: 1.4 g; Sugar: 0.4 g; Protein: 0.8 g

Stewed Calamari

Unbreaded calamari are available in the frozen section of specialty grocery stores. Garnish this dish with lemon wedges.

½ pound unbreaded calamari rings, thawed

2 tablespoons olive oil

3 tablespoons gluten-free white wine

½ cup gluten-free chicken broth

1 tomato, peeled and diced

2 tablespoons chopped fresh parsley

¼ teaspoon salt

⅛ teaspoon pepper

Wash the calamari well; drain. Heat the olive oil in a medium-size saucepan. Sauté calamari over medium-high heat for 3 minutes. Add the wine, broth, tomato, parsley, salt, and pepper; stir to blend. Cover the pan, and simmer until the calamari are tender and sauce is thickened, about 25 minutes. *Makes 4 ¾-cup servings.*

One serving–Calories: 52; Total fat: 0.7 g; Saturated fat: 0.2 g; Cholesterol: 99 mg; Sodium: 959 mg; Carbohydrates: 3.5 g; Fiber: 0.4 g; Sugar: 0.4 g; Protein: 6.9 g

Roasted Red Peppers

This dish may be served hot, cold, or at room temperature. Kept covered, the peppers can be refrigerated for up to 2 weeks.

3 red bell peppers
2 teaspoons olive oil
¼ teaspoon gluten-free white wine vinegar
Dash salt
Dash black pepper

Preheat broiler. Cut the red peppers in half; remove the seeds and membrane. Put the peppers on a baking pan; broil 12 minutes, turning occasionally, till the skins are charred all over. Put the peppers in a paper bag, folding over the top of the bag, until the peppers are cool enough to handle. Peel off the skins; cut each piece into 3 strips. Put the pepper strips in a small bowl. In a separate small bowl, stir together the olive oil, vinegar, salt, and black pepper; pour over peppers and stir gently to mix. *Makes 4 3-tablespoon servings.*

One serving—Calories: 44; Total fat: 2.5 g; Saturated fat: 0.3 g; Cholesterol: 0 mg; Sodium: 2.8 mg; Carbohydrates: 5.7 g; Fiber: 1.8 g; Sugar: 0 g; Protein: 1.1 g

Marinated Mushrooms

This recipe may be prepared in advance. Put the mushrooms in a plastic container with a lid, and store in the refrigerator for up to 1 week.

¼ pound fresh button mushrooms
1 teaspoon apple cider vinegar
¼ cup water
⅛ teaspoon salt
1 clove garlic, cut in half

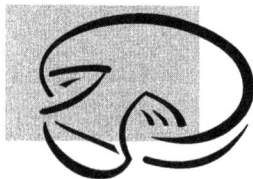

3 peppercorns

1 bay leaf

1 tablespoon olive oil

Wash the mushrooms; cut the stems close to the caps. Drop the caps into a pot of boiling water; simmer 4 minutes. Drain in a sieve for ½ hour, then put in a plastic container. In a small saucepan, combine the vinegar, water, salt, garlic, peppercorns, and bay leaf; simmer 10 minutes. Stir in the olive oil. Strain the marinade over the mushrooms. Cover and refrigerate for two days to blend flavors. To serve, remove mushrooms from marinade and place in a bowl. *Makes 4 4-mushroom servings.*

One serving—Calories: 45; Total fat: 3.7 g; Saturated fat: 0.5 g; Cholesterol: 0 mg; Sodium: 76 mg; Carbohydrates: 2.4 g; Fiber: 0.7 g; Sugar: 0 g; Protein: 1.6 g

Paella

Spain is known for its seafood, and especially for paella. When the tapas dishes have been cleared away, bring out steaming, fragrant plates of this traditional entree.

¾ cup rice

3 tablespoons salt

8 small clams

2 teaspoons olive oil

2 cloves garlic, minced

¼ pound gluten-free turkey sausage, sliced thin

2 skinless, boneless chicken breasts (4 ounces each),
    cut into ¾-inch pieces

¼ cup diced red bell pepper

¼ cup diced green bell pepper

1 small onion, cut into wedges

1½ cups gluten-free chicken broth

¼ cup minced fresh parsley

½ teaspoon oregano

½ teaspoon saffron threads

⅛ teaspoon black pepper

4 ounces fresh shrimp,
    peeled and deveined

½ cup frozen peas

1 chopped tomato

Soak the rice in a bowl of cold water for 3 hours. In a large bowl, stir together 8 cups of water and 1 tablespoon of the salt. Add the clams; let soak 15 minutes. Drain the clams, and rinse well. Discard the water and repeat the process of soaking, draining, and rinsing two more times. Heat the olive oil in a dutch oven; add the garlic, and sauté over medium heat. Add the sausage and chicken; cook over high heat until browned. Add the red and green bell peppers and the onion; cook 5 minutes, stirring often. Drain the rice well; add to the dutch oven, and sauté, stirring often, 5 minutes. Stir in the broth, parsley, oregano, saffron, and black pepper. Bring to a boil; reduce heat, cover, and simmer 15 minutes. Stir in the shrimp and clams; continue cooking until the shrimp have turned pink and the clams have opened. (Discard any unopened clams.) Stir in the peas and tomato. Heat through, and serve immediately. *Makes 4 1¼-cup servings.*

One serving—Calories: 312; Total fat: 4.8 g; Saturated fat: 1.4 g; Cholesterol: 88 mg; Sodium: 609 mg; Carbohydrates: 33 g; Fiber: 2 g; Sugar: 3.4 g; Protein: 24.5 g

Spanish Sautéed Endive

Soak the endive in water; drain, then soak again to remove all grit. Use Spanish olive oil for this dish, if available.

2 large heads endive

2 tablespoons olive oil

4 cloves garlic, minced

⅛ teaspoon salt

⅛ teaspoon black pepper

⅛ teaspoon crushed red pepper

Boil the endive until tender, about 20 minutes; drain well. Heat the olive oil in a large skillet; add the garlic, and sauté 1 minute. Add the endive, salt, black pepper, and crushed red pepper. Sauté, stirring constantly, till the endive is dry, about 5 minutes. *Makes 4 ¾-cup servings.*

One serving—Calories: 114; Total fat: 7.3 g; Saturated fat: 1.1 g; Cholesterol: 0 mg; Sodium: 131 mg; Carbohydrates: 10.8 g; Fiber: 8.4 g; Sugar: 2.2 g; Protein: 3.7 g

Spanish Caramel Flan

Spain is famous for its puddings and its custards. This is a delicious, traditional custard recipe.

1 cup plus 2 tablespoons sugar

6 eggs

1½ cups skim milk

1½ cups evaporated skim milk

2 teaspoons vanilla

⅛ teaspoon salt

Preheat oven to 325°F. Spray an 8-inch round baking pan with gluten-free nonstick spray. In a small pan, cook ½ cup of the sugar over medium-high heat until the sugar begins to melt; shake the pan frequently, but do not stir. Reduce heat to low, and cook about 5 minutes more until the sugar is melted and golden brown, stirring occasionally. Quickly pour the caramelized sugar into the round baking pan, tilting the pan to coat the bottom evenly. In a bowl, slightly beat the eggs with a whisk; stir in the milk, evaporated milk, remaining 2 tablespoons of sugar, and the vanilla and salt. Pour the milk mixture over the caramel in the pan. Set the pan inside a large baking pan, and set on an oven rack. Pour hot water into the large pan to a depth of 1 inch. Bake, uncovered, 25 minutes or till a knife inserted near the center comes out clean. Cool the flan on a rack until it reaches room temperature; cover and refrigerate for 3 to 8 hours. Loosen the flan from sides of the pan with a knife; invert onto a serving plate. *Makes 8 ½-cup servings.*

One serving—Calories: 186; Total fat: 4 g; Saturated fat: 1.2 g; Cholesterol: 162 mg; Sodium: 127 mg; Carbohydrates: 52.6 g; Fiber: 0 g; Sugar: 26.8 g; Protein: 10.2 g

Greek Dinner

If you rummage through resale shops, you can usually find some small urns and vases that look Greek. Group these in the center of the table amidst some loosely draped cloth for a centerpiece. No urns? Greece is famous for its fresh figs; fill a bowl with figs, and put large fresh leaves around the base of the bowl.

Grecian Dilled Shrimp

Spoon the shrimp into an attractive bowl, then lay a sprig of fresh dill across the side of the bowl for garnish.

1½ tablespoons minced onion

1 tablespoon minced green bell pepper

1 clove garlic, minced

1 tablespoon lemon juice

2 bay leaves

Dash salt

Dash black pepper

¼ teaspoon oregano

¼ teaspoon dill weed

½ pound boiled shrimp

In a nonmetallic bowl, stir together the onion, green bell pepper, garlic, lemon juice, bay leaves, salt, black pepper, oregano, and dill. Stir in the shrimp; cover; refrigerate 24 hours and remove bay leaves before serving. *Makes 4 3-piece servings.*

One serving–Calories: 43; Total fat: 0.6 g; Saturated fat: 0.1 g; Cholesterol: 54 mg; Sodium: 107 mg; Carbohydrates: 1 g; Fiber: 0.1 g; Sugar: 0.3 g; Protein: 8 g

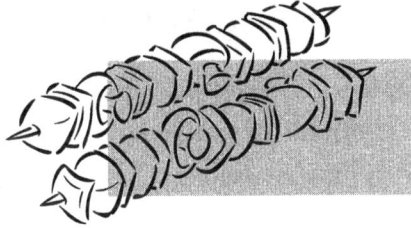

Grecian Lamb Kabobs Appetizer

The meatballs may be prepared ahead and frozen; thaw before cooking.

¼ pound lean ground lamb

1 onion

1 clove garlic, crushed

1 teaspoon minced fresh mint

1 teaspoon lemon juice

⅛ teaspoon salt

⅛ teaspoon black pepper

4 cherry tomatoes

½ green bell pepper, cut into 8 squares

Preheat broiler. Place the lamb in a medium-size bowl. Finely chop half of the onion; add to the bowl. Stir in the garlic, mint, lemon juice, salt, and black pepper. Divide the meat mixture into 8 balls of uniform size. Cut the remaining half of the onion into quarters, and separate the layers. On each skewer, thread 1 onion,

1 meatball, 1 green bell pepper, repeat, then add 1 cherry tomato. Repeat process, using 3 more skewers. Broil 10 minutes, turning frequently, till meat is browned and cooked through. *Makes 4 kabobs.*

One kabob—Calories: 89; Total fat: 4.2 g; Saturated fat: 1.7 g; Cholesterol: 26 mg; Sodium: 95 mg; Carbohydrates: 4.2 g; Fiber: 0.9 g; Sugar: 0.4 g; Protein: 6.1 g

Grecian Stewed Baked Fish

Even people who never touch fish will love *psari plaki*. Prepare it using the freshest fish possible. Cod, bass, scrod, orange roughy, or haddock may be used in place of the flounder.

4 4-ounce flounder fillets
Juice of ½ lemon
¼ teaspoon salt
¼ teaspoon pepper
1 tablespoon olive oil
2 onions, chopped
2 cloves garlic, minced
¼ cup shredded carrot
¼ cup chopped celery
1 10-ounce box frozen chopped spinach, thawed
1 8-ounce can tomato sauce
2 tablespoons chopped fresh parsley
½ cup gluten-free white wine
¼ cup water

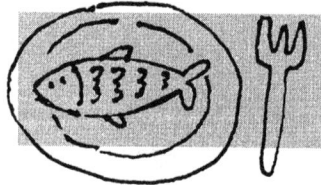

Preheat oven to 400°F. Put fish in a baking pan; sprinkle with lemon juice, salt, and pepper. Heat the olive oil in a 10-inch skillet. Add the onion, garlic, carrot, and celery; sauté until soft. Squeeze the excess water from the spinach; stir the spinach into the vegetables in the skillet. Stir in the tomato sauce, parsley, wine, and water. Spoon the vegetable mixture evenly over each piece of fish. Cover with foil, and bake 30 minutes or until fish flakes easily. *Makes 4 fillets (with ⅔ cup vegetables and sauce).*

One serving—Calories: 217; Total fat: 5.1 g; Saturated fat: 0.8 g; Cholesterol: 73 mg; Sodium: 774 mg; Carbohydrates: 14.1 g; Fiber: 2.7 g; Sugar: 5.2 g; Protein: 28.5 g

Grecian Stewed Potatoes

Cubing the potatoes gives the illusion of a larger portion, so fewer potatoes are needed. This reduces the number of calories.

3 medium russet potatoes

1½ tablespoons lemon juice

¼ cup water

1 tablespoon olive oil

1 8-ounce can tomato sauce

⅛ teaspoon salt

⅛ teaspoon pepper

¼ teaspoon garlic powder

½ teaspoon oregano

⅛ teaspoon cinnamon

1 tablespoon chopped fresh parsley

Preheat oven to 400°F. Spray an 8″ × 12″ casserole dish with gluten-free nonstick spray. Cut the potatoes into 1-inch cubes; place in the casserole dish. Sprinkle with the lemon juice. In a small saucepan, combine the water, olive oil, tomato sauce, salt, pepper, garlic powder, oregano, cinnamon, and parsley. Bring to a boil; pour the sauce over the potatoes. Bake 50 minutes, stirring occasionally. *Makes 4 ¾-cup servings.*

One serving—Calories: 173; Total fat: 3.6 g; Saturated fat: 0.5 g; Cholesterol: 0 mg; Sodium: 448 mg; Carbohydrates: 32.9 g; Fiber: 2.1 g; Sugar: 4.1 g; Protein: 4.2 g

Grecian Beets

Have a reliable mouthwash close at hand! This garlicky spread is potent—but the taste is worth it.

    1 large Idaho potato, boiled and peeled
    3 cloves garlic, crushed
    2 tablespoons olive oil
    Dash salt
    ⅛ teaspoon apple cider vinegar
    2 15-ounce cans sliced beets, drained

In a mixing bowl, whip the potatoes and garlic; slowly add the olive oil, salt, and vinegar. Whip until smooth and creamy. Cover and refrigerate 6 hours or overnight for the flavors to blend. Place the room-temperature beets on a serving dish; top with dollops of garlic spread. *Makes 4 ½-cup servings (with 3 tablespoons garlic spread).*

One serving—Calories: 166; Total fat: 7.1 g; Saturated fat: 1 g; Cholesterol: 0 mg; Sodium: 69 mg; Carbohydrates: 24.6 g; Fiber: 2.8 g; Sugar: 6 g; Protein: 2.8 g

Grecian Peasant Salad

If fresh oregano is available, use 1 tablespoon fresh instead of the ¼ teaspoon dried oregano.

    3 plum tomatoes, each cut into 8 pieces
    1 cucumber, sliced
    ½ red onion, sliced
    1 green bell pepper, chopped
    ¼ cup crumbled gluten-free feta cheese
    ⅛ teaspoon black pepper
    ¼ teaspoon dill weed
    ¼ teaspoon oregano

¼ teaspoon lemon juice

1 ½ tablespoons olive oil

2 teaspoons apple cider vinegar

In a bowl, gently toss all the ingredients together until evenly coated. *Makes 4 1-cup servings.*

One serving—Calories: 120; Total fat: 8.5 g; Saturated fat: 2.8 g; Cholesterol: 13 mg; Sodium: 169 mg; Carbohydrates: 7.9 g; Fiber: 2 g; Sugar: 0 g; Protein: 3.5 g

Grecian Flat Bread

Both sides of the bread should be nicely browned, but watch closely while it cooks so it doesn't burn.

1 cup Gluten-Free Flour Mixture (See the Hints chapter.)

¼ teaspoon salt

⅛ teaspoon oregano

⅛ teaspoon basil

Dash garlic powder

⅔ cup water

Sift the flour mixture and salt into a medium-size bowl; stir in the oregano, basil, and garlic powder. Make a well in the center, and gradually pour in the water, mixing well with a fork to form a supple dough. Knead the dough about 4 minutes, adding a tiny bit more flour mixture as needed. Set the dough aside for 10 minutes. Divide the dough into four equal portions. Roll out or pat each piece to form a large circle. Preheat a nonstick 8-inch skillet. Place one flat bread in the pan; cook until it starts to bubble, then turn it over. Carefully press down on the bread with a flat spatula, and turn it over again. Remove the bread from the pan. Repeat the cooking process with the remaining three breads. *Makes 4 flat breads.*

One flat bread—Calories: 100; Total fat: 0 g; Saturated fat: 0 g; Cholesterol: 0 mg; Sodium: 148 mg; Carbohydrates: 22 g; Fiber: 1 g; Sugar: 1 g; Protein: 3 g

Grecian Custard Rolls

Rice papers are available at Asian markets. To keep the scalding milk from scorching, rinse the pan with hot water before heating the milk. These rolls must be served as soon as they are removed from the oven. If allowed to cool, the rice paper will become rubbery and tough to cut. When served warm, the rice paper looks, cuts, and tastes like phyllo dough.

1 egg, slightly beaten

¼ cup sugar

2 tablespoons Cream of Rice

¾ cup skim milk

1 teaspoon gluten-free margarine

¼ teaspoon vanilla

4 sheets rice paper

Honey Syrup

¼ cup sugar

¼ cup water

1 cinnamon stick

1 tablespoon honey

1 orange slice

Cinnamon

Preheat oven to 350°F. Generously spray a shallow baking pan with gluten-free nonstick spray. Whip together the eggs, sugar, and Cream of Rice in a small mixing bowl. Heat the milk; slowly add hot milk to the egg mixture, stirring constantly. Return the milk and egg mixture to the pan; cook over medium heat, stirring constantly, for 7 minutes or until the mixture thickens. Remove from heat; stir in the margarine and vanilla. Cool. Soak the rice papers in water for 3 minutes to soften. Working with one sheet at a time, spray one side with gluten-free nonstick spray. Place 2 tablespoons of the custard at the edge; roll once, fold in the sides, and continue to roll. Set the roll, seam side down, in the greased baking pan. Repeat with the remaining 3 sheets of rice paper. Spray the top of the rolls with gluten-free nonstick spray. (The rolls may be covered and refrigerated at this point.) Bake 20 minutes or until the rice paper is crisp. Meanwhile, make the Honey Syrup. Simmer the sugar, water, cinnamon stick, honey, and orange slice in a saucepan for 15 minutes or until a syrup is formed. Cool. Pour syrup over warm rolls, then sprinkle with cinnamon. *Makes 4 custard rolls.*

One custard roll—Calories: 162; Total fat: 2.1 g; Saturated fat: 0.1 g; Cholesterol: 54 mg; Sodium: 63 mg; Carbohydrates: 31 g; Fiber: 0.1 g; Sugar: 20.9 g; Protein: 4.4 g

Italian Dinner

With a red-and-white checkered cloth on the table, group wine bottles of varying sizes and shapes with ivy or grape leaves in the center of your table; lay a corkscrew alongside. (Of course, the wines should be American made so you can be certain of their gluten-free status!)

Italian Baked Mussels

A small bowl of gluten-free cocktail sauce may accompany the appetizer of mussels. Garnish the mussels with thin wedges of lemon.

- 1 teaspoon olive oil
- 1 dozen fresh mussels, cleaned
- 1 tablespoon gluten-free margarine

2 cloves garlic, minced

2 tablespoons gluten-free white wine

1 teaspoon minced fresh parsley

Preheat oven to 450°F. Rub an 8″ × 11″ baking dish with the olive oil, and arrange the mussels in the dish in a single layer. Bake 5 to 10 minutes, until the shells open. (Do not overcook, or the mussels will get tough.) Throw away any shells that do not open. Remove the upper shells. Melt the margarine in a small saucepan; add the garlic, and sauté until it begins to brown. Slowly add the wine. Stir in the parsley and any liquid from the baking pan. Drizzle the sauce over the mussels. *Makes 4 3-mussel servings.*

One serving—Calories: 292; Total fat: 9.9 g; Saturated fat: 1.9 g; Cholesterol: 84 mg; Sodium: 918 mg; Carbohydrates: 12.1 g; Fiber: 0 g; Sugar: 1 g; Protein: 35.8 g

Spaghetti Bolognese

If you are having an Italian dinner, it is a given that spaghetti will be served. Rice pasta has few calories and cooks quicker than corn pasta, but corn pasta holds together better. Whichever you use, add 1 tablespoon of corn oil to the water to prevent "boil-overs" while cooking gluten-free pasta. After the food is placed on the dishes, sprinkle minced parsley all over the dishes, including the rim of each dish. This simple gesture has a dramatic effect.

1 onion, chopped

1 clove garlic, crushed

⅔ cup water

1 cube gluten-free beef bouillon

½ pound 93% lean ground beef

½ cup gluten-free white wine

1 14-ounce can diced tomatoes

2 tablespoons tomato paste

⅛ teaspoon salt

⅛ teaspoon pepper

2 tablespoons chopped fresh parsley

½ teaspoon oregano

⅛ teaspoon rosemary

½ pound gluten-free corn spaghetti

Put the onion, garlic, water, and bouillon cube in a saucepan; bring to a boil, breaking up the bouillon cube with a fork. Simmer 5 minutes or until the stock is reduced. Add the ground beef; cook quickly to brown, breaking up the meat with a fork. Drain off any fat in the pan. Add the wine, diced tomatoes with their juice, tomato paste, salt, pepper, parsley, oregano, and rosemary. Bring to a boil; cover and simmer for 1 hour. Cook the pasta al dente according to the package directions; drain well. Spoon the spaghetti onto dishes, and top with the sauce. *Makes 4 ¾-cup spaghetti servings (with ¾ cup sauce).*

One serving—Calories: 333; Total fat: 5.2 g; Saturated fat: 1.3 g; Cholesterol: 44 mg; Sodium: 637 mg; Carbohydrates: 57.2 g; Fiber: 9.8 g; Sugar: 1.1 g; Protein: 16.9 g

Italian Lemon Veal Cutlets

Cook these cutlets after your guests arrive to retain the integrity of this entree. To garnish, sprinkle lightly with shreds of lemon zest.

3 tablespoons Gluten-Free Flour Mixture
   (See the Hints chapter.)

⅛ teaspoon salt

¼ teaspoon pepper

4 veal cutlets (4 ounces each)

2 tablespoons gluten-free margarine

½ cup water

1 cube gluten-free beef bouillon

1 tablespoon freshly squeezed lemon juice

½ teaspoon sage

Combine the flour mixture, salt, and pepper in a plastic bag. Pound the cutlets to ¼-inch thickness; put in the bag with the flour mixture, and shake to coat evenly. In a large skillet, melt the margarine. Add the veal, and brown 1 minute per side; transfer the meat to a platter. Add the water, beef bouillon, lemon juice, and sage to the skillet; heat 1 minute, mashing the bouillon cube and stirring up any browned bits. Return the veal to the pan, and heat through, about 2 minutes. *Makes 4 4-ounce servings.*

One serving—Calories: 184; Total fat: 7.9 g; Saturated fat: 2.1 g; Cholesterol: 85 mg; Sodium: 395 mg; Carbohydrates: 4.6 g; Fiber: 0.2 g; Sugar: 0.2 g; Protein: 22.1 g

Italian Zucchini Bake

This casserole may be made with yellow squash or eggplant instead of the zucchini.

2 medium zucchini, cut into ¼-inch pieces

1 onion, sliced thin

½ green bell pepper, sliced thin

2 medium tomatoes, sliced

¼ teaspoon salt

⅛ teaspoon black pepper

¼ teaspoon garlic powder

¼ teaspoon basil

¼ teaspoon oregano

1 tablespoon chopped fresh parsley

2 tablespoons olive oil

3 ounces shredded gluten-free cheddar cheese

Preheat oven to 350°F. Spray a baking dish with gluten-free non-stick spray. Spread the zucchini slices in the baking dish. Top with the onion slices, green bell pepper slices, and tomato slices. Sprinkle with the salt, black pepper, garlic powder, basil, oregano, and

parsley. Drizzle with the olive oil; sprinkle with the cheese. Bake 45 minutes. *Makes 4 ¾-cup servings.*

One serving—Calories: 188; Total fat: 14.1 g; Saturated fat: 5.2 g; Cholesterol: 22 mg; Sodium: 288 mg; Carbohydrates: 9.3 g; Fiber: 2.6 g; Sugar: 0 g; Protein: 7.3 g

Antipasto Salad

When arranging vegetables, group like kinds together. For added color, roll the cheese strips in paprika.

3 tablespoons gluten-free red wine vinegar

2 tablespoons olive oil

¼ teaspoon basil

1 tablespoon chopped fresh parsley

Dash salt

Dash pepper

4 large leaves leaf lettuce

8 fresh asparagus spears

2 tomatoes, cut into thin wedges

1 15-ounce can artichoke hearts, drained

1 6½-ounce can water-packed tuna, drained

1 8-ounce can button mushrooms, drained

3 ounces gluten-free mozzarella cheese, cut into 8 long strips

4 large green olives

Combine the vinegar, olive oil, basil, parsley, salt, and pepper in a bowl; set aside. Arrange the lettuce leaves on four salad plates. Cook the asparagus in ¼ cup water for 3 minutes; rinse under cold water, and drain. Place two asparagus spears on each lettuce leaf. Arrange the tomato wedges, artichoke hearts, tuna, mushrooms, and cheese strips on the lettuce. Drizzle with the dressing. *Makes 4 1-cup servings.*

One serving—Calories: 238; Total fat: 12.1 g; Saturated fat: 1 g; Cholesterol: 8 mg; Sodium: 410 mg; Carbohydrates: 12.2 g; Fiber: 2.6 g; Sugar: 1.2 g; Protein: 21.4 g

Tuscany Pudding

When buying dried fruits, be certain the fruits have not been dusted with flour to keep them from sticking. If you are cutting up the fruits yourself, use scissors dipped in hot water. These mini puddings may be served warm or chilled. They will keep in the refrigerator 2 to 3 days. For a garnish, top each pudding with a light dusting of cinnamon and a few shreds of orange zest.

½ cup diced mixed dried fruits

1 cup gluten-free, low-fat cottage cheese

3 egg yolks

¾ teaspoon vanilla

2 tablespoons superfine sugar

1½ teaspoons cinnamon

Preheat oven to 350°F. Lightly spray four small custard cups with gluten-free nonstick spray. Put the dried fruit in a bowl; cover with warm water. Let the fruit soak 10 minutes; drain. In a large bowl, beat the cottage cheese with the egg yolks and vanilla. Stir in the sugar and cinnamon till blended. Stir in the fruit. Spoon the mixture into the custard cups. Bake 15 minutes or till tops are firm to the touch but not browned. When ready to serve, unmold onto serving dishes. *Makes 4 ½-cup servings.*

One serving—Calories: 154; Total fat: 4.2 g; Saturated fat: 1.5 g; Cholesterol: 159 mg; Sodium: 193 mg; Carbohydrates: 18 g; Fiber: 1.5 g; Sugar: 16 g; Protein: 10.5 g

Korean Dinner

Korea is filled with totem poles and color. For a centerpiece, use paper towel tubes covered in bright paper and decorated with felt-tipped markers as totem poles. Group them in the center of the table.

Korean Bok Choy Soup

Bok choy, available at most groceries, is part of the cabbage family. It has white stalks and spoon-shaped green leaves.

- 1 onion, minced
- 1 carrot, shredded
- 2 tablespoons minced fresh parsley
- 1 rib celery, minced
- 6 cups water
- 1/4 pound bok choy
- 1 small red chili, diced
- 2 teaspoons gluten-free soy sauce
- 1/4 teaspoon salt
- 1/4 teaspoon pepper
- 1 tablespoon gluten-free dry sherry

In a large saucepan, stir together the onion, carrot, parsley, celery, and water. Bring to a boil, cover, and simmer 30 minutes. Wash the bok choy thoroughly; drain, and pat dry with paper towels. Trim the stems, dice, and shred the leaves; add stems and leaves to the vegetable stock. Stir in the chili pepper, soy sauce, salt, and pepper; simmer, covered, 15 minutes. Stir in the sherry; simmer 3 minutes. *Makes 4 1½-cup servings.*

One serving–Calories: 35; Total fat: 0.3 g; Saturated fat: 0 g; Cholesterol: 0 mg; Sodium: 368 mg; Carbohydrates: 7.5 g; Fiber: 2.7 g; Sugar: 1.6 g; Protein: 1.4 g

Korean Soy Honey Salmon

To adorn this dish, select 4 small onions of uniform size. Peel them, and cut off the sprout end of each onion, leaving the root end intact. Cut each onion almost in half. Make another cut close to the first one; continue doing this until the entire onion is in thin strips, connected at the bottom. (To avoid cutting through the root end of the onion, insert a skewer 1/4 inch from the bottom before slicing. Your knife will stop each time it hits the skewer.) Place the onions in ice water that has been colored with beet juice; cover and refrigerate overnight. Drain the "chrysanthemums," and place one on a piece of kale at the side of each plate.

> 4 salmon fillets (4 ounces each)
> 1 tablespoon honey
> Dash hot red pepper flakes
> 1 tablespoon gluten-free soy sauce
> 2 teaspoons sesame oil
> 2 teaspoons minced fresh ginger
> Dash black pepper
> ¼ teaspoon minced garlic

Carefully remove the skin from the salmon. Wash the fish, then place in a reclosable, quart-size plastic bag. Stir together the honey, red pepper flakes, soy sauce, sesame oil, ginger, black pepper, and garlic. Pour the marinade into the bag. Seal the bag, and gently push the salmon around till evenly coated with marinade. Refrigerate 2 hours. Preheat broiler or prepare grill. Remove the fish from the bag; discard remaining marinade. Broil or grill for 10 to 15 minutes or till the fish flakes easily, turning the fish once. *Makes 4 4-ounce servings.*

One serving—Calories: 257; Total fat: 15.3 g; Saturated fat: 3.1 g; Cholesterol: 68 mg; Sodium: 288 mg; Carbohydrates: 4.7 g; Fiber: 0 g; Sugar: 4 g; Protein: 24 g

Korean Soy Rice

In America, we either put rice on a plate then top it with a piece of meat or put rice on the side of the plate with the meat beside it. In Korea, rice is not served on the dinner plate; traditionally, it is served family style in a separate bowl so guests may spoon out their own portions. To make rice fluffy and whiter, add 1 teaspoon of lemon juice to each quart of water before adding the rice.

1 cup short-grain rice

1 cup water

½ teaspoon gluten-free beef bouillon granules

¼ teaspoon gluten-free soy sauce

2 teaspoons chopped salt-free peanuts

Soak the rice in a bowl filled with water for 4 hours; drain and rinse with cold water until the water runs clear. In a saucepan, boil 1 cup of water. Stir in the beef bouillon, soy sauce, peanuts, and rice. Lower the heat to medium-low; cover the pan, and cook 20 minutes or until all moisture is absorbed. *Makes 4 ½-cup servings.*

One serving—Calories: 147; Total fat: 1.2 g; Saturated fat: 0.2 g; Cholesterol: 0 mg; Sodium: 219 mg; Carbohydrates: 30.1 g; Fiber: 0 g; Sugar: 0 g; Protein: 3.1 g

Korean Vegetable Salad

To enhance eye appeal, lay a few bok choy leaves on the platter before arranging the vegetables.

2 tablespoons gluten-free mayonnaise

1 teaspoon lemon juice

1½ teaspoons gluten-free soy sauce

1½ teaspoons water

3 teaspoons sesame oil

Dash red pepper flakes

4 cups fresh spinach leaves torn into bite-sized pieces

1 onion, sliced thin

3 ounces fresh mushrooms, sliced

8 cherry tomatoes, halved

2 teaspoons sesame seeds, toasted

In a bowl, whisk together the mayonnaise, lemon juice, soy sauce, water, sesame oil, and red pepper flakes; cover and refrigerate for 2 hours to blend flavors. Divide the spinach among four salad plates. Top each salad with one-fourth of the onion, mushrooms, tomatoes, and sesame seeds. Drizzle with the dressing just before serving. *Makes 4 1⅓-cup servings.*

One serving—Calories: 80; Total fat: 16.2 g; Saturated fat: 1 g; Cholesterol: 0 mg; Sodium: 195 mg; Carbohydrates: 6.1 g; Fiber: 1.8 g; Sugar: 0.7 g; Protein: 2.3 g

Korean Fruit Dessert

To find all the ingredients, you may have to go to an Asian grocery. Garnish each serving with thinly sliced mint leaves.

    2 tablespoons gluten-free dry sherry
    Juice and zest of ½ lemon
    1½ cups water
    2 tablespoons sugar
    1 whole clove
    1 cinnamon stick, broken in half
    1 vanilla bean, sliced lengthwise
    Dash cinnamon
    Dash nutmeg
    1 star anise pod
    1-inch piece fresh gingerroot, sliced
    1 tablespoon chopped unsalted cashews
    2 kiwis
    1 carambola (star fruit)
    ½ pint strawberries
    1 14-ounce can lychees, drained
    1 piece preserved ginger, drained and sliced

In a saucepan, stir together the sherry, lemon juice and zest, and water. Stir in the sugar, clove, cinnamon stick, vanilla bean, cinnamon, nutmeg, star anise, and gingerroot. Warm over medium heat, stirring constantly, until the sugar has dissolved. Raise heat; bring to a boil, then lower heat and simmer for 5 minutes. Set aside to cool. When completely cooled, strain into a small bowl;

discard flavorings. Stir in the cashews; cover, and refrigerate 1 hour. Peel, halve, and slice the kiwis. Peel and slice the carambola. Hull and slice the strawberries. Put the prepared fruits into a medium-size bowl. Add the lychees and preserved ginger; stir gently to mix. Spoon into small dessert bowls; pour the syrup over the fruit. *Makes 4 1-cup servings.*

One serving—Calories: 67; Total fat: 0.1 g; Saturated fat: 0 g; Cholesterol: 0 mg; Sodium: 77 mg; Carbohydrates: 18.8 g; Fiber: 2.4 g; Sugar: 3.4 g; Protein: 1.1 g

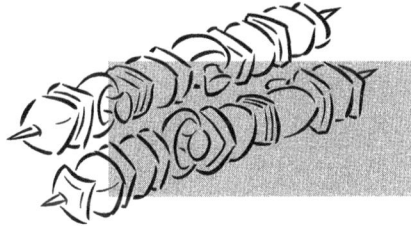

Chinese Dinner

Use straw placemats, and place chopsticks at each setting. Your centerpiece may be as simple as a painted teapot and teacups on a straw mat with whole tea leaves or bamboo leaves strategically placed.

Asian Appetizer Kabobs

Fresh rosemary looks like a cluster of thin pine needles on a twig. It is attractive, aromatic, and sturdy; therefore, it is ideal to use as a skewer for soft foods, as in this recipe. Fresh rosemary may be found in the herb section of most groceries.

    4 rosemary sticks for skewers
    4 large, raw shrimp, cleaned and deveined
    4 bay scallops, cleaned and halved
    2 green onions, cut into 1-inch pieces
    4 baby corn cobs, cut in half
    ¼ red bell pepper, cut into 8 pieces

1 tablespoon gluten-free soy sauce

⅛ teaspoon gluten-free chili powder

¼ teaspoon powdered ginger

1 clove garlic, minced

¼ teaspoon salt

⅛ teaspoon black pepper

2 teaspoons sesame oil

½ teaspoon honey

1 tablespoon gluten-free sweet sherry

½ teaspoon light brown sugar

Soak the rosemary sticks in water for ½ hour. Thread the shrimp, scallops, green onions, corn cobs, and bell pepper onto the rosemary sticks; place in a shallow pan. Whisk together the soy sauce, chili powder, ginger, garlic, salt, black pepper, sesame oil, honey, sherry, and brown sugar. Brush the marinade on the kabobs. Cover and refrigerate 2 hours. Preheat broiler. Uncover the dish; brush marinade over all sides of the kabobs again. Broil 2 to 3 minutes per side till shrimp turn pink and scallops are opaque. *Makes 4 skewers.*

One skewer—Calories: 66; Total fat: 2.5 g; Saturated fat: 0.4 g; Cholesterol: 11 mg; Sodium: 430 mg; Carbohydrates: 3.9 g; Fiber: 0.5 g; Sugar: 1.6 g; Protein: 4.8 g

Szechuan Chicken with Cashews

Select a carbon steel wok for stir-frying; it is less expensive than stainless steel, and it distributes the heat more evenly.

4 boneless, skinless chicken breasts (3 ounces each)

1 egg white

2 tablespoons cornstarch

2 teaspoons gluten-free soy sauce

1 tablespoon plus ¼ cup cold water

  2 tablespoons sesame oil

  1 onion, cut into 1-inch pieces

  2 cloves garlic, minced

  ¼ pound fresh bamboo shoots

  1 green bell pepper, cut into 1-inch pieces

  1 teaspoon dried chili pepper, finely chopped

  1 teaspoon gluten-free chicken bouillon granules

  ¼ cup salt-free cashews

Cut the chicken into ¼-inch cubes. Mix the egg white, 1 tablespoon of the cornstarch, and 1 teaspoon of the soy sauce in a large bowl. Stir in the chicken; marinate 20 minutes. In a small bowl, mix the remaining 1 tablespoon of cornstarch, 1 tablespoon of the water, and the remaining 1 teaspoon of soy sauce. Heat the sesame oil in a large skillet or wok. Cook the chicken, stirring, till the meat turns white; remove chicken. Cook the onion and garlic in the same pan till the garlic turns golden. Stir in the chicken, bamboo shoots, green bell pepper, and chili pepper. Stir-fry 1 minute. Stir in the remaining ¼ cup of water and the bouillon. Stir in the cornstarch mixture, and cook, stirring, till the sauce thickens. Stir in the cashews. *Makes 4 1¼-cup servings.*

One serving—Calories: 301; Total fat: 13.9 g; Saturated fat: 2.8 g; Cholesterol: 72 mg; Sodium: 325 mg; Carbohydrates: 10.6 g; Fiber: 1.3 g; Sugar: 1 g; Protein: 29.9 g

Crystallized Orange Peel

Orange peel is the perfect color and taste accent for most Asian or meat dishes.

  1 large orange, quartered

  1 cup granulated sugar

  1 cup water

  ½ teaspoon superfine sugar

Cut the pulp from the rind, removing the white pith. Slice the rind into very thin julienned strips. Boil the granulated sugar and water in a saucepan for 10 minutes. Add the strips of orange peel; boil until the strips are tender and translucent. Remove the strips from the syrup; drain. Spread the strips on waxed paper. Sprinkle with superfine sugar, and let set till dried, about an hour. *Makes 4 2-tablespoon servings.*

One serving—Calories: 84; Total fat: 0.1 g; Saturated fat: 0.1 g; Cholesterol: 0 mg; Sodium: 2 mg; Carbohydrates: 21.5 g; Fiber: 6 g; Sugar: 7.2 g; Protein: 0.8 g

Fried Brown Rice

To prevent the kernels from sticking together, make sure the rice is cold from the refrigerator before stir-frying.

1 tablespoon peanut oil
1 teaspoon minced garlic
1 onion, chopped
½ pound mushrooms, sliced
1 carrot, grated
2 cups cold cooked brown rice
1 tablespoon gluten-free soy sauce
¼ teaspoon powdered ginger

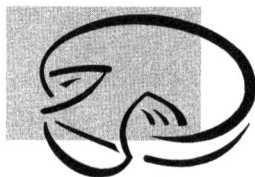

Heat the peanut oil in a large nonstick skillet. Add the garlic, onion, mushrooms, and carrot; sauté until golden. Remove vegetables. Add the rice to the pan, and fry it, stirring frequently, till it turns golden. Add the vegetables, soy sauce, and ginger; heat through. *Makes 4 ¾-cup servings.*

One serving—Calories: 175; Total fat: 4.6 g; Saturated fat: 0.8 g; Cholesterol: 0 mg; Sodium: 244 mg; Carbohydrates: 29.7 g; Fiber: 3.7 g; Sugar: 1.2 g; Protein: 5.2 g

Chinese Garlic Spinach

To garnish, sprinkle with a few strands of grated lemon peel.

- 2 pounds fresh spinach
- 2 tablespoons peanut oil
- 2 cloves garlic, crushed
- ⅛ teaspoon salt
- 1 tablespoon grated lemon zest
- 1 tablespoon gluten-free soy sauce
- ½ teaspoon light brown sugar

Remove the stems from the spinach leaves and discard. Rinse the leaves well; drain thoroughly on paper towels. Heat the peanut oil in a skillet or wok until almost smoking. Reduce heat; add garlic, spinach, and salt. Stir-fry 2 minutes till leaves are just barely wilted. Stir in the lemon zest, soy sauce, and brown sugar. Stir-fry 3 minutes. *Makes 4 1-cup servings.*

One serving—Calories: 86; Total fat: 5.1 g; Saturated fat: 0.6 g; Cholesterol: 0 mg; Sodium: 475 mg; Carbohydrates: 9.2 g; Fiber: 6.1 g; Sugar: 1 g; Protein: 8.2 g

Mandarin Orange Yogurt

Serve in small dessert bowls with a sprig of fresh mint and a mandarin orange section on the side.

- 2 cups gluten-free vanilla frozen yogurt, slightly softened
- 2 teaspoons gluten-free orange marmalade
- ½ cup mandarin orange sections, drained and chopped
- ¼ teaspoon almond extract
- 2 tablespoons chopped almonds

In a bowl, stir together the frozen yogurt, orange marmalade, orange sections, and almond extract. Spoon into an 8-inch square pan. Sprinkle almonds on top; cover, and freeze. Thaw 5 minutes before serving. To serve, scoop yogurt into balls. *Makes 4 ⅔-cup servings.*

One serving—Calories: 161; Total fat: 6.1 g; Saturated fat: 2.6 g; Cholesterol: 1 mg; Sodium: 65 mg; Carbohydrates: 25 g; Fiber: 0.6 g; Sugar: 6.6 g; Protein: 3.6 g

Japanese Dinner

Consider having your guests sit on the floor on large pillows. Spread out a large, bright-colored cloth; roll the silverware in a napkin tied with raffia. Lay a thin strip of gold material down the center of your fabric; in the center, place a bonsai tree surrounded by wisteria flowers. Hang paper lanterns.

Japanese Orange Roughy Soup

When washing the fish fillet, feel for any hidden bones, and remove them. The soup should be served very hot.

4 cups water
¼ teaspoon salt
⅛ teaspoon pepper
1½ teaspoons gluten-free
   chicken bouillon granules
2 green onions, sliced thin
1 tablespoon minced fresh parsley
5 ounces frozen chopped spinach
1 orange roughy fillet (3 ounces)

In a large saucepan, combine the water, salt, pepper, chicken bouillon, green onions, parsley, and spinach. Bring to a boil. Lower heat; simmer, covered, until spinach is thawed. Cut fish

into ½-inch pieces; add to soup. Cover; simmer for 5 minutes or until the fish flakes easily. *Makes 4 1¼-cup servings.*

One serving—Calories: 28; Total fat: 8.6 g; Saturated fat: 0 g; Cholesterol: 6 mg; Sodium: 321 mg; Carbohydrates: 0.2 g; Fiber: 0.5 g; Sugar: 0 g; Protein: 4.9 g

Japanese Steak Stir-Fry

Garnish one side of each dish with thin slices of pomegranates and oranges placed on 3 green onion stems.

    ¾ pound lean boneless Boston strip steak

    3 tablespoons gluten-free soy sauce

    ¼ teaspoon black pepper

    3 tablespoons gluten-free dry sherry

    1 medium zucchini

    1 green bell pepper

    1 carrot

    2 tablespoons sesame oil

    I cup sliced onion

    1 cup sliced mushrooms

    1 teaspoon sesame seeds

Thinly slice the steak across the grain; put into a reclosable, sandwich-size plastic bag. Add the soy sauce, black pepper, and sherry; seal the bag, and refrigerate for 3 to 8 hours. Cut the zucchini, green bell pepper, and carrot into thin strips 2½ inches long. Heat the sesame oil in a skillet or wok. Remove the steak from the bag, reserving the marinade; stir-fry the steak 2 minutes, turning and tossing the meat frequently. Add the zucchini, green bell pepper, carrot, onion, and mushrooms; stir-fry 2 minutes. Pour the marinade over the meat and vegetables; sprinkle with sesame seeds; cook 2 minutes more. *Makes 4 1-cup servings.*

One serving—Calories: 284; Total fat: 16.6 g; Saturated fat: 4.4 g; Cholesterol: 68 mg; Sodium: 482 mg; Carbohydrates: 8.2 g; Fiber: 2.6 g; Sugar: 2 g; Protein: 26.1 g

Japanese Fried Rice with Bean Sprouts

When you stir-fry rice, the rice should be cold, and the oil hot.

- 2 tablespoons gluten-free dry white wine
- 2 tablespoons gluten-free soy sauce
- 1 tablespoon water
- ⅛ teaspoon pepper
- 1 egg
- 2 teaspoons sesame oil
- ½ cup sliced celery
- ½ cup peas
- 2 green onions, sliced
- ½ cup fresh bean sprouts
- 2 cups boiled white rice, well chilled

Mix the wine, soy sauce, water, and pepper in a bowl; set aside. In another bowl, whisk the egg till frothy. Brush the inside of a large skillet or wok with 1 teaspoon of the sesame oil. Pour in the egg; cook, stirring, till the egg is cooked through and in tiny pieces; remove egg. Add the remaining 1 teaspoon of oil to the skillet; stir-fry the celery, peas, and green onions 2 minutes till just tender-crisp. Add the bean sprouts; stir-fry 1 minute. Add the rice and egg; drizzle the wine mixture over the rice. Cook, stirring, for 4 minutes or till heated through. *Makes 4 1-cup servings.*

One serving—Calories: 169; Total fat: 3.8 g; Saturated fat: 0.8 g; Cholesterol: 5 mg; Sodium: 586 mg; Carbohydrates: 27.5 g; Fiber: 1.5 g; Sugar: 1.7 g; Protein: 6.2 g

Japanese Rice Coconut Pudding

Prerinsing the rice is vital to keep the pudding from becoming pasty.

⅓ cup short-grain rice

3 cups skim milk

¼ cup brown sugar

½ teaspoon cinnamon

⅛ teaspoon cloves

1 whole egg

1 egg white

3 tablespoons unsweetened coconut milk

1¼ teaspoons vanilla

1 tablespoon coconut, toasted

Soak the rice in a bowl of water for 3 hours; rinse well, then drain. In a large saucepan, scald the milk. Add the rice, sugar, cinnamon, and cloves. Simmer, uncovered, 20 minutes till rice is tender, stirring occasionally. In a small bowl, beat the egg, egg white, and coconut milk. Whip in half of the hot rice 1 tablespoon at a time. Stir this mixture back into the rice in the pan; stir over medium heat until very thick, about 1 minute. Remove the pan from the heat; stir in the vanilla. Spoon the pudding into serving bowls; sprinkle with toasted coconut. Serve chilled. *Makes 4 1-cup servings.*

One serving—Calories: 235; Total fat: 3.4 g; Saturated fat: 1.9 g; Cholesterol: 56 mg; Sodium: 129 mg; Carbohydrates: 21.6 g; Fiber: 0.1 g; Sugar: 16 g; Protein: 7.8 g

Jamaican Dinner

"Don't worry . . . Be happy!" Weather permitting, set your table outdoors. A centerpiece? Try an arrangement of whole pineapples and bananas or a bowl of fresh tropical flowers floating in water.

Caribbean Oysters on the Half Shell

Some form of seafood is a must for a Caribbean evening. Even guests who don't care for oysters will love this recipe. Be sure the oysters are fresh.

    12 oysters on the half shell
    1 tablespoon gluten-free margarine
    ½ teaspoon freshly squeezed lemon juice
    1 teaspoon gluten-free Worcestershire sauce
    Dash red pepper flakes
    ⅛ teaspoon black pepper
    1 slice gluten-free bacon, finely crumbled

Preheat broiler. Arrange the cleaned oysters (on their half shells) in a baking pan. In a saucepan, warm the margarine, lemon juice, Worcestershire sauce, red pepper flakes, and black pepper; spoon over the oysters. Sprinkle each oyster with bacon. Broil 3 minutes or until the oysters are plump and the bacon is crisp. Serve immediately. *Makes 4 3-oyster servings.*

One serving—Calories: 54; Total fat: 3.5 g; Saturated fat: 0.7 g; Cholesterol: 23 mg; Sodium: 143 mg; Carbohydrates: 2.2 g; Fiber: 0 g; Sugar: 0 g; Protein: 3.5 g

Jamaican Chicken

Your tongue will certainly be aware that you are eating Jamaican food! Adorn the dishes with Belgian endive, kale, grape leaves, or squash blooms.

½ cup water

½ onion, minced

1 teaspoon thyme

½ teaspoon allspice

½ teaspoon black pepper

¼ teaspoon salt

2 dried chili peppers, crumbled

¼ teaspoon crushed red pepper flakes

¼ cup gluten-free dry white wine

6 thin slices gingerroot

4 boneless, skinless chicken breasts (4 ounces each), cut into
1-inch cubes

Put the water, onion, thyme, allspice, black pepper, salt, chili peppers, red pepper flakes, wine, and gingerroot into a blender; puree. Thread the chicken on skewers; lay in a flat glass pan. Pour the marinade over the meat; cover, and refrigerate for 4 hours, turning the meat frequently. Preheat broiler. Remove the meat from the marinade; lay on a broiler pan. Broil 10 to 15 minutes, turning the chicken once, until opaque and tender. *Makes 4 skewers.*

One skewer—Calories: 196; Total fat: 4 g; Saturated fat: 1 g; Cholesterol: 96 mg; Sodium: 279 mg; Carbohydrates: 2.1 g; Fiber: 0.3 g; Sugar: 0.5 g; Protein: 35.3 g

Caribbean Black Beans and Rice

This is a staple dish on Caribbean menus.

1 tablespoon olive oil

1 onion, chopped

½ red bell pepper, minced

2 cloves garlic, minced

1½ cups water

2 gluten-free chicken bouillon cubes

1 10-ounce can black beans, rinsed and well drained

½ cup rice

¼ teaspoon red pepper flakes

¼ teaspoon thyme

1 bay leaf

¼ cup shredded gluten-free cheddar cheese

In a large saucepan, heat the olive oil. Sauté the onion, red bell pepper, and garlic, stirring, until the onion is soft. Add the water and bouillon cubes; mash the bouillon with the back of a spoon till dissolved. Add the black beans, rice, pepper flakes, thyme, and bay leaf. Bring to a boil. Lower heat; cover, and simmer 20 minutes or till moisture has been absorbed. Remove the bay leaf. Sprinkle with the shredded cheese. *Makes 4 1¼-cup servings.*

One serving—Calories: 211; Total fat: 6.2 g; Saturated fat: 2.1 g; Cholesterol: 8 mg; Sodium: 708 mg; Carbohydrates: 33.7 g; Fiber: 4.1 g; Sugar: 1.2 g; Protein: 7.8 g

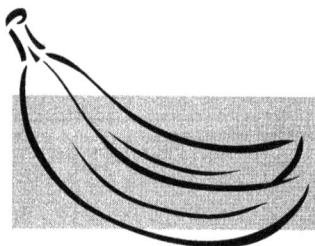

Caribbean Fried Plantain

Plantain looks like a large, dark banana and is available in most grocery stores. The taste is wonderfully tropic and not quite as sweet as a banana. In the Caribbean, plantain is served beside the entree.

1 plantain, peeled

1 teaspoon gluten-free margarine

1 tablespoon honey

1 teaspoon dark brown sugar

Slice the plantain in half lengthwise, then slice crosswise to make four pieces. Spray a skillet with gluten-free nonstick spray. Melt the margarine in the skillet. Add the plantain, honey, and brown sugar. Heat over medium heat, turning once, until the plantain is glazed and browned. *Makes 4 pieces.*

One piece—Calories: 70; Total fat: 0.7 g; Saturated fat: 0.2 g; Cholesterol: 0 mg; Sodium: 14 mg; Carbohydrates: 16.9 g; Fiber: 0.2 g; Sugar: 4.6 g; Protein: 0.2 g

Caribbean Avocado Salsa Salad

While avocados have some fat, they have zero cholesterol. Select a ripe avocado for this recipe.

1 ripe avocado
2 small tomatoes, finely chopped
1 small onion, minced
¾ teaspoon paprika
¼ teaspoon salt
¼ teaspoon pepper
Juice of ½ lemon
½ head romaine lettuce
1 tablespoon chopped fresh parsley

Halve the avocado; peel and dice into small pieces. In a shallow bowl, mash the avocado, tomatoes, and onion with a fork. Add the paprika, salt, pepper, and lemon juice; mix well. Cover and chill 1 hour. Wash the lettuce; drain well. Break into bite-sized pieces. Wrap the lettuce pieces in paper towels; put in a plastic bag, and chill 1 hour. Divide the lettuce among four salad plates. Put one-fourth of the avocado mixture on top of each salad. Sprinkle with parsley. *Makes 4 ¾-cup servings.*

One serving—Calories: 100; Total fat: 7.7 g; Saturated fat: 1.1 g; Cholesterol: 0 mg; Sodium: 158 mg; Carbohydrates: 8.1 g; Fiber: 3.4 g; Sugar: 0 g; Protein: 2.2 g

Caribbean Spicy Corn Muffins

For variety (and a tad more fat, cholesterol, and sodium), add 2 tablespoons of shredded cheddar cheese to the batter.

½ cup yellow cornmeal

½ cup Gluten-Free Flour Mixture (See the Hints chapter.)

2½ teaspoons gluten-free baking powder

3 teaspoons sugar

¼ teaspoon salt

½ cup buttermilk

2 egg whites

⅛ teaspoon red pepper flakes

2 tablespoons corn oil

Preheat oven to 375°F. Sift together the cornmeal, flour mixture, baking powder, sugar, and salt. With a whisk, stir in the buttermilk, egg whites, red pepper flakes, and corn oil. Beat for 1½ minutes. Spray muffin tins with gluten-free nonstick spray. Pour the batter into the muffin tins. Bake 20 minutes or till lightly browned. *Makes 4 muffins.*

One muffin—Calories: 188; Total fat: 7.9 g; Saturated fat: 0.7 g; Cholesterol: 0 mg; Sodium: 193 mg; Carbohydrates: 25 g; Fiber: 1.2 g; Sugar: 1.7 g; Protein: 5.2 g

Jamaican Lemon Coconut Ice

Lemon ice should be served "slushy."

3 lemons

Scant 1 cup fresh lemon juice

½ cup sugar

2¼ cups cold water

2 tablespoons coconut

Finely grate the zest of the lemons. Place the zest, 1 cup lemon juice, and sugar in a medium-size saucepan; bring to a boil. Lower heat; simmer 6 minutes or till thick and syrupy. Remove from heat. When cooled, stir in the water and coconut. Pour into a shallow freezer container with a lid. Cover and freeze 5 hours, stirring occasionally to break up the ice. *Makes 4 ¾-cup servings.*

One serving–Calories: 87; Total fat: 0.8 g; Saturated fat: 0.7 g; Cholesterol: 0 mg; Sodium: 2 mg; Carbohydrates: 21.3 g; Fiber: 0.7 g; Sugar: 14.5 g; Protein: 0.7 g

French Dinner

French cooking is famous for its rich sauces and calorie-laden desserts. Low-calorie and French cooking are mutually exclusive, so the recipes for this dinner are lower-calorie versions of authentic French cuisine.

French Green Olive Pâte

If you love olives, you will *love* this pâte. Serve the pâte surrounded by gluten-free crackers or freshly cut vegetables.

1 6-ounce jar pitted green olives, drained

2 green onions, finely chopped

1 anchovy

1 tablespoon chopped fresh parsley

⅛ teaspoon pepper

½ teaspoon freshly squeezed lemon juice

3 tablespoons olive oil

In a food processor or blender, combine all the ingredients. Blend until the pâte is of a coarse paste consistency. *Makes 4 3-tablespoon servings.*

One serving–Calories: 104; Total fat: 11.6 g; Saturated fat: 1.5 g; Cholesterol: 0 mg; Sodium: 213 mg; Carbohydrates: 0.5 g; Fiber: 0 g; Sugar: 0 g; Protein: 0.5 g

Coq au Vin Blanc (Chicken with White Wine)

Tuck a few green leek leaves under the chicken rounds, and garnish the top with a sprig of fresh dill.

4 4-ounce skinless, boneless chicken breasts

2 leeks

1 tablespoon olive oil

4 green onions, sliced

16 fresh spinach leaves, chopped

8 mushrooms, chopped

1/8 teaspoon salt

1/8 teaspoon pepper

8 tablespoons gluten-free white wine

2 cups gluten-free chicken broth

1 cup water

1/3 cup gluten-free sour cream

2 tablespoons 1% milk

1 1/2 teaspoons gluten-free prepared mustard

1 teaspoon dill weed

Preheat oven to 375°F. Cut four pieces of heavy-duty foil into 8-inch squares; spray the shiny side of each square with gluten-free nonstick spray. Flatten the chicken breasts between sheets of waxed paper; remove waxed paper and place one breast on each of the foil squares. Soak the leeks in cold water; separate and rinse well under cold running water to remove any sand. Finely slice the green portion. Heat the olive oil in a large skillet. Add the leeks, green onions, spinach, and mushrooms; sauté 30 seconds, stirring. Place one-fourth of the vegetable mixture on top of each breast; sprinkle with the salt, pepper, and wine. Roll up each chicken breast; wrap the foil to seal completely. Pour chicken broth and 1 cup of water into an 8″ × 11″ baking dish. Place the packets in the baking dish. Bake 35 minutes or till chicken is cooked through. Place the sour cream, milk, mustard, and dill in a small saucepan; warm, stirring frequently. Unwrap the packets; slice each roll into ½-inch rounds. Set on a plate, and drizzle with the dill sauce. *Makes 4 1-packet servings (with 2 tablespoons dill sauce).*

One serving—Calories: 298; Total fat: 11 g; Saturated fat: 3.7 g; Cholesterol: 106 mg; Sodium: 595 mg; Carbohydrates: 8.9 g; Fiber: 2 g; Sugar: 2.9 g; Protein: 39 g

Pommes de Terre (Potatoes)

Frequent stirring is needed to keep the potatoes from sticking to the bottom of the pan.

- 2 tablespoons olive oil
- 1 onion, chopped
- 2 green onions, chopped
- 2 slices gluten-free bacon
- ½ teaspoon chopped fresh thyme
- 1 bay leaf
- 2 teaspoons cornstarch
- ½ cup gluten-free chicken broth
- 3 russet potatoes, peeled and cut into 1-inch chunks
- ¼ teaspoon salt
- ⅛ teaspoon pepper
- 1 tablespoon chopped fresh parsley

Heat the olive oil in a saucepan; add the onion, green onions, bacon, thyme, and bay leaf; sauté 10 minutes. Sprinkle the cornstarch over the bacon and vegetable mixture; stir until browned. Stir in the broth, potatoes, salt, and pepper. Cover and simmer slowly 35 minutes, stirring frequently, till the potatoes are cooked through. Add a little water if needed. Remove and discard the bacon. To serve, garnish with chopped parsley. *Makes 4 ¾-cup servings.*

One serving—Calories: 223; Total fat: 8.7 g; Saturated fat: 1.5 g; Cholesterol: 3 mg; Sodium: 358 mg; Carbohydrates: 31.9 g; Fiber: 3.5 g; Sugar: 0.6 g; Protein: 5.6 g

Asparagus with Egg Sauce

This recipe alters the traditional high-calorie creamed egg sauce without sacrificing taste.

> 1 egg
> ¼ teaspoon salt
> ¼ teaspoon pepper
> 2 teaspoons gluten-free margarine, melted
> 1 green onion, minced
> 1½ pounds fresh asparagus
> 1 tablespoon diced pimiento

Soft-boil the egg. When the egg is cool enough to handle, remove the shell. In a small bowl, mash the egg with the salt, pepper, and 1 teaspoon of the margarine; keep warm. Add the remaining 1 teaspoon of margarine and the green onion; sauté till onion is limp. Stir into the egg mixture. In a large skillet, steam the asparagus 3 minutes or till just tender-crisp; drain. Place the asparagus on a serving dish; spoon the egg sauce over the top, and sprinkle with the pimiento. *Makes 4 7-spear servings (with 1¼ tablespoons sauce).*

One serving—Calories: 53; Total fat: 2.9 g; Saturated fat: 0.8 g; Cholesterol: 53 mg; Sodium: 190 mg; Carbohydrates: 4.3 g; Fiber: 1.7 g; Sugar: 0 g; Protein: 3.6 g

French Sweet and Sour Relish

The dried fruits traditionally used in this recipe are raisins, apricots, and prunes. Experiment by adding dried figs, cranberries, or cherries. Use a noncorrosive pan to cook the relish; an aluminum pan will react with the vinegar.

> 1 tablespoon olive oil
> 1 pound red onions, sliced very thin
> 1 tablespoon sugar

1 tablespoon gluten-free white wine vinegar

¼ teaspoon salt

¼ teaspoon pepper

¼ cup dried fruit, finely chopped

½ cup gluten-free white wine

Heat the olive oil in a medium-size saucepan. Add the onions, and sauté, stirring occasionally, until they are limp. Stir in the sugar, vinegar, salt, pepper, and fruit. Cover the pan, reduce heat to low; simmer, stirring frequently, about 15 minutes until the onions and fruit have a jamlike consistency. Remove from heat; stir in the wine. *Makes 4 ⅓-cup servings.*

One serving—Calories: 108; Total fat: 3.7 g; Saturated fat: 0.5 g; Cholesterol: 0 mg; Sodium: 218 mg; Carbohydrates: 27.2 g; Fiber: 2.8 g; Sugar: 9.1 g; Protein: 1.5 g

French Nasturtium Salad

Nasturtiums are edible flowers. To be eaten safely, they must be fresh and pesticide free. Consider planting some in your garden in the spring so you will have a ready supply for this salad.

3 tablespoons olive oil

1 tablespoon grated gluten-free Parmesan cheese

4 teaspoons gluten-free white wine vinegar

1 teaspoon freshly squeezed lemon juice

¼ teaspoon dry mustard

1 teaspoon basil, crushed

1 teaspoon sugar

¼ teaspoon pepper

1 tablespoon minced fresh parsley

1 clove garlic, minced

¼ cup thin strips gluten-free ham (cut 1½ inches long)

4 cups assorted greens

8 nasturtium flowers

In a small bowl, whisk together 2 tablespoons of the olive oil and the Parmesan cheese, vinegar, lemon juice, mustard, basil, sugar, pepper, and parsley. Heat the remaining 1 tablespoon of oil in a small skillet. Add the garlic, and sauté 20 seconds. Add the ham; sauté 15 seconds till heated through. Divide the greens among four salad plates. Top with the ham, drizzle with dressing, and garnish with the flowers. *Makes 4 1-cup servings.*

One serving—Calories: 121; Total fat: 11 g; Saturated fat: 1.8 g; Cholesterol: 3 mg; Sodium: 109 mg; Carbohydrates: 2.7 g; Fiber: 1 g; Sugar: 0.6 g; Protein: 3 g

French Meringue Custard

The French are famous for using heavy cream and egg yolks in their dessert recipes, so it is challenging to create a reduced-calorie authentic French dessert. Remove all white pith from the orange peel before adding to the pudding.

1¾ cups 1% milk
½ teaspoon orange juice
1 3" × 1" strip orange zest
1 vanilla bean, split lengthwise
4 tablespoons sugar
2 teaspoons cornstarch
2 egg whites plus 1 egg white, at room temperature
Nutmeg

Combine 1¼ cups of the milk, the juice, and the orange zest in a saucepan. Scrape in the seeds from the vanilla bean; add the bean. Bring the mixture to a slow simmer. (Do not allow it to boil.) Stir together 3 tablespoons of sugar and cornstarch in a bowl; whisk in 2 egg whites. Gradually add the hot milk mixture, whisking constantly. Return the mixture to the pan. Cook over medium heat, stirring constantly, till the mixture almost simmers and thickens enough to coat a spoon (about 8 minutes). Do not permit it to boil. Strain into a shallow bowl, and refrigerate 2 hours. Beat 1 egg white till soft peaks form. Gradually add 1 tablespoon of sugar; whip until the meringue is very stiff but not dry. Place the remaining ½ cup of milk in a large skillet. Add enough water to bring the depth to 1½ inches. Bring the liquid to a gentle simmer. Using 2 soupspoons, dip the spoons in cold water, then form four puffs from the meringue; drop each puff into the simmering liquid. The meringues will expand and puff up during cooking. Cook about 30 seconds. Using a slotted spoon, transfer the meringues to a kitchen towel. Arrange the meringues on top of the chilled custard, then sprinkle generously with nutmeg. This dessert may be made up to 8 hours ahead and refrigerated. *Makes 4 ¾-cup servings.*

One serving—Calories: 92; Total fat: 1.1 g; Saturated fat: 0.6 g; Cholesterol: 4 mg; Sodium: 96 mg; Carbohydrates: 13.9 g; Fiber: 0 g; Sugar: 12.5 g; Protein: 6 g

African Dinner

Pick up a remnant piece of leopard-print material, and drape it across the dinner table. Your centerpiece may be a collection of wooden vases or boxes.

Nigerian Peanut Soup

Africa is a large continent; the foods vary greatly from one country to the next. However, one common ingredient is used throughout Africa—peanut butter!

- 4 cubes gluten-free chicken bouillon
- 4 cups boiling water
- 2 small, dried green chili peppers, finely minced

½ cup diced green bell pepper

½ cup chopped onion

2 tablespoons gluten-free chunky peanut butter

In a large saucepan, dissolve the bouillon in the water. Add the chili peppers, and bring the mixture to a boil. Stir in the bell pepper and onion. Reduce heat; cover, and simmer for 20 minutes, till the vegetables are tender. Reduce heat to simmer; stir in peanut butter, and cook, stirring constantly, until it has melted. Serve immediately. *Makes 4 1-cup servings.*

One serving—Calories: 71; Total fat: 4.8 g; Saturated fat: 0.6 g; Cholesterol: 0 mg; Sodium: 776 mg; Carbohydrates: 4.8 g; Fiber: 1.2 g; Sugar: 0.5 g; Protein: 3.3 g

Ethiopian Braised Chicken

The skin helps keep the chicken moist, but to reduce calories further, remove the skin from the chicken before cooking.

1 8-ounce can tomato sauce

2 tablespoons paprika

1 cup gluten-free dry white wine

1 tablespoon grated gingerroot

Dash red pepper flakes

⅛ teaspoon cinnamon

⅛ teaspoon nutmeg

⅛ teaspoon ground cloves

⅛ teaspoon allspice

¼ teaspoon turmeric

¼ teaspoon salt

⅛ teaspoon black pepper

2 tablespoons chopped fresh parsley

1 tablespoon olive oil

2 onions, chopped

1 clove garlic, minced

1 broiler chicken, cut into pieces, skin removed

In a bowl, stir together the tomato sauce, paprika, wine, ginger-root, red pepper flakes, cinnamon, nutmeg, cloves, allspice, turmeric, salt, black pepper, and parsley. Heat the olive oil in a large skillet. Add the onion and garlic; sauté over medium heat until the onion is tender but not browned. Stir in the tomato sauce mixture. Add the chicken pieces, spooning the sauce over the meat. Bring to a boil; reduce heat, cover, and simmer 45 minutes or till chicken is tender, turning the chicken pieces often. *Makes 4 5-ounce servings (with ¼ cup sauce).*

One serving—Calories: 224; Total fat: 11.1 g; Saturated fat: 2.6 g; Cholesterol: 78 mg; Sodium: 782 mg; Carbohydrates: 9.3 g; Fiber: 0.8 g; Sugar: 5.1 g; Protein: 27.4 g

Kenya Raisin Rice

When cooked, short-grain rice is more "puffy" than long-grain rice. As it absorbs flavorings from the liquid, it tends to become stickier. Fluff up cooked short-grain rice with a fork just before serving.

- 2½ cups water
- 1 cup short-grain rice
- ¼ teaspoon cinnamon
- ⅛ teaspoon saffron
- 1 teaspoon gluten-free margarine
- ⅛ teaspoon turmeric
- 2 teaspoons sugar
- ¼ teaspoon salt
- 2 tablespoons raisins

Bring the water to a boil. Add the rice, cinnamon, saffron, margarine, turmeric, sugar, salt, and raisins. Cover, reduce heat, and simmer slowly 25 minutes or till the rice is tender. *Makes 4 ⅔-cup servings.*

One serving—Calories: 207; Total fat: 1 g; Saturated fat: 0.3 g; Cholesterol: 0 mg; Sodium: 161 mg; Carbohydrates: 44.7 g; Fiber: 0.2 g; Sugar: 4.8 g; Protein: 1.4 g

Zimbabwe Greens

The greens used in Africa are not available in America, but collard greens are very close in texture and taste.

    1 pound collard greens, washed
    2 cups water
    1 tomato, chopped
    5 green onions, sliced
    ⅛ teaspoon salt
    ⅛ teaspoon pepper
    1 tablespoon gluten-free smooth peanut butter

Finely shred the greens, discarding tough stems. Place the greens and the water in a saucepan. Bring to a boil and cook at a brisk simmer, stirring occasionally, till the greens are tender-crisp. Drain, reserving liquid. Return the greens to the pan; stir in the tomato, onions, salt, and pepper. Heat through, stirring occasionally. With a fork, whip together the peanut butter and ¾ cup of the reserved cooking liquid; add to the vegetables. Heat till the greens have a creamy consistency, adding more liquid if the sauce becomes too thick. *Makes 4 1-cup servings.*

One serving—Calories: 52; Total fat: 2.7 g; Saturated fat: 0.2 g; Cholesterol: 0 mg; Sodium: 106 mg; Carbohydrates: 5.9 g; Fiber: 3.1 g; Sugar: 0.2 g; Protein: 3.2 g

Moroccan Carrot Orange Salad

Not only is this salad healthful, but it holds well. Kids love this salad, so pack any leftovers in lunch boxes. If you are short on time, substitute canned (and drained) mandarin oranges for the fresh orange sections.

    ¼ cup raisins
    2 seedless oranges, peeled and pith removed
    ½ pound carrots, shredded

1 tablespoon olive oil

Juice of ½ lemon

1 small onion, sliced

2 tablespoons chopped walnuts

⅛ teaspoon black pepper

⅛ teaspoon red pepper flakes

Soak the raisins in a bowl of warm water for 10 minutes; drain, and place in a large bowl. Separate the orange sections; add to the raisins. Stir in the carrots, olive oil, lemon juice, onion, walnuts, black pepper, and red pepper flakes; toss till evenly coated. Cover and refrigerate 1 hour. *Makes 4 ⅓-cup servings.*

One serving—Calories: 224; Total fat: 12.3 g; Saturated fat: 1.2 g; Cholesterol: 0 mg; Sodium: 42 mg; Carbohydrates: 27.3 g; Fiber: 5.3 g; Sugar: 19 g; Protein: 3.9 g

Algerian Fruit Bowl

To serve, cut sections of a large palm leaf to set under each dessert dish. For an added garnish, insert a cinnamon stick on the side of each dish.

1 seedless orange, peeled and pith removed

1 apple, cored

1 cup chopped dates

¼ cup chopped dried figs

¼ cup chopped dried apricots

  2 bananas, sliced

  1 cinnamon stick

  ½ cup orange juice

  1 tablespoon chopped pistachios

Cut the orange and apple into bite-sized pieces; place in a bowl. Stir in the dates, figs, apricots, bananas, cinnamon stick, and orange juice. Cover, and refrigerate for 2 hours for the flavors to blend. Spoon into dishes; sprinkle with the pistachios. *Makes 4 1-cup servings.*

One serving—Calories: 135; Total fat: 1.4 g; Saturated fat: 0.2 g; Cholesterol: 0 mg; Sodium: 5 mg; Carbohydrates: 31.7 g; Fiber: 3.6 g; Sugar: 8.2 g; Protein: 1.5 g

Irish Dinner

The color scheme for an Irish dinner is an easy choice: green!

Killarney Soup

If you don't have gluten-free chicken broth, use water in place of the broth and add 2 teaspoons of gluten-free chicken bouillon granules.

  1 leek

  2 sprigs fresh thyme

  2 sprigs parsley

  1 bay leaf

  2 bone-in chicken thighs (3 ounces each)

  2 cups gluten-free chicken broth

  3 cups water

  ½ teaspoon salt

  ¼ teaspoon pepper

1 potato, peeled and cut into ½-inch cubes

¼ cup diced gluten-free ham

¼ cup diced prunes

Cut the dark green leaves from the leek; reserve one leek green, and discard the remaining greens. Wash the leek and the reserved leek green; slice the light green and white part of the leek. Wrap the thyme, parsley, and bay leaf into the fold of the leek green, and tie it closed with string. Place the chicken, sliced leeks, broth, water, salt, pepper, and herb-filled leek green in a large saucepan. Bring to a boil; skim off the foam that rises to the surface. Lower heat; cover, and simmer for 1¼ hours. Lift the chicken out of the pan; add the potato, and simmer 30 minutes. Discard the chicken skin and bones; cut the meat into small pieces, and return them to the soup. Add the ham and prunes; simmer gently 10 minutes. Remove the stuffed leek green before serving. *Makes 4 1½-cup servings.*

One serving—Calories: 195; Total fat: 4.7 g; Saturated fat: 1.7 g; Cholesterol: 41 mg; Sodium: 805 mg; Carbohydrates: 13 g; Fiber: 0.7 g; Sugar: 2.4 g; Protein: 14.3 g

Traditional Irish Stew

Originally, Irish stew was made with mutton, which is a much tougher and stronger-tasting variety of lamb.

1 pound boneless lamb shoulder, trimmed of fat, cut into ¾-inch pieces

1 tablespoon chopped fresh parsley

½ teaspoon thyme

½ teaspoon salt

¼ teaspoon pepper

3 cups gluten-free chicken broth

1½ pounds red potatoes, peeled and quartered

1 onion, chopped

½ pound carrots, peeled, cut into ½-inch pieces

2 ribs celery, cut into ½-inch pieces

3 tablespoons cornstarch

In a dutch oven, simmer the lamb, parsley, thyme, salt, and pepper in 2 cups of the broth, covered, for 1½ hours. Add a little water if needed to keep meat covered. Stir in the potatoes, onion, carrots, and celery, and the remaining 1 cup of broth. Simmer, covered, 45 minutes. In a small bowl, whisk together the cornstarch and 3 tablespoons of broth from the stew. Stir the cornstarch mixture into the stew until well blended. Simmer, uncovered, 3 minutes till thickened, stirring constantly. *Makes 4 1¼-cup servings.*

One serving—Calories: 351; Total fat: 4.8 g; Saturated fat: 2.1 g; Cholesterol: 83 mg; Sodium: 1,008 mg; Carbohydrates: 47.8 g; Fiber: 2.7 g; Sugar: 3.7 g; Protein: 28.2 g

Leprechaun Bread

Sultanas (white raisins) may be used instead of the currants (small black raisins).

2 cups Gluten-Free Flour Mixture (See the Hints chapter.)

½ teaspoon salt

1 teaspoon gluten-free baking powder

½ teaspoon cinnamon

¼ teaspoon nutmeg

1 tablespoon sugar

1 tablespoon cold gluten-free margarine

¼ cup currants

2 eggs

1 cup buttermilk

1 tablespoon gluten-free, low-fat mayonnaise

2 teaspoons baking soda

Preheat oven to 375°F. Sift the flour mixture, salt, baking powder, cinnamon, nutmeg, and sugar into a large bowl. With two knives, cut in the margarine until fine. Stir in the currants. In a small bowl, whip the eggs till frothy; stir in the buttermilk, mayonnaise, and baking soda. Add the egg mixture to the dry ingredients, and mix lightly with a fork until blended. Turn the dough onto a flat surface sprinkled with Gluten-Free Flour Mixture; knead the dough lightly for 10 seconds. Spray a baking sheet with gluten-free nonstick spray. Shape the dough into a ball, and place on the baking sheet. Shape the ball into a 5-inch loaf. Spray a knife with gluten-free nonstick spray; cut three ¼-inch-deep slits from edge to edge to mark the loaf into six sections. Spray the top of the loaf with gluten-free nonstick spray. Bake 35 minutes or until golden. *Makes 6 1½-inch wedges.*

One wedge—Calories: 232; Total fat: 4.8 g; Saturated fat: 1 g; Cholesterol: 71 mg; Sodium: 285 mg; Carbohydrates: 39.3 g; Fiber: 1.7 g; Sugar: 8.7 g; Protein: 7.7 g

Blarney Chocolate Mousse

Strawberries make the perfect garnish. Dip the bottom half of each strawberry into melted chocolate, and lay it on waxed paper to dry.

1 packet gluten-free unflavored gelatin

¾ cup 1% milk

¾ cup semisweet chocolate chips

1 teaspoon vanilla

2 tablespoons gluten-free apricot brandy

2 cups gluten-free, frozen nondairy whipped topping, thawed

In a saucepan, sprinkle the gelatin over the milk; let stand 1 minute. Over low heat, stir until the gelatin dissolves, about 5 minutes. Add the chocolate chips; stir till completely melted. Remove from heat; stir in the vanilla and brandy. Cool till mixture mounds; fold in the whipped topping. Spoon into dessert bowls or a serving bowl; cover and refrigerate 4 hours. *Makes 4 ¾-cup servings.*

One serving—Calories: 299; Total fat: 16.2 g; Saturated fat: 10.8 g; Cholesterol: 2 mg; Sodium: 28 mg; Carbohydrates: 36.8 g; Fiber: 2.5 g; Sugar: 28.2 g; Protein: 3.3 g

Scandinavian Dinner

Decorate your table to reflect the sea culture of Finland, Norway, and Sweden. On a white tablecloth, gather a piece of royal blue material in the center of the table. Within the folds of the cloth, nestle 2 or 3 boats with masts and sails. After your guests have eaten their soup, bring out a Swedish *smorgasbord*, a light buffet of assorted foods. Group the Stuffed Snow Peas, Swedish Meatballs, Norwegian Fried Trout, Swedish Herring, Cucumber Salad, and Artichoke Appetizers on a couple of platters. Set the platters near the center of your table for guests to help themselves.

Finnish Seafood Soup

Almost any fish or shellfish may be used to make this soup.

5 cups water

¼ pound fresh salmon fillet

½ teaspoon salt

⅛ teaspoon black pepper

2 bay leaves

3 whole allspice seeds

1 large red potato, diced

1 carrot, diced

½ onion, sliced

½ red cabbage, sliced thin

1 rib celery, chopped

⅛ green bell pepper, minced

1 slice gluten-free bacon, diced

1 6½-ounce can minced clams

6 fresh medium shrimp, deveined and chopped

¼ cup chopped fresh mushrooms

⅛ teaspoon cumin

⅛ teaspoon thyme

⅛ teaspoon oregano

⅛ teaspoon rosemary, crushed

⅛ teaspoon red pepper flakes

¾ cup 2% milk

Bring 2 cups of the water to a boil in a small saucepan. Add the salmon, salt, and black pepper. Simmer till the fish is almost cooked through. Remove the salmon, reserving the fish stock. Break the fish into 1-inch pieces. Add the bay leaves and allspice to the stock in the saucepan. Add the potato, carrot, onion, cabbage, celery, and green bell pepper. Cover, and simmer till the vegetables are almost tender. In a small skillet, cook the bacon until crisp; drain and crumble. Put the bacon, salmon, clams with broth, shrimp, remaining 3 cups of water, mushrooms, cumin, thyme, oregano, rosemary, and red pepper flakes in the stock. Stir in the milk, a few tablespoons at a time. Cover and simmer for 1 hour. *Makes 6 1½-cup servings.*

One serving—Calories: 107; Total fat: 3.2 g; Saturated fat: 1 g; Cholesterol: 33 mg; Sodium: 272 mg; Carbohydrates: 10.2 g; Fiber: 1.1 g; Sugar: 2.4 g; Protein: 11.5 g

Stuffed Snow Peas

To keep snow peas crisp, wash them, then drain; put them in a small plastic bag with a paper towel folded on the bottom; refrigerate for at least an hour (or up to two days).

    3 tablespoons gluten-free cottage cheese
    1 tablespoon gluten-free cream cheese, softened
    1 tablespoon finely grated radish
    2 teaspoons minced green onion
    ⅛ teaspoon pepper
    ¼ teaspoon dill
    12 fresh snow peas

Stir together the cottage cheese, cream cheese, radish, green onion, pepper, and dill. Split the snow peas open lengthwise. Stuff with the cheese filling; cover and refrigerate for 1 to 8 hours. *Makes 6 servings (2 stuffed snow peas each).*

One serving—Calories: 23; Total fat: 1 g; Saturated fat: 0.7 g; Cholesterol: 3 mg; Sodium: 48 mg; Carbohydrates: 1.3 g; Fiber: 0.4 g; Sugar: 0.9 g; Protein: 2.3 g

Swedish Meatballs

Swedish meatballs are almost always to be found at a smorgasbord. Sprinkle the sauce with additional chopped parsley before serving.

¼ cup fresh gluten-free bread crumbs

3 tablespoons plus ¼ cup 2% milk

3 teaspoons gluten-free margarine

2 tablespoons minced onion

¼ pound 93% lean ground beef

¼ pound lean ground veal

1 egg

1 tablespoon minced fresh parsley

¼ teaspoon nutmeg

½ teaspoon paprika

½ teaspoon salt

½ teaspoon pepper

1 tablespoon cornstarch

½ teaspoon gluten-free beef bouillon granules

1 tablespoon dill weed

¼ cup water

¼ cup gluten-free sour cream

In a large bowl, soak the bread crumbs in 3 tablespoons of the milk for 5 minutes. Melt 1 teaspoon of the margarine in a non-stick skillet; add the onion, and sauté until limp. Add the onion to the bread crumbs. With your hands, mix in the ground beef, veal, egg, parsley, nutmeg, paprika, ¼ teaspoon of the salt, and ¼ teaspoon of the pepper. Cover; refrigerate 2 hours. Preheat oven to 350°F. Spray a cookie sheet with gluten-free nonstick spray. Shape tablespoons of the meat mixture into balls; lay on the cookie sheet. Bake 15 minutes till cooked through, turning often. In a saucepan, melt the remaining 2 teaspoons of marga-rine. Stir in the cornstarch, bouillon, dill, and the remaining ¼ teaspoon of salt and ¼ teaspoon of pepper. Slowly stir in the water and the remaining ¼ cup of milk. Cook over medium heat, stirring constantly, till thickened; stir in the sour cream. Spoon the sauce into a shallow dish; top with the meatballs. *Makes 6 4-meatball servings.*

One serving—Calories: 86; Total fat: 4.7 g; Saturated fat: 2.1 g; Cholesterol: 50 mg; Sodium: 250 mg; Carbohydrates: 2.5 g; Fiber: 0.1 g; Sugar: 0.7 g; Protein: 7.3 g

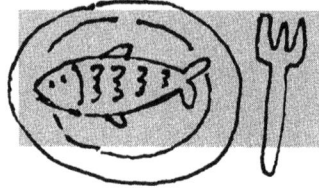

Norwegian Fried Trout

Sprinkle the fish with grated lemon zest just before serving. Set a bowl filled with the sour cream sauce on the side.

    2 fresh trout (½ pound each), cleaned and filleted
    ¼ teaspoon salt
    ¼ cup Gluten-Free Flour Mixture (See the Hints chapter.)
    4 teaspoons gluten-free margarine
    1 tablespoon olive oil
    ¼ cup gluten-free sour cream
    ¼ teaspoon lemon juice

Wash the fish under cold running water; pat dry. Sprinkle the salt inside and out. Cut the fish into bite-sized pieces. Put the flour mixture into a plastic bag. Add the fish pieces, and shake to coat evenly. Spray a skillet with gluten-free nonstick spray. Melt 2 teaspoons of the margarine and the olive oil together; add the fish, and fry 8 minutes or until browned, gently turning the pieces frequently with a large spatula. Remove the fish pieces to a serving platter. Add the remaining 2 teaspoons of margarine to the pan; over low heat, scrape up the browned pan drippings with a spoon. Stir in the sour cream, and continue cooking over very low heat for 2 minutes; do not let the sour cream boil. Stir in the lemon juice. Drizzle a little sauce over the fish; put the remaining sauce into a small bowl. *Makes 6 ⅓-cup servings.*

One serving—Calories: 205; Total fat: 11.8 g; Saturated fat: 3 g; Cholesterol: 56 mg; Sodium: 182 mg; Carbohydrates: 4 g; Fiber: 0.2 g; Sugar: 0.5 g; Protein: 19.7 g

Swedish Herring

In place of salted herring, 2 6-ounce cans of herring fillets may be used. Make this 3 days before you plan to serve it so flavors can blend. Use a noncorrosive saucepan for the vinegar mixture.

¾ cup gluten-free white wine vinegar

½ cup water

¼ cup sugar

1 salted herring (1½ pounds), cleaned, scraped, and soaked in
   cold water for 12 hours

2 small onions, thinly sliced

1½-inch piece of fresh horseradish root, shredded

1 carrot, thinly sliced

3 bay leaves

2¼ teaspoons whole allspice seeds

¾ teaspoon yellow mustard seeds

In a saucepan, boil the vinegar, water, and sugar, stirring constantly, till the sugar is dissolved. Remove from heat, and cool. Cut the herring into ¾-inch-thick pieces. Arrange one-third of the onions in a 1-quart glass dish. Top with one-third of the herring slices. Sprinkle with one-third of the horseradish and carrots, 1 bay leaf, ¾ teaspoon of the allspice, and ¼ teaspoon of the mustard seeds. Repeat the layers twice more. Pour the cooled vinegar mixture over the top. Cover with plastic wrap, and refrigerate 3 days. *Makes 6 ⅔-cup servings.*

One serving—Calories: 220; Total fat: 10.3 g; Saturated fat: 2.3 g; Cholesterol: 68 mg; Sodium: 181 mg; Carbohydrates: 10.7 g; Fiber: 1 g; Sugar: 5.7 g; Protein: 20.9 g

Cucumber Salad

If small, tender cucumbers are available, use 5 cucumbers, and do not peel their skins.

    1 teaspoon sugar
    ¼ teaspoon salt
    ¼ cup gluten-free, low-fat sour cream
    1 tablespoon grated onion
    1 teaspoon lemon juice
    2 large cucumbers, pared and sliced thin

In a bowl, stir together the sugar, salt, sour cream, onion, and lemon juice; fold in the cucumbers. Cover and chill 2 hours. *Makes 6 ⅓-cup servings.*

One serving—Calories: 32; Total fat: 1.8 g; Saturated fat: 1.2 g; Cholesterol: 3 mg; Sodium: 105 mg; Carbohydrates: 3.6 g; Fiber: 0.8 g; Sugar: 0.7 g; Protein: 1 g

Artichoke Appetizers

For the most eye appeal, put a different topping on each appetizer. On the side of each topping, insert accent greens such as parsley, cilantro, fresh dill, basil, rosemary, thyme, watercress, or short, thin slices of green onion (green part only).

    1 15-ounce can artichoke hearts, drained
    1½ tablespoons gluten-free, fat-free Italian dressing
    3 ounces gluten-free cream cheese, softened
    Garnishes—your choice of red or black caviar, shrimp, rolled
        cucumber slice, roasted red or yellow pepper, rolled anchovy,
        green or black olive slices, mushroom slice, button
        mushroom, cherry tomato slice, radish slice, grapes (green,
        red, or black), rolled lox, rolled dried beef, pimiento, browned
        chopped onion, shreds of zucchini

Cut each artichoke heart in half, and set the halves on a platter. Drizzle with the dressing. Whip the cream cheese till fluffy; put a dollop of cheese on each artichoke heart. Garnish each dollop with something different. *Makes 6 ¼-cup servings.*

One serving (without garnishes)—Calories: 97; Total fat: 5.1 g; Saturated fat: 3.1 g; Cholesterol: 14 mg; Sodium: 164 mg; Carbohydrates: 11.4 g; Fiber: 1.2 g; Sugar: 4.9 g; Protein: 3 g

Norwegian Potato Pancake Bread

Oddly enough, this bread turns out better if the potatoes are old—the older the better. The quicker you work with the potatoes, the lighter the bread will be. These pancake breads are traditionally used as a wrapper for cheese or thick slices of smoked ham, or on a smorgasbord.

2 medium golden potatoes
¾ teaspoon salt
¼ teaspoon sugar
¼ cup Gluten-Free Flour Mixture (See the Hints chapter.)

Cook the potatoes in their skins in a pot of boiling water. When cooked through, remove from water, and cool. Peel; mash with the salt and sugar. Sift the flour mixture; add to potatoes, and mix to form a dough. Add a little more flour only if needed, keeping in mind that the less flour used, the lighter the bread. Form the dough into a long sausage shape; cut into six slices. With a rolling pin, roll the slices into ⅛-inch-thick pancakes. Preheat a nonstick skillet on the stove; spray with gluten-free nonstick spray. Fry the pancake breads, turning once, until golden. *Makes 6 slices.*

One slice—Calories: 64; Total fat: 0.1 g; Saturated fat: 0 g; Cholesterol: 0 mg; Sodium: 310 mg; Carbohydrates: 14.9 g; Fiber: 1.2 g; Sugar: 0.3 g; Protein: 1.5 g

Finnish Fruit Soup

To garnish, dip 6 thin slices of lemon in cinnamon. Use the tip of a sharp knife to start a hole in the center of the 6 slices; insert a cinnamon stick through each hole, then lay on top of each fruit bowl. This soup may be served warm, cold, or at room temperature.

⅓ cup dried apricots

2 tablespoons raisins

½ cup prunes

3 cups cold water

2 cinnamon sticks

1 ½-inch-thick lemon slice

2 tablespoons tapioca

½ cup sugar

2 McIntosh apples, peeled, cored, and cut into ½-inch slices

In a large saucepan, soak the apricots, raisins, and prunes in the water for 30 minutes. Stir in the cinnamon sticks, lemon, tapioca, and sugar; bring to a boil. Reduce heat; cover and simmer 10 minutes, stirring frequently with a wooden spoon. Stir in the apples; simmer 5 minutes more or until the apples are tender but not mushy. Pour into a large bowl; let cool to room temperature. Remove the cinnamon stick; cover with plastic wrap, and refrigerate 3 hours to let the flavors blend. Spoon into fruit bowls to serve. *Makes 6 1-cup servings.*

One serving—Calories: 132; Total fat: 0.2 g; Saturated fat: 0 g; Cholesterol: 0 mg; Sodium: 5 mg; Carbohydrates: 33.8 g; Fiber: 2.7 g; Sugar: 24.2 g; Protein: 0.7 g

Picnics and Barbecues

icnics and barbecues are synonymous with "easy" foods. While picnics primarily involve precooked or reheatable foods, barbecues involve cooking foods on a grill. Marinating meats before grilling will impart both tenderness and added flavor. To help prevent foods from sticking to the grates, spray cold grill grates with gluten-free nonstick spray. These menus offer a wide variety. Make all the recipes for a crowd, or pick and choose for a smaller group.

Fried Chicken and Salads Picnic

Homemade Salsa

Picnics and barbeques lend themselves to snacking. Homemade salsa with gluten-free nacho chips for dipping combine for the perfect snack.

  1 tablespoon olive oil
  10 green onions, chopped

¼ cup green bell peppers, chopped

2 cloves garlic, minced

3 cups very ripe tomatoes, chopped

½ teaspoon oregano

2 tablespoons chopped canned jalapeño peppers

3 tablespoons chopped canned green chilies

3 tablespoons gluten-free white wine vinegar

3 tablespoons chopped fresh parsley

1 teaspoon sugar

1 teaspoon freshly squeezed lime juice

½ teaspoon salt

¼ teaspoon black pepper

Heat the olive oil in a large skillet. Add the green onions, bell peppers, and garlic; sauté till tender but not browned. Add the tomatoes and oregano; sauté 2 minutes. Stir in the jalapeño peppers, green chilies, vinegar, parsley, sugar, lime juice, salt, and black pepper. Transfer to a bowl; cover and refrigerate overnight to blend the flavors. *Makes 16 ¼-cup servings.*

One serving—Calories: 17; Total fat: 0.9 g; Saturated fat: 0.1 g; Cholesterol: 0 mg; Sodium: 109 mg; Carbohydrates: 2.1 g; Fiber: 0.5 g; Sugar: 0.7 g; Protein: 0.4 g

Spicy Chicken Wings

For a picnic, broil the wings just before leaving the house. If you are not going to be eating within an hour, cool the wings, wrap in foil, place in a reclosable, quart-size plastic bag, and put them in a cooler with ice. When it is time to eat, remove the foil packet from the plastic bag, and eat the chicken cold. Or you can warm the wings, in the foil, on a grill.

32 chicken wings

2 teaspoons olive oil

2 teaspoons cayenne

2 teaspoons paprika

¼ teaspoon salt

⅛ teaspoon black pepper

Dash red pepper flakes

½ teaspoon dill

¼ teaspoon cumin

2 tablespoons gluten-free balsamic vinegar

8 ounces apricot preserves

1 tablespoon gluten-free soy sauce

Preheat broiler. Separate the chicken wings at the joints, and remove and discard the wing tips. In a bowl, combine the olive oil, cayenne, paprika, salt, black pepper, and red pepper flakes; add the wings, and turn until well coated. Place the wings on a broiler pan rack; broil, turning occasionally, about 20 minutes or until crisp and golden. In a small bowl, stir together the dill, cumin, vinegar, apricot preserves, and soy sauce; serve with the wings as a dipping sauce. *Makes 16 4-piece servings.*

One serving—Calories: 160; Total fat: 9.3 g; Saturated fat: 2.4 g; Cholesterol: 44 mg; Sodium: 138 mg; Carbohydrates: 9.3 g; Fiber: 0.2 g; Sugar: 0 g; Protein: 10.2 g

Oven-Fried Chicken

What is a picnic without fried chicken? For the crumbs in the recipe, make Corn Muffins (see Index), then let two muffins air-dry for 2 days, covered lightly with waxed paper. When dry, crumble or whirl in a blender.

3 tablespoons Gluten-Free Flour Mixture (See the Hints chapter.)

¼ teaspoon salt

¼ teaspoon paprika

¼ teaspoon black pepper

¼ teaspoon thyme

¼ teaspoon garlic powder

⅛ teaspoon cayenne

⅛ teaspoon red pepper flakes

8 chicken drumsticks

1 egg white, beaten

3 tablespoons cold water

1 teaspoon olive oil

¾ cup Corn Muffin crumbs (See Index.)

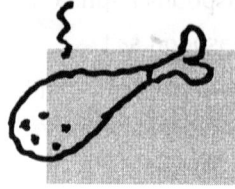

Preheat oven to 350°F. Sift together the flour mixture, salt, paprika, black pepper, thyme, garlic powder, cayenne, and red pepper flakes; transfer to a plastic bag. Add the drumsticks, and shake until evenly coated. In a shallow bowl, whisk together the egg white, water, and olive oil. Sprinkle the corn muffin crumbs on a plate. Spray a shallow baking sheet with gluten-free nonstick spray. Dip the drumsticks in the egg mixture, then in the bread crumbs. Set on the baking sheet. Bake 20 minutes; turn the chicken, and continue baking about 20 minutes or until golden and cooked through. (To ensure the chicken stays moist, do not overbake.) *Makes 4 2-piece servings.*

One serving—Calories: 334; Total fat: 13.1 g; Saturated fat: 6.5 g; Cholesterol: 93 mg; Sodium: 356 mg; Carbohydrates: 10.9 g; Fiber: 0.4 g; Sugar: 2.2 g; Protein: 21.1 g

Greek Pasta Salad

This salad is best made with ziti, but a gluten-free version of this small pasta is difficult to find. Elbow macaroni is suggested because it is readily available, but use the smallest form of gluten-free pasta available.

8 ounces gluten-free elbow macaroni or smaller pasta

2 large tomatoes, chopped

4 green onions, sliced

2 small cucumbers, cut lengthwise in half, then into ¼-inch slices

4 ounces gluten-free feta cheese, crumbled

½ green bell pepper, chopped

4 teaspoons dill weed

2 tablespoons minced fresh parsley

6 tablespoons olive oil

½ teaspoon salt

¼ teaspoon black pepper

1 teaspoon oregano

½ teaspoon garlic powder

Cook the macaroni al dente following package directions; rinse with cold water, and drain well. Put the macaroni in a large bowl, and add the tomatoes, onions, cucumbers, cheese, and green bell pepper. In a small bowl, whisk together dill, parsley, olive oil, salt, black pepper, oregano, and garlic powder; pour over pasta and toss to coat evenly. Cover; refrigerate 3 hours for flavors to blend. *Makes 8 ½-cup servings.*

One serving—Calories: 246; Total fat: 13.5 g; Saturated fat: 3.6 g; Cholesterol: 13 mg; Sodium: 824 mg; Carbohydrates: 25.5 g; Fiber: 1 g; Sugar: 0 g; Protein: 5.4 g

Greek Potato Salad

This is the perfect picnic salad. It won't wilt, it may be left out without refrigeration for at least 2 hours, and there is no dressing or sauce to spill during transport to the picnic site.

2 pounds Idaho potatoes, boiled, peeled, and cooled

1 thinly sliced onion

½ cup chopped celery

½ cup chopped green bell pepper

2 tablespoons chopped fresh parsley

6 tablespoons olive oil

4 tablespoons apple cider vinegar

½ teaspoon salt

¼ teaspoon black pepper

Dice the potatoes into a large bowl. Add the onion, celery, green bell pepper, parsley, olive oil, vinegar, salt, and black pepper; mix very gently till evenly coated. Cover, and refrigerate 2 hours to allow flavors to blend. Toss again just before serving. *Makes 8 ¾-cup servings.*

One serving—Calories: 205; Total fat: 10.3 g; Saturated fat: 1.5 g; Cholesterol: 0 mg; Sodium: 226 mg; Carbohydrates: 26.8 g; Fiber: 1.5 g; Sugar: 0.5 g; Protein: 2.8 g

Marinated Bean Salad

Make this salad at least 6 hours before serving to allow the flavors to blend. At a picnic, the salad will hold several hours without refrigeration.

> 1 14-ounce can kidney beans
> 1 14-ounce can black beans
> 1 14-ounce can lima beans
> 1 14-ounce can Great Northern beans
> 1 14-ounce can garbanzo beans
> 2 onions, sliced
> 1 green bell pepper, chopped
> 1 tablespoon dill
> ¼ teaspoon mint
> ¼ teaspoon garlic powder
> ¼ teaspoon salt
> ¼ teaspoon black pepper
> ¼ teaspoon oregano
> 4 tablespoons olive oil
> 2 tablespoons gluten-free balsamic vinegar

Rinse the beans in a colander, then drain; transfer the beans to a bowl. Add the onions and green bell pepper. In a smaller bowl, whisk together the dill, mint, garlic powder, salt, black pepper, oregano, olive oil, and vinegar. Pour the dressing over the vegetables, and toss till the beans are evenly coated. Cover and refrigerate for 6 hours. *Makes 16 ⅓-cup servings.*

One serving—Calories: 112; Total fat: 3.8 g; Saturated fat: 0.5 g; Cholesterol: 0 mg; Sodium: 282 mg; Carbohydrates: 16.4 g; Fiber: 3.9 g; Sugar: 0.7 g; Protein: 5.2 g

Baked Beans

To warm baked beans at a picnic, put them in a foil pan, cover with foil, then set on the grill, stirring occasionally, till warmed.

    2 16-ounce cans gluten-free pork and beans
    4 tablespoons unsulfured molasses
    4 slices gluten-free bacon, cooked crisp, then crumbled
    1 teaspoon light brown sugar
    1 teaspoon gluten-free Worcestershire sauce

Preheat oven to 350°F. Stir together all ingredients in an 8-inch square glass baking dish. Cover with foil, and bake 30 minutes. *Makes 8 ½-cup servings.*

One serving—Calories: 116; Total fat: 2 g; Saturated fat: 0.5 g; Cholesterol: 3 mg; Sodium: 338 mg; Carbohydrates: 20.6 g; Fiber: 0.2 g; Sugar: 2.6 g; Protein: 4.5 g

Vegetable Pasta Salad

Rinsing chick-peas washes away much of the "gas" element—but also nutrients. You decide whether to rinse or not.

    8 ounces gluten-free elbow macaroni
    1 16-ounce can chick-peas, rinsed and drained
    ½ bunch broccoli, cut into small florets
    ½ cup frozen peas
    ½ green bell pepper, chopped
    6 green onions, sliced
    16 cherry tomatoes, cut in half

6 tablespoons olive oil

4 tablespoons apple cider vinegar

½ teaspoon minced garlic

½ teaspoon salt

¼ teaspoon black pepper

½ teaspoon dill weed

Cook the macaroni al dente according to the package directions; rinse with cold water, and drain well. Transfer to a bowl. Add the chick-peas, broccoli, peas, green bell pepper, green onions, and tomatoes. In another bowl, whisk the olive oil, vinegar, garlic, salt, black pepper, and dill. Pour the dressing over the salad, and toss till the pasta and vegetables are evenly coated. Cover, and refrigerate for 3 hours to blend flavors. *Makes 4 1-cup servings.*

One serving—Calories: 155; Total fat: 11.6 g; Saturated fat: 1.4 g; Cholesterol: 0 mg; Sodium: 775 mg; Carbohydrates: 31.8 g; Fiber: 3.9 g; Sugar: 0 g; Protein: 6.4 g

Asian Broccoli Salad

Cover and refrigerate overnight to blend flavors. This salad is so colorful, it doesn't need a garnish.

2 pounds broccoli florets

2 14-ounce cans baby corn, drained

2 red bell peppers, cut into thin strips

4 tablespoons slivered blanched almonds

2 tablespoons sesame seeds

4 tablespoons peanut oil

4 cloves garlic, crushed

4 teaspoons gluten-free soy sauce

4 teaspoons honey

4 teaspoons lemon juice

¼ teaspoon salt

¼ teaspoon black pepper

Blanch the broccoli by boiling 3 minutes or till tender-crisp. Drain; rinse with cold water, then drain again. Transfer to a large bowl; add the corn, red pepper, and almonds. Warm a dry skillet and add the sesame seeds. Cook over medium heat about 1 minute, stirring constantly, until lightly browned. Whisk together the peanut oil, garlic, soy sauce, honey, lemon juice, salt, and black pepper; stir in the sesame seeds. Pour the dressing over the salad, and toss. Cover, and refrigerate for 2 hours. *Makes 8 1-cup servings.*

One serving—Calories: 140; Total fat: 7.3 g; Saturated fat: 1 g; Cholesterol: 0 mg; Sodium: 424 mg; Carbohydrates: 15.1 g; Fiber: 4.1 g; Sugar: 7.3 g; Protein: 7 g

Asian Cole Slaw

If you don't have rice vinegar, substitute apple cider vinegar.

½ cup rice vinegar

1½ tablespoons sesame oil

2 teaspoons olive oil

½ teaspoon salt

¼ teaspoon pepper

1 head savoy cabbage, thinly sliced and tough ribs discarded

1 pound carrots, shredded

5 green onions, thinly sliced

½ cup chopped fresh parsley

1 tablespoon poppy seeds

In a large bowl, whisk together the vinegar, sesame and olive oils, salt, and pepper. Add the cabbage, carrots, green onions, parsley, and poppy seeds, tossing well to coat evenly. Cover, and refrigerate for 2 hours. *Makes 8 ¾-cup servings.*

One serving—Calories: 67; Total fat: 4 g; Saturated fat: 0.7 g; Cholesterol: 0 mg; Sodium: 178 mg; Carbohydrates: 7.9 g; Fiber: 4.2 g; Sugar: 2.5 g; Protein: 1.3 g

Jalapeño Corn Bread

No flour is used in this recipe. When chopping jalapeño peppers, wear plastic gloves to avoid burning your fingers.

    3 cups yellow cornmeal
    ½ cup sugar
    ½ teaspoon salt
    2 cups boiling water
    3 tablespoons corn oil
    1 cup skim milk
    2 eggs, slightly beaten
    ¼ cup shredded gluten-free sharp cheddar cheese
    ¼ cup minced red bell pepper
    ¼ cup minced onion
    1½ tablespoons gluten-free baking powder
    1 teaspoon minced jalapeño pepper
    ⅛ teaspoon red pepper flakes

Preheat oven to 400°F. In a bowl, combine the cornmeal, sugar, and salt. Stir in the water and corn oil, then the milk and eggs, mixing well. Stir in the cheese, bell pepper, onion, baking powder, jalapeño pepper, and red pepper flakes. Spray a 9″ × 13″ pan with gluten-free nonstick spray. Spoon the batter into the pan. Bake 40 minutes or until a toothpick inserted in the center comes out clean. Cut into 24 pieces. *Makes 24 3- by 1½-inch servings.*

One serving—Calories: 87; Total fat: 3 g; Saturated fat: 0.6 g; Cholesterol: 19 mg; Sodium: 67 mg; Carbohydrates: 13.5 g; Fiber: 0.7 g; Sugar: 2.9 g; Protein: 2.1 g

Mandarin Orange Salad

This is more of a dessert than a salad. For a picnic, put plenty of ice in the cooler; the salad needs to be kept cold. The canned fruits should be packed in juice (not heavy syrup).

- 1 14-ounce can sliced peaches
- 1 14-ounce can sliced pears
- 1 14-ounce can apricot halves
- 1 14-ounce can pineapple tidbits
- 1 14-ounce can mandarin oranges
- ½ cup chopped walnuts
- 1½ cups gluten-free miniature marshmallows
- 1 8-ounce container gluten-free, frozen nondairy whipped topping, thawed

Drain the peaches, pears, apricots, pineapple, and oranges. Cut the peaches, pears, and apricots into bite-sized pieces. In a bowl, gently fold all ingredients together. Cover, and chill for 3 hours before serving. *Makes 18 ½-cup servings.*

One serving—Calories: 88; Total fat: 2.3 g; Saturated fat: 2.1 g; Cholesterol: 0 mg; Sodium: 4 mg; Carbohydrates: 12.3 g; Fiber: 0.8 g; Sugar: 10.4 g; Protein: 0.4 g

Baby Back Ribs Barbecue

Grilled Baby Back Ribs

While this entree is not exactly low in calories, it has far fewer calories than conventionally prepared ribs. By boiling the ribs first, you reduce the fat and ensure that the meat will be cooked through. Usually a low-calorie entree (meat, fish, poultry) weighs about 5 ounces; with ribs, you have to allow more per person because of the weight of the bones. This recipe is equally good when you substitute 2 pounds bone-in chicken pieces for the ribs.

    2 pounds lean baby back ribs
    ⅛ teaspoon salt
    ¼ teaspoon pepper
    ¼ teaspoon garlic powder
    1 teaspoon minced fresh parsley
    1 tablespoon lemon juice
    2 teaspoons gluten-free soy sauce
    1 tablespoon gluten-free Worcestershire sauce
    2 tablespoons olive oil
    2 tablespoons light brown sugar
    ¼ cup gluten-free ketchup

Cut off any visible fat from the ribs; cut each slab in half. Put the ribs in a large pot, cover with water, and bring to a boil. Lower heat, and simmer 20 minutes; drain. Line a baking sheet with plastic wrap; place the ribs on the baking sheet. In a bowl, whisk together the salt, pepper, garlic powder, parsley, lemon juice, soy sauce, Worcestershire sauce, and olive oil. Brush the marinade on both sides of the meat. Cover with plastic wrap, and refrigerate 3 hours. Prepare grill. In a small bowl, stir together the brown sugar and ketchup, adding remaining marinade from the rib pan.

Place the ribs on the grill, and cook over medium heat about 25 minutes, turning and basting frequently with sauce. *Makes 6 ⅓-pound servings.*

One serving—Calories: 389; Total fat: 22.3 g; Saturated fat: 6.7 g; Cholesterol: 105 mg; Sodium: 384 mg; Carbohydrates: 5.5 g; Fiber: 0.2 g; Sugar: 5.1 g; Protein: 29 g

Foil Potatoes and Vegetables

Potatoes may be cut the day before; put the cut potatoes in a bowl of water, cover, and refrigerate till ready to use.

    6 medium red potatoes, cut into eighths
    16 baby carrots
    4 ribs celery, cut in quarters
    2 medium onions, cut in eighths
    2 zucchini, cut in quarters
    2 tablespoons chopped fresh parsley
    4 teaspoons olive oil
    2 tablespoons gluten-free white wine
    1 teaspoon lemon juice
    2 teaspoons dill weed
    ½ teaspoon oregano
    ½ teaspoon garlic powder
    ¼ teaspoon pepper
    ¼ teaspoon salt
    1 teaspoon paprika

Prepare grill. Cut four pieces of foil, each approximately 8″ × 10″. Place the potatoes, carrots, celery, onions, and zucchini on the foil sheets, dividing evenly. Whisk together the parsley, olive oil, wine, lemon juice, dill, oregano, garlic powder, pepper, salt, and paprika; drizzle over the vegetables. Seal the foil packets well; place on grill, and cook over medium heat about 25 minutes, turning packets occasionally, until the potatoes are tender. *Makes 8 ⅔-cup servings.*

One serving—Calories: 159; Total fat: 2.6 g; Saturated fat: 0.4 g; Cholesterol: 0 mg; Sodium: 104 mg; Carbohydrates: 30.6 g; Fiber: 5 g; Sugar: 3.5 g; Protein: 2.7 g

Grilled Tomato Salad

Use only firm tomatoes for this salad. Garnish by tucking a few watercress sprigs around the edge of the salad.

½ cup orange juice

8 teaspoons olive oil

½ teaspoon basil

4 large tomatoes, cut into ½-inch slices

2 medium red onions, cut into ½-inch slices

¼ teaspoon salt

¼ teaspoon pepper

10 ounces gluten-free mozzarella cheese,
    cut into ¼-inch slices

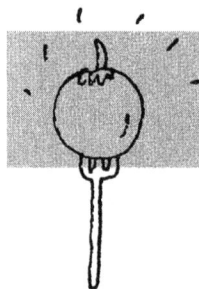

Prepare grill. In a small saucepan, bring the juice to a boil; reduce heat; simmer till juice is reduced to 2 tablespoons. Remove from heat; whisk in 5 teaspoons of the olive oil and the basil. Brush the tomato and onion slices on both sides with the remaining 3 teaspoons of oil; sprinkle with the salt and pepper. Grill the tomato and onion slices on high heat for 2 minutes per side or just till charred. Arrange overlapping slices of tomato, onion, and mozzarella on a serving platter. Drizzle with the orange dressing. *Makes 8 ¾-cup servings.*

One serving—Calories: 175; Total fat: 10.8 g; Saturated fat: 4.5 g; Cholesterol: 19 mg; Sodium: 346 mg; Carbohydrates: 9.3 g; Fiber: 1.5 g; Sugar: 1.6 g; Protein: 10.9 g

Autumn Fruit Kabobs

Dip cut apples and pears in lemon juice before threading on the skewers. The lemon juice prevents the fruits from browning.

  1 orange, peeled, membrane removed, and sections separated
  2 Delicious apples, each cut into 6 wedges
  2 Bartlett pears, each cut into 6 wedges
  1 teaspoon lemon juice
  2 teaspoons corn oil
  1 tablespoon honey
  1 tablespoon light corn syrup
  ¼ teaspoon cinnamon
  ⅛ teaspoon ground cloves

Prepare grill. Alternately thread the fruits onto skewers. Mix the lemon juice, corn oil, honey, corn syrup, cinnamon, and cloves. Grill the kabobs over high heat for 5 minutes, turning frequently and brushing with the marinade, till lightly browned. *Makes 6 kabobs.*

One kabob—Calories: 104; Total fat: 2 g; Saturated fat: 0.2 g; Cholesterol: 0 mg; Sodium: 5 mg; Carbohydrates: 23.4 g; Fiber: 3.2 g; Sugar: 10.5 g; Protein: 0.7 g

Chicken Barbecue

Maple Barbecued Chicken

Marinating poultry not only tenderizes the meat but allows the chicken to absorb the flavors.

  2 tablespoons gluten-free white wine vinegar
  1 tablespoon lemon juice
  ½ teaspoon salt
  ½ teaspoon pepper

2 tablespoons olive oil

4 4-ounce bone-in chicken breasts

1 small onion, minced

2 teaspoons gluten-free Worcestershire sauce

¼ cup gluten-free chicken broth

1 teaspoon gluten-free brown mustard

2 tablespoons gluten-free ketchup

1 tablespoon apple cider vinegar

2 tablespoons maple syrup

In a bowl, whisk together the wine vinegar, lemon juice, salt, pepper, and olive oil. Put the chicken in a reclosable, quart-size plastic bag; add the marinade. Seal the bag, and refrigerate for 3 hours. Light the grill and spray it with gluten-free nonstick spray. Remove the chicken from the marinade. Pour the marinade into a bowl, and stir in the onion, Worcestershire sauce, chicken broth, mustard, ketchup, cider vinegar, and maple syrup. Grill the chicken, turning once, 10 minutes per side or until the chicken is cooked through. During cooking, frequently baste the chicken with the maple syrup sauce. *Makes 4 breasts.*

One breast—Calories: 250; Total fat: 11.3 g; Saturated fat: 2 g; Cholesterol: 49 mg; Sodium: 616 mg; Carbohydrates: 11.1 g; Fiber: 0.6 g; Sugar: 8.5 g; Protein: 25.4 g

Apricot Yams

Use a wide metal spatula to turn the sweet potatoes. Turn the sweet potatoes frequently to prevent them sticking to the grates.

2 yams

¼ cup reduced-sugar apricot preserves, pureed

2 tablespoons gluten-free white wine

2 cloves garlic, minced

¼ teaspoon salt

¼ teaspoon pepper

Prepare grill. Prick the sweet potatoes with a fork, and microwave on high for 5 minutes (or bake at 350°F for 30 minutes) till partially cooked. Peel the sweet potatoes, and quarter them lengthwise. Mix the preserves and wine. Mash the garlic with the salt and pepper to form a paste; stir into the preserves. Brush the grill with corn oil to prevent the sweet potatoes from sticking. Grill the sweet potatoes over medium-high heat for 2 minutes. Brush the grilled surface of the sweet potatoes with the glaze, and continue to grill for a total of 20 minutes, turning and brushing with glaze every 2 minutes until the sweet potatoes are shiny and crisp on the outside and tender on the inside. *Makes 4 half-potato servings.*

One serving—Calories: 194; Total fat: 0.2 g; Saturated fat: 0 g; Cholesterol: 0 mg; Sodium: 120 mg; Carbohydrates: 48.4 g; Fiber: 0.2 g; Sugar: 1 g; Protein: 3.1 g

Grilled Portobello Salad

For a special touch, add toasted sesame or sunflower seeds to the salad.

1 tablespoon olive oil

1 clove garlic, minced

½ teaspoon gluten-free brown mustard

2 teaspoons lemon juice

2 teaspoons gluten-free balsamic vinegar

⅛ teaspoon salt

⅛ teaspoon black pepper

1 tablespoon minced fresh parsley

2 portobello mushrooms

1 red bell pepper, quartered

4 cups mixed salad greens

2 ounces goat cheese, crumbled

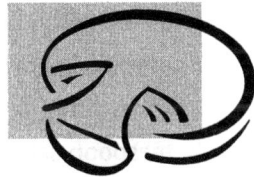

Prepare grill. In a bowl, whisk together the olive oil, garlic, mustard, lemon juice, vinegar, salt, black pepper, and parsley. Add the mushrooms and bell pepper, and stir to distribute the marinade evenly. Let set for 15 minutes. Remove the bell pepper and mushrooms from the marinade; and grill a few minutes per side over high heat till slightly charred, turning once. Slice the mushrooms. Divide the salad greens among four salad plates. Top the salads with the mushrooms and bell peppers. Drizzle the remaining marinade over the salads. Sprinkle with the goat cheese. *Makes 4 1¾-cup servings.*

One serving—Calories: 106; Total fat: 8 g; Saturated fat: 3.4 g; Cholesterol: 11 mg; Sodium: 156 mg; Carbohydrates: 5.7 g; Fiber: 2.2 g; Sugar: 0.8 g; Protein: 5 g

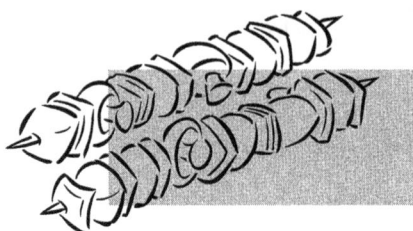

Kabob Barbecue

Lamb Kabobs

After grilling the lamb (or any meat or fish), place the food on a warm platter, and keep it warm in a 175°F oven for 5 minutes to let the juices flow from the center of the food to the outside.

- 3 tablespoons gluten-free white wine
- 3 tablespoons olive oil
- 3 cloves garlic, minced
- ¼ teaspoon salt
- ¼ teaspoon black pepper
- 1 teaspoon minced fresh parsley
- ⅛ teaspoon mint, crushed

1½ pounds lean leg of lamb, cut into 1-inch cubes

2 tablespoons lemon juice

1 large green bell pepper, cut into 12 pieces

1 red onion, cut into 12 pieces

Whisk together the wine, olive oil, garlic, salt, black pepper, parsley, and mint. Put the meat in a reclosable, quart-size plastic bag; pour the marinade over the meat. Seal the bag, and refrigerate the meat overnight. Prepare grill. Add the lemon juice to the bag, and let the meat marinate 30 minutes at room temperature. Thread the lamb, green pepper, and onion alternately on six skewers; lay in a pan lined with plastic wrap. Brush any remaining marinade over the kabobs. Place on the grill over highest setting, turning the kabobs, for about 2 minutes until seared on all sides. Lower the heat to medium on a gas grill, or move the coals to the edges of the grill to cook with indirect heat, and cook about 8 minutes, turning frequently, until the meat is just cooked through. *Makes 6 kabobs.*

One kabob—Calories: 290; Total fat: 17.8 g; Saturated fat: 5.4 g; Cholesterol: 63 mg; Sodium: 176 mg; Carbohydrates: 5.2 g; Fiber: 1.1 g; Sugar: 0.8 g; Protein: 18.7 g

Garlic Potato Kabobs

Select potatoes that are uniform in size for even cooking. Prick the potato skins several times before cooking.

3 garlic cloves, peeled

¼ teaspoon salt

½ teaspoon pepper

⅛ teaspoon gluten-free chili powder

¼ teaspoon paprika

¼ teaspoon dill weed

2 tablespoons olive oil

12 small whole red potatoes

Smash the garlic cloves with the wide part of a knife. Place the garlic cloves, salt, pepper, chili powder, paprika, and dill in a bowl, then add the olive oil. Cover and store in a dark place for two days to ferment. Prepare grill. Cut the potatoes in half. Thread the potatoes on four skewers; grill on high heat until crispy, basting frequently with the garlic oil. *Makes 4 3-potato servings.*

One serving—Calories: 249; Total fat: 7.1 g; Saturated fat: 1 g; Cholesterol: 0 mg; Sodium: 164 mg; Carbohydrates: 41.9 g; Fiber: 4.3 g; Sugar: 3.7 g; Protein: 5 g

Vegetable Kabobs

If using wooden skewers, soak them in water 1 hour before threading with vegetables. This prevents the skewers from scorching during grilling.

  1 zucchini, cut into 8 slices

  1 yellow squash, cut into 8 slices

  1 red bell pepper, cut into 8 pieces

  8 cherry tomatoes

  8 button mushrooms

  8 canned artichoke hearts

  1 tablespoon olive oil

  1 tablespoon gluten-free balsamic vinegar

  1 clove garlic, crushed

  ½ teaspoon oregano

  ⅛ teaspoon salt

  ¼ teaspoon black pepper

Thread the zucchini, yellow squash, bell pepper, tomatoes, mushrooms, and artichoke hearts on eight skewers; place on a baking sheet lined with plastic wrap. Whisk together the olive oil, vinegar, garlic, oregano, salt, and black pepper; pour over the kabobs. Cover with plastic wrap, and refrigerate 2 hours.

Prepare grill. Place the skewers on the grill, and cook 3 minutes on each side over very high flame. The vegetables should be tender-crisp. *Makes 8 kabobs.*

One kabob—Calories: 43; Total fat: 2 g; Saturated fat: 0.3 g; Cholesterol: 0 mg; Sodium: 110 mg; Carbohydrates: 6.2 g; Fiber: 2.3 g; Sugar: 0.2 g; Protein: 1.9 g

Salmon Barbecue

Honey Mustard Salmon

No oil is used in this recipe. Grill the fish over medium-high heat. If the fire is not hot enough, it will not caramelize the honey, which is needed to form a shiny crust. Too hot a fire will burn the outside before the inside is cooked through.

- 1 tablespoon gluten-free soy sauce
- 1 tablespoon dry mustard
- 2 teaspoons apple cider vinegar
- 4 tablespoons honey
- 4 4-ounce salmon fillets

Prepare grill. Whisk together the soy sauce, mustard, vinegar, and honey; warm in a small pan. Remove the skin from the salmon. Grill over medium-high heat, turning once. When the fish is about halfway cooked, begin brushing with the honey mustard sauce. *Makes 4 4-ounce servings.*

One serving—Calories: 285; Total fat: 13 g; Saturated fat: 2.5 g; Cholesterol: 68 mg; Sodium: 289 mg; Carbohydrates: 17.7 g; Fiber: 0 g; Sugar: 16 g; Protein: 24 g

Foil Potatoes

These may be assembled and refrigerated several hours before grilling.

    2 14-ounce cans sliced potatoes, drained
    2 tablespoons minced green onion
    1½ tablespoons olive oil
    ¼ teaspoon garlic powder
    ¼ teaspoon gluten-free chili powder
    1 tablespoon paprika
    ⅛ teaspoon salt
    ¼ teaspoon pepper

Prepare grill. Divide the potatoes among four 12-inch-square pieces of foil. Sprinkle each with green onion. Stir together the olive oil, garlic powder, chili powder, paprika, salt, and pepper; drizzle over the potatoes. Seal the packets well. Grill over high heat 10 minutes, turning frequently. *Makes 4 ½-cup servings.*

One serving—Calories: 192; Total fat: 5.2 g; Saturated fat: 0.7 g; Cholesterol: 0 mg; Sodium: 83 mg; Carbohydrates: 34.2 g; Fiber: 0.7 g; Sugar: 0 g; Protein: 3 g

Baby Eggplant Parmigiana

Baby eggplants are seasonal and a different treat to offer your guests. They usually weigh less than ¼ of a pound each and are very tender and sweet.

    4 baby eggplants
    1½ tablespoons olive oil
    2 tablespoons gluten-free white wine
    1 tablespoon plus 2 teaspoons chopped fresh parsley
    1 small clove garlic, minced
    ¼ teaspoon salt
    ¼ teaspoon pepper

¼ teaspoon oregano

¼ teaspoon basil

2 ounces shredded gluten-free mozzarella cheese

4 tablespoons gluten-free spaghetti sauce, warmed

Prepare grill. Cut the eggplants into fans by making ¼-inch-thick lengthwise cuts beginning at the bottom ends and cutting toward the stem ends, leaving the stems intact. Press down with the heel of your hand at the stem end of each eggplant to gently fan the slices. In a small bowl, combine the olive oil, wine, 1 tablespoon of the parsley, and the garlic, salt, pepper, oregano, and basil. Brush both sides of the eggplant slices with the dressing. Grill about 5 minutes on high heat, turning once, basting frequently. Sprinkle the cheese on the eggplant, and grill 1 minute more to allow the cheese to melt. Transfer to a platter, and drizzle with the spaghetti sauce. Sprinkle with the remaining 2 teaspoons of chopped parsley. *Makes 4 baby eggplants.*

One baby eggplant—Calories: 123; Total fat: 8.3 g; Saturated fat: 0.8 g; Cholesterol: 0 mg; Sodium: 346 mg; Carbohydrates: 7.9 g; Fiber: 2.9 g; Sugar: 0.9 g; Protein: 4.8 g

Tomato Feta Salad

Cubanelle peppers are abundant in the summer and fall. If you don't mind a few extra calories and a little more sodium, add 3 or 4 kalamata olives to each salad.

1 head Bibb lettuce

4 cubanelle peppers

4 plum tomatoes

¼ teaspoon salt

¼ teaspoon black pepper

4 teaspoons olive oil

1 tablespoon minced fresh parsley

2 tablespoons crumbled gluten-free feta cheese

Prepare grill. Divide the lettuce evenly among four salad plates. Slice the cubanelle peppers and the tomatoes in half lengthwise. Grill the peppers over high heat, turning several times, 10 minutes or until lightly charred. Grill the tomatoes about 1 minute on each side, or until lightly charred. Lay the peppers and tomatoes on top of the lettuce, dividing evenly. Sprinkle with the salt and black pepper; drizzle with the olive oil. Sprinkle with the parsley and feta cheese. *Makes 4 1¼-cup servings.*

One serving—Calories: 92; Total fat: 6.4 g; Saturated fat: 1.9 g; Cholesterol: 6.2 mg; Sodium: 235 mg; Carbohydrates: 7.6 g; Fiber: 2.1 g; Sugar: 0 g; Protein: 2.5 g

7

Desserts

Often the most difficult part of gluten-free and reduced-calorie eating is dessert. But it doesn't have to be that way—try some of these tasty treats. Desserts of different ethnicities are in Chapter 5's ethnic dinners, so be sure to look there, too.

Fruit-Based Desserts

Spiced Peaches

This light and refreshing dessert may be made ahead and stored, covered, in the refrigerator for several days. Merely reheat the peaches on the stove when ready to serve. Spiced Peaches are excellent served over vanilla yogurt.

2 20-ounce cans sliced peaches, packed in juice

¼ teaspoon cinnamon

1 teaspoon light brown sugar

Drain the peaches, reserving 5 tablespoons of the juice. Put the peaches, reserved juice, cinnamon, and brown sugar in a medium-size saucepan; warm, stirring occasionally to blend ingredients. Serve warm. *Makes 6 ⅓-cup servings.*

One serving—Calories: 75; Total fat: 0 g; Saturated fat: 0 g; Cholesterol: 0 mg; Sodium: 7 mg; Carbohydrates: 14.1 g; Fiber: 2.1 g; Sugar: 11.5 g; Protein: 1 g

Layered Fruit Bowls

Use any fresh fruits that are in season, or substitute canned fruit (drain canned fruit before using it).

1 cup gluten-free, low-fat cottage cheese

¼ cup sliced fresh strawberries

1 kiwi, peeled and sliced

¼ cup black raspberries

¼ cup apricot nectar

Divide the cottage cheese among four fruit dishes. Place the strawberries, kiwi slices, and raspberries on top of the cottage cheese; drizzle the nectar over the top. *Makes 4 ½-cup servings.*

One serving—Calories: 83; Total fat: 0.6 g; Saturated fat: 0.2 g; Cholesterol: 0 mg; Sodium: 182 mg; Carbohydrates: 11.1 g; Fiber: 1 g; Sugar: 6.2 g; Protein: 8.4 g

Cinnamon Apples

Almonds or walnuts may be used in place of the pecans.

- 1 McIntosh cooking apple
- 1 teaspoon corn oil
- 1 teaspoon gluten-free margarine
- 2 tablespoons chopped pecans
- ¼ teaspoon cinnamon

Cut the apple in half, and core it. Cut each half into 4 wedges. Heat the corn oil and margarine in a nonstick skillet until foamy. Add the apple wedges, and sauté over high heat 1 minute. Sprinkle with pecans and cinnamon; cook another 3 to 4 minutes until the apples are glazed and crisp-tender. Serve warm. *Makes 4 2-wedge servings.*

One serving–Calories: 60; Total fat: 4.4 g; Saturated fat: 0.4 g; Cholesterol: 0 mg; Sodium: 12 mg; Carbohydrates: 5.8 g; Fiber: 1.2 g; Sugar: 4.1 g; Protein: 0.2 g

Apricot Cherry Compote

Juice-packed peach halves may be substituted for the apricots, and pear halves may be substituted for the cherries.

- 1 15-ounce can apricot halves with syrup
- ⅓ cup apricot nectar
- 2 teaspoons cornstarch
- 1 tablespoon cold water
- 3 teaspoons light brown sugar
- 4 pitted prunes
- 1 15-ounce can pitted sweet cherries, drained
- 2 tablespoons unsweetened coconut

Pour 1 cup of syrup from the canned apricots into a saucepan. Add the apricot nectar, and boil till the volume is reduced to

½ cup. In a small bowl, stir together the cornstarch and water; stir into the syrup with a whisk. Stir in the brown sugar. Simmer the syrup, stirring constantly, 20 seconds or until thickened. Add the prunes, drained apricots, and drained cherries. Simmer, uncovered, 5 minutes or until heated through. Spoon into 6 fruit dishes. Toast the coconut, and sprinkle on top of the compotes. *Makes 6 ½-cup servings.*

One serving—Calories: 96; Total fat: 1 g; Saturated fat: 0.2 g; Cholesterol: 0 mg; Sodium: 5 mg; Carbohydrates: 25.3 g; Fiber: 0.8 g; Sugar: 8.3 g; Protein: 1 g

Brandied Cherry Compote

If you prefer to leave out the brandy, stir in 1 teaspoon of gluten-free almond extract instead.

⅔ cup dried cherries

¼ cup sugar

1 ½ cups plus 1 tablespoon cold water

1 ¼ teaspoons cornstarch

¼ cup finely chopped walnuts

3 tablespoons gluten-free brandy

2 cups gluten-free frozen cherry yogurt

In a small saucepan, stir together the cherries, sugar, and 1½ cups of the water; simmer 10 minutes or until the liquid is reduced to 1 cup. Dissolve the cornstarch in 1 tablespoon of cold water; add it to the cherry mixture. Simmer, stirring, 2 minutes. Stir in the walnuts. Remove from heat; stir in the brandy. Spoon the yogurt into 4 dessert bowls; spoon the cherry sauce over the top. *Makes 4 ½-cup servings (with ½ cup topping).*

One serving—Calories: 268; Total fat: 8.5 g; Saturated fat: 2.9 g; Cholesterol: 1 mg; Sodium: 65 mg; Carbohydrates: 44.6 g; Fiber: 1.2 g; Sugar: 21 g; Protein: 3.9 g

Berry Pecan Cobbler

This cobbler may be assembled ahead, then covered and refrigerated for up to 24 hours before baking.

¾ cup sugar

3 tablespoons cornstarch

1 cup chopped fresh strawberries

1 cup fresh red raspberries

1 cup fresh blueberries

2 egg whites

⅛ teaspoon salt

1½ cups pecans, finely chopped

Preheat oven to 350°F. In a bowl, stir together ½ cup of the sugar and the cornstarch; add the berries, and toss to coat. Spoon the mixture into a 9-inch pie plate. Whip the egg whites till foamy; gradually add the remaining ¼ cup of sugar and the salt; beat just until stiff peaks form. Fold in the pecans. Drop teaspoonfuls of pecan mixture over the top of the cobbler. Bake 30 minutes. If the crust browns too quickly during last 15 minutes of baking, cover the cobbler loosely with a sheet of foil that has been sprayed with gluten-free nonstick spray. *Makes 8 ⅔-cup servings.*

One serving–Calories: 238; Total fat: 16.2 g; Saturated fat: 1.4 g; Cholesterol: 0 mg; Sodium: 53 mg; Carbohydrates: 22.7 g; Fiber: 4.1 g; Sugar: 13 g; Protein: 3.3 g

Waldorf Salad

For added color, use red, green, and black seedless grapes.

2 large Delicious apples

2 large Bartlett pears

1 banana, sliced

1 tablespoon lemon juice

1 cup seedless grapes

½ cup diced celery

2 tablespoons raisins

¼ cup coarsely chopped walnuts

½ cup chopped dates

3 ounces gluten-free, low-fat cream cheese, softened

Core the apples and pears, and cut them into small pieces. In a large bowl, toss the apples, pears, and banana with lemon juice. Stir in the grapes, celery, raisins, walnuts, and dates. With fingers, gently blend in the cream cheese. Cover and refrigerate. *Makes 4 1-cup servings.*

One serving—Calories: 210; Total fat: 7.5 g; Saturated fat: 2.2 g; Cholesterol: 10 mg; Sodium: 101 mg; Carbohydrates: 34.6 g; Fiber: 4.1 g; Sugar: 8.9 g; Protein: 3.7 g

Fruit Tart

This is the perfect summer dessert—the base is light and it uses the bountiful fruits of summer.

2 eggs, separated

½ cup plus 2 teaspoons sugar

½ teaspoon grated lemon zest

½ teaspoon almond extract

⅓ cup Gluten-Free Flour Mixture (See the Hints chapter.)

⅛ teaspoon salt

¾ teaspoon gluten-free baking powder

4 cups sliced fresh fruit (kiwi, strawberries, peaches, blueberries,
  seedless grapes)

1 tablespoon plus 1 teaspoon cornstarch

¾ cup orange juice

1 tablespoon gluten-free orange liqueur

Preheat oven to 375°F. In a small bowl, beat the egg yolks until thick and lemon colored. Gradually beat in ¼ cup of the sugar. Beat in the lemon zest and almond extract. In another bowl, using clean, dry beaters, beat the egg whites until foamy. Gradually beat in 2 teaspoons of the sugar; continue beating until glossy soft peaks form. With a whisk, fold the egg white mixture into the egg yolk mixture. Sift the flour mixture, salt, and baking powder over the egg mixture. Carefully fold the dry ingredients into the eggs. Spray an 8″ × 12″ pan with gluten-free nonstick spray. Spoon the batter into the pan. Bake 12 to 15 minutes until lightly browned. Cool the tart in the pan at least 1 hour; remove from pan to a platter. Arrange the fruit attractively on the cooled tart. In a saucepan, combine the remaining ¼ cup of sugar and the cornstarch. Stir in the orange juice. Bring to a boil over medium heat, stirring constantly; boil 1 minute. Remove from heat; stir in liqueur. Cool the glaze to room temperature, stirring occasionally. Spoon the glaze over the fruit. Refrigerate until serving time. *Makes 8 ¾-cup servings.*

One serving—Calories: 142; Total fat: 1.6 g; Saturated fat: 0.4 g; Cholesterol: 53 g; Sodium: 61 mg; Carbohydrates: 29.7 g; Fiber: 2.5 g; Sugar: 18.5 g; Protein: 3 g

Nectarine Roll-Ups

Almost any fresh fruit may be used in place of the nectarines. The filling may be prepared up to 3 days in advance.

2 tablespoons gluten-free light rum

3 tablespoons sugar

¼ cup peach preserves

½ teaspoon grated lemon zest

¼ teaspoon cinnamon

⅛ teaspoon nutmeg

1¼ pounds very ripe nectarines, pitted and chopped fine

¼ cup slivered almonds, toasted

8 rice papers

Preheat oven to 400°F. In a medium-size skillet, heat the rum, sugar, preserves, lemon zest, cinnamon, and nutmeg until the sugar and preserves have dissolved. Remove from heat, and stir in the nectarines and almonds. Soak the rice papers in water for 3 minutes to soften; pat dry. Spray the rice papers with gluten-free nonstick spray. Divide the fruit filling among the rice papers. Fold the sides of each rice paper into the center, then roll the rice paper into a cylinder. Spray a baking sheet with gluten-free non-stick spray. Lay the rolls on the baking sheet. Spray the top of the rolls with gluten-free nonstick spray. Bake 15 minutes or until heated through. Serve warm. *Makes 8 roll-ups.*

One roll-up—Calories: 168; Total fat: 4.3 g; Saturated fat: 0.2 g; Cholesterol: 0 mg; Sodium: 25 mg; Carbohydrates: 27.5 g; Fiber: 1.6 g; Sugar: 11.6 g; Protein: 4.2 g

Classic Desserts Redefined

Crêpes Suzette à l'Orange

Try substituting peach nectar for the orange juice and gluten-free peach brandy for the orange liqueur.

1 cup skim milk

½ cup Gluten-Free Flour Mixture, sifted (See the Hints chapter.)

2 tablespoons sugar

2 egg whites

½ teaspoon vanilla

¼ teaspoon finely grated orange zest

⅓ cup orange juice

¼ cup light corn syrup

2 tablespoons gluten-free, unsalted margarine

1 tablespoon gluten-free orange liqueur

1 tablespoon gluten-free brandy

In a large bowl, combine the milk, flour mixture, sugar, egg whites, and vanilla; whisk till well mixed. Add a little more milk if needed to form a loose batter. Spray a 6-inch skillet with gluten-free nonstick spray; heat the skillet over medium heat. Remove from heat, and spoon in 2 tablespoons of the batter; lift and tilt the skillet to spread the batter evenly. Return to heat; brown one side, then carefully turn to brown the second side. Invert the pan over paper towels, and remove the crepe. Repeat with the remaining batter to make 8 crepes. (The skillet may need more nonstick spray. Do not spray a hot skillet; remove the pan from the heat, and let cool slightly before respraying.) Fold each crepe in half; fold in half again, forming a triangle. Set the crepes aside. In a larger skillet, combine the orange zest, orange juice, corn syrup, margarine, orange liqueur, and brandy. Cook, stirring, just until bubbly. Arrange the folded crepes in the sauce; simmer 3 minutes just till heated through, spooning the sauce over the crepes. *Makes 8 crepes.*

One crepe—Calories: 108; Total fat: 2.1 g; Saturated fat: 0 g; Cholesterol: 1 mg; Sodium: 78 mg; Carbohydrates: 18.9 g; Fiber: 0.2 g; Sugar: 4 g; Protein: 2.8 g

White Chocolate Mousse

Shred a piece of semisweet chocolate to sprinkle over the top of the mousse before serving.

  3 ounces white chocolate, chopped fine

  1 tablespoon water

  2 cups gluten-free nondairy whipped topping

Melt the chocolate with the water in the top of a double boiler over barely simmering water until the chocolate is melted, stirring frequently. Remove from heat; cool, stirring occasionally. Fold in half of the whipped topping until completely blended, then gently fold in the remainder of the whipped topping. Spoon into bowls. *Makes 4 ½-cup servings.*

One serving—Calories: 74; Total fat: 4.4 g; Saturated fat: 3.9 g; Cholesterol: 1 mg; Sodium: 4 mg; Carbohydrates: 6.5 g; Fiber: 0 g; Sugar: 4.6 g; Protein: 0.2 g

Crustless Pumpkin Pie

This dessert serves 10, so you can enjoy delicious leftovers.

  2 envelopes gluten-free unflavored gelatin

  2 tablespoons cold water

  2¼ cups evaporated skim milk

  1 16-ounce can solid-pack pumpkin

  6 tablespoons light brown sugar

  ½ teaspoon cinnamon

  ¼ teaspoon nutmeg

  ⅛ teaspoon ground ginger

  ⅛ teaspoon ground cloves

  1 teaspoon vanilla

  10 teaspoons gluten-free nondairy whipped topping

  Cinnamon

In a medium bowl, sprinkle the gelatin over the cold water to soften; set aside. In a small saucepan, heat 1 cup of the evaporated milk to just boiling. Slowly stir the hot milk into the gelatin, stirring until the gelatin is dissolved. Stir in the remaining 1¼ cups of milk and the pumpkin, sugar, cinnamon, nutmeg, ginger, cloves, and vanilla. Spray a 10-inch pie plate with gluten-free nonstick spray. Pour the pumpkin mixture into the pie plate. Chill until firm. To serve, top each slice with a teaspoon of whipped topping, then sprinkle the topping lightly with cinnamon. *Makes 10 slices.*

One slice—Calories: 112; Total fat: 0.9 g; Saturated fat: 0.8 g; Cholesterol: 2 mg; Sodium: 71 mg; Carbohydrates: 15 g; Fiber: 1 g; Sugar: 14.1 g; Protein: 6.3 g

Frozen Treats

Peach Daiquiri Ice

Imagine—a luscious dessert with zero fat and zero cholesterol!

1 16-ounce can peach slices, packed in juice

¼ cup sugar

2 tablespoons gluten-free light rum

¼ teaspoon finely shredded lime zest

1 tablespoon lime juice

⅛ teaspoon mint

Drain the peaches, reserving 2 tablespoons of juice. In a blender, combine the peach slices and reserved peach juice with the sugar, rum, lime zest, lime juice, and mint. Cover and blend till smooth. Pour into an 8½″ × 4½″ loaf pan. Cover and freeze at least 4 hours till firm. Let stand at room temperature about 10 minutes before serving. *Makes 4 ⅓-cup servings.*

One serving–Calories: 136; Total fat: 0 g; Saturated fat: 0 g; Cholesterol: 0 mg; Sodium: 7 mg; Carbohydrates: 38 g; Fiber: 1.5 g; Sugar: 35.2 g; Protein: 0.7 g

Banana Sundaes

Freeze the bananas at least 8 hours before making this dessert. Remove the peel, then wrap bananas separately in foil to freeze. To make a pretty garnish, dip 4 thin slices of banana halfway into melted chocolate. Set 1 slice on top of each sundae. An easy way to melt the chocolate for the garnish is to put semisweet chocolate chips in a custard cup, then set the cup in a pan of barely simmering water. (The water should come about ⅔ of the way up the custard cup.) Stir the chocolate chips till melted.

¾ cup sugar

7 tablespoons unsweetened cocoa

1 teaspoon cornstarch

½ cup skim milk

½ teaspoon vanilla

6 frozen overripe bananas

In a saucepan, whisk together the sugar, cocoa, cornstarch, and ¼ cup of the milk to form a paste. Over medium heat, stir in the remaining ¼ cup of milk. Simmer, stirring constantly, 5 minutes or until smooth and slightly thick. Remove from heat. Stir in ¼ teaspoon of the vanilla; cool 5 minutes. Break each banana into 4 or 5 pieces, and place the banana pieces in a blender. Add the remaining ¼ teaspoon of vanilla to the blender, and blend until smooth. Immediately spoon the bananas into four champagne glasses, and drizzle the cocoa sauce over the top of each. *Makes 4 1¼-cup servings.*

One serving–Calories: 224; Total fat: 1.1 g; Saturated fat: 0 g; Cholesterol: 0 mg; Sodium: 12 mg; Carbohydrates: 49.7 g; Fiber: 4.7 g; Sugar: 15.5 g; Protein: 3.45 g

Mint Ice Milk

This ice milk will taste refreshing after a meal on a hot summer day. Garnish it with a sprig of fresh mint.

¾ cup sugar

1 envelope gluten-free unflavored gelatin

1 12-ounce can evaporated skim milk

1 egg

1 egg white

2½ cups skim milk

2 teaspoons vanilla

2 tablespoons gluten-free white crème de menthe

In a large saucepan, stir together the sugar, gelatin, and evaporated milk. Cook, stirring, over medium-low heat until the sugar and gelatin dissolve and the mixture almost boils; remove from heat. In a small bowl, whisk the egg and egg white slightly; very slowly, while whisking, stir in half of the hot sugar mixture. Stir the egg mixture back into the saucepan. Cook and stir over low heat 2½ minutes; do not boil. Stir in the skim milk, vanilla, and crème de menthe. Transfer mixture to a mixing bowl; cover, and freeze about 2 hours or until almost frozen. When almost frozen, remove from freezer; whip at high speed with a mixer. Return to freezer for about 2 hours until almost frozen again, then whip one more time. Cover and freeze for 4 hours. *Makes 4 1-cup servings.*

One serving–Calories: 65; Total fat: 0.3 g; Saturated fat: 0.1 g; Cholesterol: 15 mg; Sodium: 43 mg; Carbohydrates: 10.3 g; Fiber: 0 g; Sugar: 8.8 g; Protein: 3.3 g

Peanut Butter and Jelly Sundaes

Peanut butter and jelly never tasted so good! Boiled peanuts are available in the health food section of most grocery stores. Gluten-free frozen chocolate yogurt may be used in place of the vanilla yogurt.

> 2 tablespoons gluten-free peanut butter
> 2 cups gluten-free frozen vanilla yogurt, slightly softened
> 10 ounces fresh strawberries, hulled and chopped
> ¼ cup sugar
> ½ teaspoon vanilla
> 1 tablespoon boiled peanuts, chopped fine

Stir the peanut butter into the yogurt until mostly blended in, leaving a few white streaks. Cover and refreeze. Put the strawberries, sugar, and vanilla in a small saucepan; bring to a boil over high heat, stirring frequently. Reduce heat; simmer 5 minutes. Pour the strawberry mixture into a blender, and puree; cover and refrigerate. To serve, spoon the yogurt mixture into four dessert bowls, drizzle with the strawberry sauce, and sprinkle with the peanuts. *Makes 4 ¾-cup servings.*

One serving—Calories: 208; Total fat: 8.6 g; Saturated fat: 3 g; Cholesterol: 1 mg; Sodium: 107 mg; Carbohydrates: 29.3 g; Fiber: 1.3 g; Sugar: 7.9 g; Protein: 5.6 g

Cookies, Cakes, and Other Delicious Baked Treats

Date Cornflake Cookies

These cookies may also be rolled in chopped nuts, cocoa, or confectioner's sugar instead of coconut. Store the cookies in an airtight container.

½ cup chopped dates

1 egg

¼ cup sugar

Dash salt

¾ teaspoon vanilla

½ cup gluten-free cornflakes

½ cup gluten-free puffed-rice cereal

½ cup chopped walnuts

½ cup coconut

Combine the dates, egg, sugar, salt, and vanilla in a small skillet. Cook over medium heat till the mixture pulls away from the side of the pan. Continue cooking 3 minutes, stirring constantly. In a large bowl, combine the corn and rice cereals and the nuts. Add the cereal mixture to the date mixture. Using hands dipped into cold water, roll tablespoons of the mixture into balls. Roll the balls in the coconut. *Makes 20 cookies.*

One cookie—Calories: 251; Total fat: 10.5 g; Saturated fat: 4.8 g; Cholesterol: 53 mg; Sodium: 71 mg; Carbohydrates: 37.7 g; Fiber: 2.9 g; Sugar: 8 g; Protein: 4.5 g

Chocolate Chip Rum Cookies

If you prefer not to use rum, substitute 2 teaspoons of orange juice.

1 cup Gluten-Free Flour Mixture (See the Hints chapter.)

½ teaspoon baking soda

⅛ teaspoon salt

2 tablespoons gluten-free margarine, softened

½ cup light brown sugar

1 whole egg

1 egg white

2 teaspoons gluten-free light rum

½ teaspoon vanilla

½ cup mini semisweet chocolate chips

Preheat oven to 375°F. Sift together the flour mixture, baking soda, and salt. Whip the margarine and brown sugar 3 minutes till soft and fluffy. Add the egg, egg white, rum, and vanilla. Beat 1 minute. Gradually add the dry ingredients; beat until blended. Stir in the chocolate chips. Spray baking sheets very lightly with gluten-free nonstick spray. Place tablespoonfuls of dough on the baking sheets. Bake 12 minutes. *Makes 20 cookies.*

One cookie—Calories: 73; Total fat: 2.7 g; Saturated fat: 1.3 g; Cholesterol: 27 mg; Sodium: 50 mg; Carbohydrates: 11 g; Fiber: 0.2 g; Sugar: 5.9 g; Protein: 1.1 g

Almost Fat-Free Chocolate Cookies

These cookies make an excellent base for many desserts. If you need a chocolate pie crust, let these cookies dry out at room temperature overnight, then grind them in a blender; add melted gluten-free margarine, and press into a pie plate.

¾ cup Gluten-Free Flour Mixture (See the Hints chapter.)
¼ cup sugar
¼ cup unsweetened cocoa
½ teaspoon baking soda
¼ teaspoon salt
⅓ cup light corn syrup
2 egg whites, slightly beaten
3 ounces semisweet chocolate pieces

Preheat oven to 350°F. Sift the flour mixture, sugar, cocoa, baking soda, and salt into a bowl. Stir in the corn syrup and egg whites until blended. (The dough will be thick and slightly sticky.) Spray a cookie sheet with gluten-free nonstick spray. Drop the dough by teaspoonfuls onto the cookie sheet. Bake 7 minutes or just until set; do not overbake. Cool on a wire rack. Melt the chocolate pieces in a double boiler over barely simmering water; lightly drizzle the chocolate over the cookies. *Makes 16 cookies.*

One cookie—Calories: 77; Total fat: 1.7 g; Saturated fat: 1 g; Cholesterol: 0 mg; Sodium: 52 mg; Carbohydrates: 15.4 g; Fiber: 0.7 g; Sugar: 5.9 g; Protein: 1 g

Prune Brownies

These cake-like brownies will hold several days if kept well covered.

½ cup Gluten-Free Flour Mixture (See the Hints chapter.)

⅓ cup unsweetened cocoa

½ teaspoon gluten-free baking powder

¼ teaspoon salt

1 4-ounce jar baby food prunes

⅔ cup sugar

2 teaspoons vanilla

1 whole egg

2 egg whites

1 tablespoon gluten-free mayonnaise

Preheat oven to 350°F. Sift the flour mixture, cocoa, baking powder, and salt. Whip together the prunes, sugar, vanilla, egg, egg whites, and mayonnaise until light. Stir in the dry ingredients just until blended. Spray an 8-inch baking pan with gluten-free nonstick spray. Pour the batter into the pan. Bake 20 minutes or until the edges look dry. Cool completely before cutting. *Makes 12 brownies.*

One brownie—Calories: 72; Total fat: 1.2 g; Saturated fat: 0.4 g; Cholesterol: 18 mg; Sodium: 74 mg; Carbohydrates: 11.1 g; Fiber: 1.3 g; Sugar: 6.6 g; Protein: 2.1 g

Almond Jam Bars

Spread the egg whites to the edge of the pan, sealing the top completely to keep it from shrinking during baking.

> 1 cup Gluten-Free Flour Mixture (See the Hints chapter.)
> 6 tablespoons sugar
> 1/8 teaspoon salt
> 2 eggs, divided
> 3 tablespoons gluten-free margarine, softened
> 1/4 cup all-fruit raspberry jam
> 1/4 teaspoon almond extract
> 1/4 cup coconut
> 1/4 cup chopped slivered almonds

Preheat oven to 375°F. Sift the flour mixture, 3 tablespoons of the sugar, and the salt into a bowl. Make a well in the center; add the egg yolks and margarine. Work the dough with the hands until well blended. Spray an 8-inch square baking pan with gluten-free nonstick spray. Press the dough into the pan. Bake 12 minutes. Remove from oven, and let the crust cool a little. Spread the jam over the crust. Whip the egg whites until soft peaks form. Gradually add the remaining 3 tablespoons of sugar, then the almond extract; continue whipping until stiff peaks form. Fold in the coconut. Spread the meringue over the jam; sprinkle the almonds over the top. Bake 8 more minutes or until the top is lightly browned. Cool completely before cutting into bars. *Makes 16 bars.*

One bar—Calories: 85; Total fat: 3.6 g; Saturated fat: 1 g; Cholesterol: 27 mg; Sodium: 54 mg; Carbohydrates: 11.4 g; Fiber: 0.5 g; Sugar: 5 g; Protein: 1.9 g

Chocolate Liqueur Cake

This cake takes only minutes to assemble. To save on calories, instead of frosting, dust the top with confectioner's sugar.

¾ cup Gluten-Free Flour Mixture (See the Hints chapter.)

1 cup sugar

⅓ cup unsweetened cocoa

¾ teaspoon gluten-free baking powder

¾ teaspoon baking soda

¼ teaspoon salt

1 egg

¼ cup corn oil

1 teaspoon gluten-free, low-fat mayonnaise

1 teaspoon vanilla

5 teaspoons gluten-free coffee liqueur

½ cup boiling water

Chocolate Liqueur Glaze

1¾ cups confectioner's sugar

¼ cup unsweetened cocoa

¼ cup skim milk

1 tablespoon honey

1 teaspoon gluten-free coffee liqueur

¾ teaspoon vanilla

Preheat oven to 350°F. Over a bowl, sift together the flour mixture, sugar, cocoa, baking powder, baking soda, and salt. Make a well in the center, and add the egg, corn oil, mayonnaise, vanilla, and coffee liqueur. Stir together with a wire whisk. Slowly pour in the water; stir with the whisk till blended thoroughly. Spray a 9-inch square pan baking dish with gluten-free nonstick spray. Pour the batter into the baking dish. Bake 20 minutes or till a toothpick inserted near the center comes out clean. Set the cake on a wire rack to cool. To make the Chocolate Liqueur Glaze, combine the sugar and cocoa in a small saucepan. Whisk in the milk and honey. Cook over low heat 1 to 2 minutes, stirring constantly, just until smooth. Do not overcook the glaze, or it will become grainy. Remove from stove, and stir in the liqueur and vanilla. Frost the cool cake with the warm glaze. *Makes 9 3-inch-square servings.*

One serving—Calories: 286; Total fat: 7.7 g; Saturated fat: 1.4 g; Cholesterol: 24 mg; Sodium: 77 mg; Carbohydrates: 52 g; Fiber: 2.1 g; Sugar: 37.9 g; Protein: 3 g

Pineapple Peach Cake

For a dramatic presentation, press sliced almonds around the outside edge of the cake.

    4 eggs, separated
    ½ cup sugar
    2 teaspoons gluten-free, low-fat mayonnaise
    1 teaspoon vanilla
    2 teaspoons gluten-free baking powder
    ½ cup Gluten-Free Flour Mixture (See the Hints chapter.)
    ¼ cup minced almonds
    1 14-ounce can sliced peaches
    1 8-ounce can crushed pineapple
    8 ounces gluten-free nondairy frozen whipped topping, thawed
    6 strawberries, cut in half

Preheat oven to 350°F. Beat the egg whites until foamy. Slowly add the egg yolks to the whites, one at a time, beating well after each addition. Add the sugar, mayonnaise, and vanilla. Sift together the baking powder and flour mixture; gradually add to the egg mixture, mixing well. Stir in the almonds. Line a 10-inch round cake pan with waxed paper, cut to fit. Spray gluten-free nonstick spray on the waxed paper. Pour the batter into the pan. Bake 20 minutes. Remove the cake from the pan, and cool on a wire rack. When cool, remove the waxed paper, and place the cake on a serving plate. Drain the peaches, reserving 3 tablespoons of peach juice. Spread the pineapple over the top of the cake. Spread a thin layer of whipped topping over the pineapple. Arrange the peach slices and strawberries attractively on top of the whipped topping. Drizzle with the reserved peach juice. Frost the sides of the cake with the remaining whipped topping. *Makes 12 slices.*

One slice—Calories: 157; Total fat: 6.3 g; Saturated fat: 3.7 g; Cholesterol: 71 mg; Sodium: 32 mg; Carbohydrates: 14 g; Fiber: 1.2 g; Sugar: 10.6 g; Protein: 3.4 g

Macaroon Cupcakes

Instead of using frosting, dust the tops of the cupcakes with sifted confectioner's sugar.

    6 tablespoons gluten-free margarine, softened
    ⅔ cup sugar
    3 eggs, separated
    1 teaspoon almond extract
    ½ teaspoon vanilla
    1½ cups Gluten-Free Flour Mixture (See the Hints chapter.)
    2¼ teaspoons gluten-free baking powder
    ⅛ teaspoon salt
    ⅔ cup skim milk
    ½ cup shredded coconut

Preheat oven to 350°F. Cream the margarine. Gradually add ½ cup of the sugar, beating till the mixture is light and fluffy. Add the egg yolks, almond extract, and vanilla; beat well. With clean, dry beaters, whip the egg whites until soft peaks form; gradually add the remaining 3 tablespoons of sugar, beating until the egg whites are stiff but not dry. Sift the flour mixture, baking powder, and salt together; add to the margarine and sugar mixture alternately with the milk, beating until blended. Fold in the coconut and egg whites. Line muffin cups with paper cupcake liners. Spoon the batter into the liners, filling each two-thirds full.

Bake 15 minutes or until a toothpick inserted in the center of a cupcake comes out clean. Cool completely, then dust the tops with confectioner's sugar. *Makes 18 cupcakes.*

One cupcake—Calories: 93; Total fat: 4.4 g; Saturated fat: 1.6 g; Cholesterol: 36 mg; Sodium: 80 mg; Carbohydrates: 12.4 g; Fiber: 0.5 g; Sugar: 4.8 g; Protein: 2.5 g

Carrot Snack Cake

This dessert has less than half the calories of traditional carrot cake. For a pretty effect, place a paper doily over the top of the cooled cake, then dust with sifted confectioner's sugar.

¼ cup gluten-free margarine, softened

½ cup sugar

2 eggs

1 egg white

1 tablespoon gluten-free, low-fat mayonnaise

¼ cup skim milk

½ teaspoon vanilla

½ cup finely shredded carrot

¼ cup finely chopped walnuts

1 cup Gluten-Free Flour Mixture (See the Hints chapter.)

1¾ teaspoons gluten-free baking powder

¼ teaspoon cinnamon

⅛ teaspoon salt

Dash nutmeg

Preheat oven to 350°F. Cream the margarine and sugar until blended. Beat in the eggs, egg white, mayonnaise, milk, and vanilla. Stir in the carrot and walnuts. Sift together the flour mixture, baking powder, cinnamon, salt, and nutmeg; stir into the carrot mixture until well blended. Spray an 8-inch square pan with gluten-free nonstick spray. Pour the batter into the pan. Bake

20 minutes or until a toothpick inserted in the center comes out clean. *Makes 9 2½-inch-square servings.*

One serving—Calories: 157; Total fat: 7.5 g; Saturated fat: 1.5 g; Cholesterol: 47 mg; Sodium: 139 mg; Carbohydrates: 18.7 g; Fiber: 0.9 g; Sugar: 8 g; Protein: 3.9 g

Anise Biscotti

At just 42 calories each, these are the perfect accompaniment to Peach Daiquiri Ice (see Index).

½ cup Gluten-Free Flour Mixture (See the Hints chapter.)

¾ teaspoon gluten-free baking powder

½ teaspoon finely crushed aniseed

1 tablespoon gluten-free margarine

2 tablespoons sugar

¼ teaspoon grated lemon zest

1 egg

2 tablespoons sliced almonds

Preheat oven to 375°F. Sift together the flour mixture, baking powder, and aniseed. In a large bowl, beat together the margarine, sugar, and lemon zest. Add the egg, and beat well. Stir in the dry ingredients and almonds. On waxed paper, shape the dough into a long log. Spray a baking sheet with gluten-free nonstick spray. Place the log on the baking sheet; flatten very slightly. Bake 15 to 20 minutes or till lightly browned. Cool completely on a wire rack (about 1 hour). Preheat oven to 300°F. Cut the log into ½-inch slices; arrange with one cut side down on the baking sheet. Bake 10 minutes; turn the slices over, and bake 5 to 10 minutes longer or till crisp and dry. Cool completely. *Makes 12 slices.*

One slice—Calories: 42; Total fat: 1.8 g; Saturated fat: 0.4 g; Cholesterol: 18 mg; Sodium: 17 mg; Carbohydrates: 5.2 g; Fiber: 0.3 g; Sugar: 1.4 g; Protein: 1.2 g

Index

www.ingramcontent.com/pod-product-compliance
Lightning Source LLC
Chambersburg PA
CBHW060328100426
42812CB00003B/918